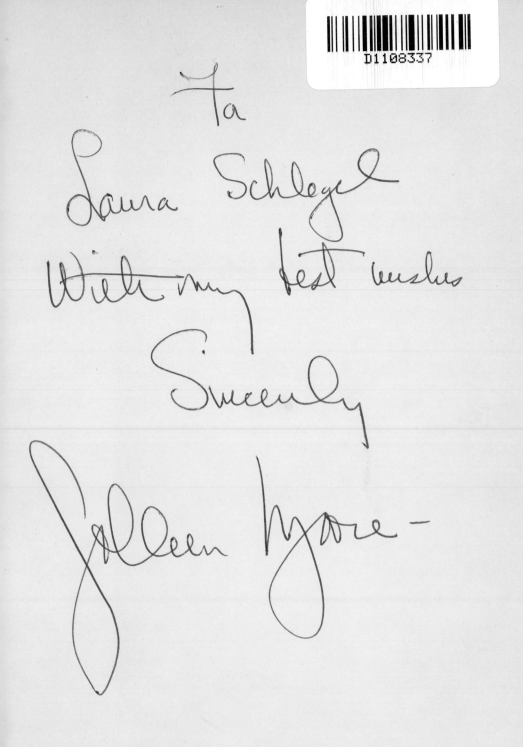

To

Laura Schlegel

With my best wishes

Sincerely

Colleen Moore —

SILENT STAR

SILENT STAR

COLLEEN MOORE

DOUBLEDAY & COMPANY, INC.
GARDEN CITY, NEW YORK
1968

LIBRARY OF CONGRESS CATALOG CARD NUMBER 68–10562
COPYRIGHT © 1968 BY COLLEEN MOORE
ALL RIGHTS RESERVED
PRINTED IN THE UNITED STATES OF AMERICA
9 8 7 6 5 4 3 2

CONTENTS

To Adela Rogers St. Johns,
my friend and mentor since
my first days in Hollywood

SILENT STAR

CHAPTER 1

THE NEVER LAND

In 1915 Hollywood was a small town adjacent to—and a world apart from—the city of Los Angeles. Tucked between the towering Hollywood Hills and the Pacific Ocean, it had been developed some years earlier by three real estate operators who bought up farm land and laid out streets in the hope of attracting some of the Easterners coming out in increasing numbers every winter to bask in Southern California's warm sunlight. Some Easterners came, but not to bask in the sun. To work in it. To write and act in and direct and produce a new art form that was changing the dreams of the world—motion pictures.

The way I always heard it, Hollywood got its first big impetus if not its start toward becoming the movie capital of the world when Cecil B. De Mille went out there in 1913 to film *The Squaw Man* and came back East exclaiming over the glorious intensity of Southern California sunshine. Filming in those days, of course, even the filming of most interior scenes, was done in sunlight, as Klieg and Cooper-Hewitt lights were not yet in general use.

I've since read another version of how Hollywood came to be chosen as the film center. It seems that in 1909, after years of bitter disputes over patent rights to various movie-making devices, those companies holding essential patents formed the Motion Picture Patents Company to keep unlicensed companies out of production and distribution. The excluded companies were determined to stay in business, and they did. But they played it safe. They moved their operations to Hollywood so they could be close to the Mexican border in case of injunction.

I rather like that version. It has a serial thriller touch to it that sounds like Hollywood.

In any case, and one after another, the pioneer movie-makers in New York and Chicago packed up and went west to Hollywood—or near enough to it (Culver City, Universal City, even Los Angeles) to say that's where they were.

By 1915 there were quite a few of them there—Griffith, Mack Sennett, Christie Comedies, and Selig in Los Angeles, Universal in Universal City, Ince in Culver City, and Paramount in Hollywood itself.

For all the bustling commerce such a listing suggests, Hollywood in 1915 was still more country than town. Few of the roads were paved, and at the corner of Hollywood Boulevard and Vine Street—the center of Hollywood even today—there was an orange grove surrounding a large Spanish house owned by a family named Stern.

The orange grove, in turn, was surrounded—or nearly so—by churches. At the side of the grove was the Episcopal Church, St. Stephen's. Across the street in front of it was the Baptist Church. Across the street in back was the Methodist Church. Considering where Hollywood ended up in the eyes of the world, it started out rather saintly!

In 1915 Hollywood was not a community as we understand and use the word today. It was several communities. Not only did actors not mix with the "private" people of Los Angeles, who might as well have been living in Europe for all Hollywood ever saw of them, actors didn't even mix much with people from studios other than their own. Each studio, though small, was almost as self-contained socially as it was artistically—which may explain why the early films showed so much originality instead of being so many copies of each other as they were later on.

Still, it was a friendly town and an exciting one, its leading citizens some of the most talented, temperamental—and explosive—individualists ever assembled together in one place.

There was, in fact, from my point of view, only one thing wrong with Hollywood in 1915.

I wasn't there.

I wasn't even anywhere nearby. I lived all the way across the country in Tampa, Florida. My only connections with Hollywood were those of any other thirteen-year-old schoolgirl at the time. Every Friday after school my girl friends and I went to the Bijou Theater to see Grace Cunard and Francis Ford in the serial *Lucille Love*. On Saturday afternoons we went to the Strand Theater to see feature films starring Mary Pickford or Marguerite Clark or Francis X. Bushman or J. Warren Kerrigan. We wrote fan letters to the stars and cut their pictures out of movie magazines and pasted them in a scrapbook.

The only difference between my movie scrapbook and those of my friends was that I left a blank page in mine for my own picture after I became a movie star. Because I didn't just hope to go to Hollywood. I intended to.

My family, while sympathetic to my ambition, was not as sold as I was on the chances of it being realized. I did a better job on the girl who lived across the street from us. She left a blank page in her scrapbook for me, too.

My dream of being an actress started when I was five years old. One Saturday afternoon my mother took me to the theater to see Maude Adams in J. M. Barrie's *Peter Pan*. The play made such an indelible impression on me that when I saw it again a few years ago I knew entrances and exits before they were made, lines before they were spoken. But the moment which not only impressed me the most but shaped my future came from a line not written in the play.

The theater was dark, the matinee audience, crowded with children, tense. The unthinkable was happening in the Never Land. Tinker Bell was dying.

Tears were running down my face as Peter Pan came down to the footlights and spoke to the audience. "All the children who believe in fairies raise their hands. If you believe, you can save Tinker Bell."

I was so carried away I jumped on my seat and, waving both hands, screamed, "I believe in fairies, I really do!"

The audience burst into laughter, turning to look at me. I stared back at them, their laughter hitting me with a force I had never felt before. And when I realized that it was I—I—who was making them laugh, a curious feeling of power came over me—as if for those few brief moments I held that audience in my hands.

That Saturday afternoon I knew—not hoped, knew—I would become an actress.

I don't mean to say that for the next ten years I concentrated so hard on being an actress that I talked and ate and slept and breathed acting—that would come later—though I did have my moments.

I read one time in *Photoplay* magazine that Norma Talmadge had said an actress must be able to weep spontaneously, so I thought the sooner I learned to cry, the better off I'd be. I certainly didn't want anybody to have to send for the glycerine bottle for me when I became a star. That would be a disgrace.

I used to practice crying while I walked to school in the morning. Whenever it rained, I took the streetcar, but that didn't stop my practicing. I'd sit there staring at one of the advertising placards, tears rolling down my cheeks.

One day a lady sitting next to me bent down to me and said in a solicitous voice, "What's the matter, little girl?"

"Oh, nothing, ma'am," I snuffled back at her, smiling through my tears. "I'm just practicing to be a movie actress."

After a long look at me she moved to another seat, turning to stare at me every few moments until she got off the streetcar. I couldn't see what there was to stare about. I was just making good use of time that would otherwise have been wasted.

I made use of more than time.

As a child I took piano lessons and showed some talent for it, enough anyhow to make my mother dream of my becoming a concert pianist—not that I suppose it takes much to start a mother dreaming where her children are concerned. Myself, I had other plans. I regarded piano the way I came to regard horseback riding, ballet, or any other skill I might learn—would it help me in my acting career?

My best times at the piano were improvising. One rainy summer afternoon when I was nine years old, I said to my seven-year-old brother Cleeve and our two English cousins who were staying with us at the time, "How would you like me to play a story on the piano for you?"

They gathered around me, and I proceeded to make up a woebe-

I came of a tradition of beautiful women—my mother was lovely;
Aunt Lib a great beauty. I don't know what happened to me.

At the age of six months I was bald, had one blue eye and one brown eye and a weight problem, but I was not above making an entrance.

gone tale about a lost child, improvising appropriate music as I went along. Soon tears began to flow down Cousin Lisbeth's cheeks. Next my brother Cleeve welled over. At last Cousin Jack started crying, too.

As I saw the effect my performance was having on them, I was filled with that same powerful thrill I had experienced at *Peter Pan*, except that this time it didn't surprise me. It did, however, spur me on to greater effort, and in a voice now trembling I began to tell them, gory detail by gory detail, how the lost child fell into the hands of savage Indians.

My greater effort proved to be my undoing. I was so touched by my own histrionics I had to abandon the child to her fate. I was sobbing too hard to go on.

On the whole, however, my childhood was just like anybody else's. Or maybe, considering what you read about the childhood of so many people in the arts, it wasn't. Mine was a happy childhood.

I was born Kathleen Morrison. I was also born a Yankee—in Port Huron, Michigan—but I lived most of my childhood in the South, first in Atlanta, Georgia, then in Tampa, Florida.

There were five of us—my father and mother, my brother Cleeve and I, and my grandmother on my mother's side, who came to live with us after she was widowed, not because she had nowhere else to go, but because in those days a Grandma who was left alone wasn't sent to a nursing home or shifted about from pillar to post but was taken into the family of one of her children and made a part of that family. Grandma had six other daughters besides my mother, but she chose to live with us, and I was glad she did.

We weren't rich, but we weren't poor, or if we were, we didn't know it. We did know, my brother and I, what it meant to be loved. My father and mother must have had differences, but they must also have argued those differences out in private. I never heard them so much as exchange a cross word. More important, they were in love with each other all their lives, and their love—and the great unity they had between them—spilled over onto Cleeve and me—so much so that when disillusionment came to me later on in my own marriage, I was shocked as well as hurt. Nothing in my experience had prepared me for it.

The years of my childhood were years in which the Victorian

influence still persisted. Girls were innocent and unsophisticated, or if they weren't they pretended to be, because this was the accepted, the ideal image. It was also the image portrayed on the screen by such stars as Mary Pickford and Marguerite Clark.

Today my children would laugh and say, "What a bunch of squares!" We were, but the hole our peg went into was square, too, so we fitted.

There was an innocence then even among adults. I remember hearing my parents say there'd never be another war because people were too civilized. With communications like the telegraph, people would understand and settle their differences quickly, and with the movies now showing one half of the world what the other half was like, war was impossible. It was not knowing enough about each other that caused wars. Mary Pickford was worth a dozen ambassadors. Charlie Chaplin was uniting the world with laughter.

Listening to them talk, I was overwhelmed with visions of my future. It was going to be even more than I had dreamed of—fame, being an actress, and now stopping wars singlehanded. What a life!

Of my mother's six sisters, three of them had—as people said in those days—married well. Because they had no children of their own, they showered me with gifts of clothes and toys from New York and Paris and London. They also began sending me doll furniture —tiny, exquisite silver cabinets and chests, Battersea enamel tables and chairs, a Sèvres china tea set. I had a doll house Dad had built for me, but the furniture from the aunts was much too elegant —and expensive—to play with. Instead it became known as Kathleen's Collection, and it was kept on display in a cabinet where I admired it and wondered from time to time what I would eventually do with it.

I had other collections—among them, of all things, water collected in little bottles from as many oceans and rivers and lakes as I or my relatives had access to—and other interests, but I never lost sight of my true goal.

One day an upright piano packed in a large wooden box was delivered to a neighbor down the street. After the front of the box was removed and the piano taken out, I took one look at the stagelike structure that was left and persuaded the neighbor's yard man to haul it over to our house and set it up in the back yard.

My young aunts, who wanted to know how I would look with hair, experimented with a curly wig. Only the ice cream bribe made this picture possible.

The American Stock Company was now in business. I wrote the plays, and my friends and I were the players, performing to audiences of other children at one cent the admission.

Business, unfortunately, was bad. We played to very small audiences, sometimes as small as one or two. But my vanity wasn't the only thing that suffered. I've always liked a paying business, and we sometimes couldn't even get the ones who did come to pay the penny we asked.

Something obviously had to be done, and we did it. Barnum & Bailey's Circus had just left town, so we organized one of our own. Cleeve and I were the acrobats, various friends were clowns, and the usual pets, of course, the caged lions and tigers. But we had something more. We had a gimmick.

For three days before the show we paraded around the neighborhood after school with signs that read, Circus in Morrison's Back Yard Saturday—No Boys Allowed.

It worked. There were so many children sitting on the fence in our back yard that Saturday they broke it down.

My Aunt Lib, the one with the bird on her hat, claimed that I was the child of her soul. I didn't know what it meant but it suited me fine.

I was so carried away by our success that when I performed an acrobatic stunt with Cleeve, hanging by my knees from a gym bar and holding him dangling, a leather book strap around his middle, and the ends of it clenched in my teeth, I twirled him around so fast I broke the edge off my new front tooth.

Even my mother was carried away by our success. She sent out cookies and lemonade for all—on the house.

Afterward we divided the vast sum of forty-three cents among us, and while I contemplated the blissful thought that a theatrical life, besides being spiritually rewarding, could also be very profitable, I contemplated the further thought that while it does indeed pay to advertise, it pays even better if the product offered is something forbidden.

The aunt who was to be instrumental in getting me to my goal was my Aunt Lib Howey in Chicago. Aunt Lib was christened Elizabeth, but when she was twelve years old she renamed herself Liberty, saying she hoped when she grew up, men would say, "Give me Liberty, or give me death!"

Aunt Lib, who was considered a great beauty with her big blue eyes, blond hair, and peaches-and-cream complexion, looked like a fairy princess to me. I used to think she should have been an actress. She thought so, too. She was, in fact, such a frustrated actress, it was an easy job for me to brainwash her about my going to Hollywood. She, in turn, brainwashed her husband, my Uncle

Walter Howey, who was an editor of the Chicago *Examiner* and was to me just as dynamic a personality as Aunt Lib was herself. (Not only to me, I might add. In 1928 two of Uncle Walter's former reporters, Ben Hecht and Charles MacArthur, wrote a play about him called *The Front Page*.)

Uncle Walter and Aunt Lib were mad about each other, but they weren't dynamic people for nothing. Sometimes they would bring me to Chicago to visit them, and I adored going, if only to watch the fights. They fought with such large and elegant words. Sometimes I think that was why they fought—to try out their vocabularies, each one hoping the other would have to stop in the middle of the fight to say, "*What* does *that* mean?"

Anyhow, they would carry on until my aunt would burst into tears. Then my uncle would swear his undying love in great poetic phrases, and they'd fall into each other's arms.

It was so exciting I wanted to clap. My parents, of course—dear, sweet, gentle souls that they were—would have been horrified if I had told them about the fights between Uncle Walter and Aunt Lib, but I was no fool. I wanted to come back and see the show again.

If they didn't have anything else to fight about, they'd fight over me, my aunt saying, "She is the child of my soul," to which my uncle would retort, "She is the child of my imagination." I'd just sit there thinking that, as we'd say down South, I was quite some punkins.

Quite some punkins I may have been, and happy child I definitely was, but as I got farther and farther into my teens, I began to get more and more restless and fired up, thinking about Hollywood and how I could ever manage to get there.

Not that the movies, it turned out, had become the salvation of the world. My parents discussed the war in Europe over and over again, upset about the fighting and disillusioned that such a thing could be happening in this day and age.

I remember my mother saying, "I don't understand how cousins like the Kaiser and King George can make war against each other, especially with Queen Victoria for a grandmother. Families should stick together."

I said, "I thought you said the movies and things like that were going to stop all wars."

My father and mother looked at each other, and then at me.

Mother said, "That's what every civilized person thought." She sighed. "But I guess with all this communication, like the wireless and the telephone and your beloved movies, maybe we'll all be too close for comfort."

I frowned at her. "Do you think if Mary Pickford went over and talked to them they'd stop?"

Mother smiled—a gentle smile—and came over and kissed me. "I'm afraid," she said, "it's too late even for Mary Pickford."

That was in 1916. It took another year before the movies, unable to change the course of the world, settled for changing at least one ardent admirer's way of life.

At church one Sunday in November of 1917 I heard a verse from the Gospel According to St. Matthew: "All things whatsoever ye ask in prayer, believing, ye shall receive."

I asked my mother if this meant that if I prayed and absolutely knew I was going to be an actress, nothing could stand in my way. My mother hesitated, but only for a minute. "Yes, darling," she said. "If you will thoroughly believe, and ask God's help, I'm sure that somehow a miracle will happen, and God Himself will send you to Hollywood."

The next nine mornings I stopped in at church for a few minutes on my way to school, lighted a candle, and with positive knowledge, prayed for God's help. On the night of the ninth day, my miracle happened.

Every night after supper we gathered in the living room around my father to listen to him read a story. That night he was reading Poe's *The Murders in the Rue Morgue,* and he had just reached the part where the gorilla was climbing over the windowsill, when the phone rang, nearly sending me flying out of my seat.

The phone kept ringing. Not the repeated short rings of a local call. The steady ring that meant long distance and—unless it was one of the aunts calling Grandma—usually bad news.

"Hurry, Chas," Mother said after an apprehensive exchange of glances between them. "It's long distance."

Suddenly, frighteningly, my knees began to shake. The call was going to be about me. I knew it. It was Hollywood calling to tell me to come west at once, I was to be a movie star.

It wasn't Hollywood. But I wasn't far off.

"Hello!" my father shouted into the phone. It was, after all,

My brother Cleeve and I were always the best of friends. Nobody had ever heard of sibling rivalry in my family.

long distance. How long a distance there was no way of telling.

He turned to us, looking scared. "It's Walter. In Chicago."

Mother went over and took Dad's hand.

He listened for a bit, and the scared look left—to be replaced by one of absolute bewilderment. "You mean to tell me D. W. Griffith will give Kathleen a six-months' contract in Hollywood?"

My heart jumped.

Dad turned to Mother. "I always told you Walter is crazy."

He turned back to the phone and listened some more. "But she's only fifteen. She has to finish school."

Mother took the receiver from Dad and spoke into the phone. "Walter, this is Agnes. Please tell me what this is all about."

My heart was pounding so hard, I shut my mouth tight for fear it would pop out.

I can't remember when I wasn't trying to act. At twelve I was striking attitudes.

As I look back on it now I wonder at my audacity in dreaming that I could become a movie star. The vogue for beauty in those days was a tiny, well-rounded, blue-eyed girl with long blond curls— Mary Pickford—or a wee, doll-like, brown-eyed brunette also with curls—Marguerite Clark. I was a skinny kid with a turned-up nose and dark red hair worn in pigtails, and I didn't have blue eyes or brown eyes either. I had one of each.

But ignorance is bliss, and since we never see ourselves as others see us, my dream of becoming a movie star wasn't the least disturbed by such mundane matters as what I looked like.

After Mother hung up the phone, she explained what had happened. My Uncle Walter, as editor of one of the Hearst newspapers, had a certain amount of influence in Chicago, and he'd been able to get first D. W. Griffith's *The Birth of a Nation* and then his *Intolerance* past the censors. When Mr. Griffith asked Uncle Walter what he could do to repay him, my blessed, brainwashed Aunt Lib spoke right up. "We have a niece—"

Mr. Griffith groaned. "Not a niece!"

Also blessed—and also brainwashed—Uncle Walter nodded. "I'm afraid so."

My brother Cleeve, when he heard that, piped up, "She's a payoff!"

I stared at him, feeling like a deflated balloon. Cleeve was right.

Hollywood wasn't sending for me. I was being sent to Hollywood—not because anybody out there thought I was any good, but simply to pay off a favor.

I stayed deflated for maybe a minute. How did I care how I got there? What mattered was I was finally going.

Or was I?

Dad was saying, "After she graduates from high school she'll have plenty of time to be an actress."

My heart sank. Then Mother spoke up.

Now my mother was always a great one for maxims. I was raised on them. And while she firmly believed that "God opens many doors in our lives," she believed just as firmly that "Opportunity only knocks once."

Right now she was saying, "Chas, all we've ever heard from this child is movies, movies, movies. Suppose life cracks up on her when she's grown up. She'll say we didn't give her the only opportunity she ever had to do the only thing she ever wanted to do."

"I understand, dearie," Dad replied. Dad always called my mother dearie, just as she always called him Chas. "But what about her education?"

Mother shrugged. "Six months in Hollywood can't be much worse than having the measles, as far as school is concerned. For that matter, she can have a tutor and have her lessons sent to her. Then when she returns she won't have lost a day's work."

"That's all very well," Dad said, "but you do have a husband and son as well as a daughter. And I have a machinery business here in Tampa. If she goes to Hollywood, who's going to take her?"

That stopped my mother cold.

It nearly stopped me, too.

Cleeve whispered to me, "I'm betting on Mother."

I wasn't. She just went on looking at Dad without any answer. My mother won most of the time, but we all knew Dad made the decisions on important things.

Grandma cleared her throat, and I turned to look at her. But not with any hope. My grandmother thought all actresses were wicked women. She was the only one in the entire family, and that included the aunts who lived in Paris, whom I hadn't sold on the idea that I was another Mary Pickford.

She sat there now ramrod straight, the way she always sat, her back not touching the chair, because my grandmother was first and foremost a lady, and a lady's back did not touch the chair she sat in. Her lips were tight, and she spoke in a firm voice. "I will take her to Hollywood."

I let out a yell and rushed to her to give her a hug and a kiss, then to Dad and Mother for the same. Then I sat down in the middle of the floor and started to cry. My father put his arm around my mother and said, "We did raise an odd one, didn't we?"

I sat on where I was, blubbering and thinking Aladdin wasn't the only one who had a magic lamp. I had one, too. Only it wasn't a lamp. It was a telephone.

A few days later we were on our way—Grandma and I and also my mother, who was going out with us to make sure we found a suitable place to live and to look the whole situation over.

We had first to go to Chicago, where Uncle Walter and Aunt Lib met us. We were hardly off the train when Uncle Walter said, "There's one hitch I didn't tell you about on the phone, because Lib wouldn't let me."

My heart sank again.

"Kathleen has to go over to the Essanay Studios, and have a test made to see if her eyes photograph the same."

I didn't see why they shouldn't. They did in still photographs. But I went and had the test.

I asked the director who was making it if I had to cry in a scene. He said no, but if I wanted to cry, it was okay with him. I was anxious to find out if all that practicing was going to pay off.

It did. And my eyes did photograph the same.

The night before we left for Hollywood, Uncle Walter took us to the College Inn to celebrate. Aunt Lib told me it was a nightclub. When I asked her what that meant, Uncle Walter said, "It's a place where they don't have lunch." Then he raised his champagne glass and said, "Here's to Colleen Moore, the newest Griffith discovery and a future movie star."

I started looking around, wondering who Colleen Moore was.

Uncle Walter beamed at me. "That's you, baby."

My own name, he explained, was too long to fit on a movie marquee. Twelve letters was the limit. And since I was going to be seeing my name up in lights one of these days, a suitable name had to be found.

Uncle Walter had taken the problem to his archrival and sometime friend Teddy Beck, editor of the Chicago *Tribune*. Over a beer in a friendly neighborhood tavern they decided the time had come for introducing an Irish actress to the movies. There was a lot of good publicity in it.

They felt very creative and had another beer.

Morrison, they decided, sounded too Scotch. Why not chop it off and make Moore out of it? You couldn't get any more Irish than that. Feeling very proud of themselves, they ordered another beer.

Kathleen, while Irish, as indeed half of me was, definitely would not do because of the famous serial queen, Kathleen Williams. Something really original was needed.

They had another beer while they went over all the Irish names they could think of. Two beers later they were slapping each other on the back and ready to order drinks all around. They'd come up with Colleen, a Gaelic word of endearment meaning little girl.

Uncle Walter beamed at me again. "Now nobody can say you're not my child. I've given you a new name."

"And I," Aunt Lib said, "gave her a career."

They glared at each other, then burst out laughing.

I laughed with them. It felt peculiar getting an entirely new name at the age of fifteen, but then everything I was doing now was new. Besides, hadn't Mary Pickford been born Gladys Smith? I began to feel quite professional.

The next day as we boarded the Santa Fe *Chief*, Uncle Walter handed me a letter. When the train pulled out, I opened it and read it.

"*Dear baby,*" it said, "*Hollywood, where you will now be living, is inhabited by a race of people called Press Agents. The studios pay them a lot of money to think up stories about the players under contract and to persuade editors like me to print their stories. So the moral of this letter is, never believe one damned word you ever read about yourself.*"

Uncle Walter knew what he was talking about. While I was reading his letter, Mother was reading the newspaper he'd handed her. In it was his own story—sent out on all the news wires—about how I became a motion picture actress.

According to the newspaper, I had been visiting Uncle Walter and Aunt Lib in Chicago that summer when D. W. Griffith came to

Here I am at thirteen (third from the left in the front row) at the Convent of the Holy Names in Tampa, Florida. My peers and I were all more interested in Photoplay Magazine *than in Latin.*

their house one night for dinner. As a hoax I put on the maid's uniform and started serving. Mr. Griffith took one look at me and said, "Mrs. Howey, you've just lost a maid, and I've gained a new movie star." Then they revealed to him that I wasn't the maid, I was their niece.

As young and unsophisticated as I was, I shuddered as I read the story. Even today I wonder how a topflight editor like Uncle Walter could have concocted anything so corny.

Yet I know. Uncle Walter was so proud of "his child" that he couldn't bear to have anyone know I was a payoff, that neither acting ability nor looks had had anything to do with my becoming a "find."

The irony of it is that Uncle Walter not only wrote that absurd story, he told it so often that—against his own advice—he finally came to believe it himself.

The trip to California took three days and three nights. I kept asking Grandma to let me look at my fifty-dollar-a-week contract "just one more time," until finally she said, "By the time we get to Hollywood, there won't be any print left," and she put it in her purse and never let me see it again.

I would go to the observation car at the rear of the train and sit on the small open platform and dream of Hollywood. I could hear the train wheels singing, "*You will be a star, you will be a star.*" Then logic would pull me back to earth as I speculated on the fact that I had no training whatever. All I knew about how silent movies were made was what I'd read in the fan magazines—interviews in which stars and directors gave advice to hopefuls—and though I'd read every magazine I could get my hands on, what did I really know? Next to nothing. I could cry now whenever I had to, but what about technique? I'd seen that word used over and over again, but what did it mean, technique?

Then my fifteen-year-old optimism would push all doubts aside. I would think, maybe it just means work, and if it does, then I'll be all right, because I love to work, I really do.

And I really did.

When we came out of the desert into California, I ran out to the observation platform to stare at the snowcapped mountains, the green orange groves, the palm trees, and the brilliant sky. I knew this was my land. This was where I belonged.

Mrs. Brown, a sort of studio chaperone, met us at the station in Los Angeles and took us to a small bungalow she had rented for us on Fountain Avenue, about a half block from the Griffith Studio.

Walking to the corner, I could see the crumbling city of Babylon—the huge, two-city-block set used in *Intolerance*—still standing. It was something to feast your eyes on.

The studio itself was a letdown. It was a large, three-story barnlike structure made of clapboard and painted dark green, and attached to it in a very makeshift manner were many small buildings. It looked to me as if when they needed more room they just got together some old boards and added on another shack. I don't know what I expected—a marble palace, maybe—but it seemed incredible to me that all the great Griffith films had been made in that ramshackle place.

In front of the studio was a cement court, with groups of people sitting around, some in make-up, some not. After I was taken inside the studio to meet Mr. Griffith's manager, Mrs. Brown brought me back to the courtyard and over to a group of girls about my age to introduce me to them.

I recognized only one of them—Bessie Love. I'd seen pictures of her in *Photoplay*, with captions saying she was a star of tomorrow. But they were all so pretty and seemed so assured, I felt shy.

The names of the other girls were Mildred Harris, Winifred West-over, Carmel Meyers, and Pauline Stark.

Pauline said to me right off the bat, "Are you going to the studio school? You have to go to school till you're sixteen, you know. It's the law."

"I'm going to have a tutor," I blurted out—and felt like a snob. But I didn't know what else to do except tell the truth.

They didn't take offense. They just said it was too bad, because the studio school was lots of fun.

Carmel said, "Have you met the Gishes?"

Mildred said, "I *adore* the Gishes, especially Lillian."

Winifred said, "Do you think it's true what they say about Lillian and Mr. Griffith—that he's madly in love with her?"

Bessie said, "Why wouldn't he be? She's the nicest person there is in the movies."

Pauline sighed. "Maybe they're secretly married."

I didn't say anything. How could I? It was all news to me, though my movie magazines had hinted that Mr. Griffith was in love with Lillian Gish.

Dorothy Gish was great, one of the girls said, and always full of funny remarks. Constance Talmadge, said another, was Dorothy's best friend. Bobby Harron, another put in, was in love with Dorothy, but she only looked on him as a brother.

Chat, chat, chat, on they went, talking about everyone at the studio. It was just like reading the fan magazines, only better. This was practically straight from the horse's mouth.

I loved it—until one of them turned to me and said, "Did Mr. Griffith really discover you?"

I may not have known what else to do except tell the truth when they asked me about going to the studio school, but I did this time. I was afraid if they found out I was a payoff, they'd blab it all over Hollywood, and I'd be out of the movies before I was even in them. I couldn't bring myself to repeat Uncle Walter's story.

My uncle, Walter Howey, a newspaper editor with the Chicago Examiner, *put me in pictures via a deal with D. W. Griffith.*

I just said Mr. Griffith saw me in Chicago, had a test made at Essanay, and gave me a contract.

Years later I found out that Carmel Meyers was a payoff, too. Her father, a rabbi, was an authority on ancient history, whom Mr. Griffith had used as a consultant on *Intolerance*. He took no pay, only a contract for Carmel.

Mildred Harris' mother, the head of wardrobe, was such an expert on costumes she was rewarded with a contract for her daughter. Winifred Westover's father was a newspaper man who'd done favors for Griffith.

We were all payoffs except Bessie Love and Pauline Stark. And none of us wanted to admit it.

Before they could ask me any more questions, Mrs. Brown rescued me. She took me inside the big barn to meet Chet Withey, a Griffith director, saying, "This is Colleen Moore, the new girl Mr. Griffith sent out from Chicago."

He looked me over—kindly, if critically—and said, "She'll do. She can play the city girl with Mildred and Bobby."

I wondered if Mildred was the girl I'd just met and if Bobby was the Robert Harron I'd seen in pictures.

As a teenager I had one fixed idea—to go to Hollywood and become a movie star but it never really occurred to me that I would go as a payoff.

"Be here, made up, at nine in the morning," he added. "We're going out by the Soldiers' Home to shoot exteriors."

I couldn't believe it. I'd only been in Hollywood six hours, and I was already in the movies.

Afterward Mrs. Brown told me yes, it was Mildred Harris, and yes, it was Robert Harron, adding that for me to have a part in a picture with him was a lucky break for me. He was a big star.

She took me upstairs to a balcony that ran the length of the studio, its back wall one long row of doors. I was to share a dressing room with Mildred Harris, she said as she opened one of the doors to a cubbyhole of a room.

I looked on the door to see if there was a star there. There wasn't even a name.

Just then a vivacious blond teenager came rushing out of another cubbyhole, her arms stacked with clothes. "Here," she said to a cleaning woman, "you can have all my clothes—the good ones, too. My sister Norma just married a millionaire—Joseph M. Schenck —so I'm getting everything new—from the skin out."

I knew who she was even before Mrs. Brown introduced me to her—Constance Talmadge, who'd just been made a star because of her performance as the Wild Girl in Griffith's *Intolerance*. Star or not, millionaire brother-in-law or not, I couldn't imagine anyone giving away all the clothes she owned.

The half block back to our rented bungalow seemed a mile, I had so much to tell Mother and Grandma. Especially about Lillian Gish and Mr. Griffith.

When I did tell them that, Mother said, "I think if I were you, I'd say no more about this. Gossip is a dreadful vice. What goes on between Mr. Griffith and Miss Gish is their own affair, not yours and the other girls'."

I was properly squelched, but I decided anyhow I'd take a good long look at them if I ever saw them together, just to see what I could see. I thought it was terribly romantic.

When Mother said she'd found a tutor for me, I told her I didn't need one, there was a school at the studio. But she said no, my lessons were to be sent to me from my convent school so that when I came home after my six months in Hollywood I'd be right up with my class.

It made sense to my mother. She didn't know, because I didn't tell her, that I wasn't ever going home. I couldn't.

In Barrie's play *Peter Pan,* the directions for locating that place of enchanting make-believe, the Never Land, were very explicit— "second to the right and then straight on till morning." And it was easy to get there. All you had to do was believe—and "think lovely, wonderful thoughts."

Explicit and easy and impossible to find, the Never Land.

Or so it had seemed to me.

For years I had believed, if not in the Never Land of Peter Pan, in the Never Land of Hollywood. Had believed, had thought lovely, wonderful thoughts, and for all that my Never Land was only a continent away, it might as well have been second to the right and then straight on till morning.

Until now. Now at last I had found it. I was right here in it, this place of enchanting make-believe. And I was going to stay here and become a star.

How could I possibly go home?

I was home.

CHAPTER 2

"PAPA, WHAT IS BEER?"

A fifteen-year-old girl going to Hollywood today would be cast in suitable teenage roles—a supporting role as a kid sister, a featured part as a problem student or a juvenile delinquent, a starring role in a *Junior Miss* type comedy, even the once-in-a-lifetime Lolita. But whatever the character, no matter how large or how meaty the part, she would be essentially a young teenager playing a young teenager.

In my first film in Hollywood, *Bad Boy*, I played a soubrette, a city girl who tries—and fails—to woo a bucolic young man away from his country sweetheart. Even in my third film, *Hands Up!*, shot about three or four weeks later, in which I was cast as the daughter of a railroad magnate, I was not a little-girl daughter. The climax of my part in the movie was a scene in which, kidnaped and being held for ransom, I was attacked by the villain. He, too, I might add, failed.

Hollywood—and, for that matter, the moviegoing public, whose wants Hollywood always found it profitable to satisfy—was not overly interested in those days in what real-life fifteen-year-olds thought and did. It was not, on the other hand, so depraved—or demented—as to be suggesting via its films that a real-life fifteen-year-old girl should woo away from or even woo, let alone be attacked. Hollywood used fifteen-year-old girls in relatively grownup roles in films of love and adventure for a very practical reason.

Klieg lights, once they came into general use, and Cooper-Hewitt lights, too—those mercury-tube forerunners of today's fluorescent lights which gave a blue cast to your skin and turned your lips purple—were crude affairs. Only the youngest, clearest, most wrinkle-free skins could stand up to the scrutiny of closeups under their harsh glare.

A fifteen-year-old beginner in those first few years of motion pictures was likely to become a star by eighteen or nineteen. She was also likely to become a has-been by twenty-two unless she took extremely good care of her complexion or, as was the case with Pauline Frederick, still a star in her early thirties, the cameraman obliged by keeping a discreet distance away.

Most of the stars when I arrived in Hollywood in 1917—female stars, at any rate—were barely in their twenties—Norma Talmadge, Blanche Sweet, and Anita Stewart, who, like Pauline Frederick, always played young marrieds caught in the bridge-or-babies con-flict—Mary Pickford, Marguerite Clark, Lillian Gish, and Mae Marsh, who always played young, pure, innocent heroines in the throes of their first love. Since Hollywood wasn't any more interested, gen-erally speaking, in the grittier problems of older marrieds, and since the public couldn't bear to see America's Sweetheart and her friends descend from the lofty—and virginal—pinnacle of ro-mance, all of these stars faced the prospect of oblivion before they were hardly more than old enough to experience in their own lives what they portrayed with such expertise on the screen.

What saved them—and all of us coming after them—was an in-novation which came, as might have been expected, from the Griffith Studio. During the filming of *Broken Blossoms* in 1919, word leaked out from the laboratory that in the rushes Lillian Gish, then an aging twenty-two, looked as fresh and young as a child of twelve. Wanting to believe it, hardly daring to, actresses clamored for in-formation. Was it some new kind of film? A new camera? Different lighting?

Nobody could find out. The set was closed to visitors. Billy Bitzer, Griffith's cameraman, was mum.

When the picture was released, we all rushed to see it. What we'd heard was true. Lillian Gish looked astonishingly young. Finally Mr. Griffith let everyone in on the secret. Billy Bitzer had covered his camera lens with black maline, a fine, silk net, the small holes in the material acting as a retouching lens.

From then on, cameramen went berserk. They made test after test, not only with black net, but with pink net, blue net, and, for blondes, gold net. They even tried layers of net, until the faces of some stars were so fuzzy it was hard to tell who they were.

Out of all this experimentation came the diffusion lens. Some of the early ones were made with circles in the glass to break up the light. Others were a crosshatch of fine lines. Eventually they became so refined that today actresses in their fifties photograph like glamour girls.

Men can look younger, too, though the public even in 1917 didn't mind seeing a line or two in a man's face. In the rags-to-riches formula of those days, any man worth his Horatio Alger salt needed firmness of purpose, and firmness of purpose was somehow more convincing in a face that looked as if it had had some prior experience at it.

There was one woman in those early days who flouted convention so far as to play two starring roles on the screen in 1912 at the unbelievable age of sixty-eight. One of the roles, that of Queen Elizabeth, might by a stretch of the imagination be considered a character part, but no stretching of anybody's imagination could make a character part out of Camille. The woman, of course, was Sarah Bernhardt, who could afford to flout convention, though I must say that when I saw *Queen Elizabeth* as a ten-year-old in Tampa, Florida, my critical reaction was she was just a fat old lady who was always flailing her arms about. I much preferred Mary Pickford.

Bernhardt, by the way, came to Los Angeles on one of her perennial farewell tours soon after I arrived there, traveling, as she always did, with a large number of people. On this occasion the whole entourage was booked into the downtown Biltmore Hotel. Bernhardt refused to stay there, saying she had to be by the sea, so she took her personal maid and went to stay at a small inn on the beach at Santa Monica.

The reason she had to be by the sea, it turned out, was she loved to fish. The innkeeper, nearly overcome at playing host to the Divine Sarah, was terrified she wouldn't catch any, but she did. She caught lots of fish. So many, in fact, that she went around afterward telling everybody that the greatest fishing in all the world was at Santa Monica, California.

During the few days of her stay there it undoubtedly was. The innkeeper, taking no chances, put a bathtub under the end of the pier, filled it with fish every morning, and stationed a man beside it to hook a catch onto her line each time it plopped down into the water.

But to get back to film-making in 1917, in particular to my venture as a fifteen-year-old making her first films. I don't know that I thought there was anything peculiar about playing a grownup kind of role. It was what I was used to seeing in the movies myself, and it was what all the other girls my age at the studio were doing.

Most of the stories themselves had an air of unreality about them, or maybe I should say an air of romanticized reality. People wanted to believe that life as it was shown in the movies was life as it could be for them if only they were pretty enough or brave enough or lucky enough; that they, too, would have adventure, find romance, pursue wealth; that no matter how scary or painful or sad any situation might become for them, it would all come out right in the end just as it did in the movies—the kidnaped girl rescued in the nick of time, the train wreck miraculously avoided, the young lovers walking hand-in-hand into the sunset to live happily ever after.

At that time I was as willing to believe in the reality of this fairytale world as anybody else.

Willing to believe in it and thrilled to my bones to be a part of it.

If I was told to be on the set at nine, I was there at seven-thirty. I hated to go home at night, and I couldn't wait for it to be morning again, so I could go back.

If I didn't happen to be in any of the scenes scheduled for that day's shooting, I went to the studio anyhow. Not just to be there where all of this magic was taking place, though that was part of it, but because I wanted to learn. I was passionate to learn my trade.

I made it through my first film, *Bad Boy*, simply by doing what the director told me to do. In a sense, this was what every actor, experienced or not, did in those days. There wasn't any script. Films

This is the first movie still of Colleen Moore. Uncle Walter decided Kathleen Morrison was too long to fit a movie marquee and he wanted my name in lights.

were shot "off my cuff," as directors used to say. The director did have an outline to follow, but it was a very sketchy outline. He had to rely on his own imagination and story sense, improvising as he went along (and doing, as I look back on it, a really tremendous job).

The actors, in turn, relied on the director to tell them what he wanted, improvising dialogue that seemed suitable to the content and intent of a scene. If, for instance, the director said to me, "You don't like this man, and you just tell him so," I would say to the man, "I don't like you! I think you're terrible! Now go away from me!" When the film was edited, an appropriate title would be inserted to convey to the audience the gist of what I was saying, or if the director happened to like—and remember—the words I'd used, he'd use them.

Films were short in those days, even a feature film no more than four or five reels. In the kind of feature film I worked in, which was called a program film—quickly and cheaply made in order to meet the constant and ever-increasing demand of theater owners for new movies to show—there was no such thing as retakes. It took only a couple of weeks to shoot an entire movie. In my first few movies, it took even less time than that to shoot the scenes I was in.

I arrived in Hollywood two days after Thanksgiving. By the end of the year I'd appeared in three movies. In that time I'd also learned a few things.

I started learning when I saw my first film, *Bad Boy*, at Talley's Theater in Los Angeles. It seemed to me it was released almost the day it was finished. Probably not, but they didn't waste any more time distributing a movie in those days than they did making it.

My part in it as the second lead was small. It had taken up no more than three or four days of the total shooting time. (That didn't bother the homefolks back in Tampa, where a big sign was put up outside the Bijou Theater—COLLEEN MOORE, THE FORMER KATHLEEN MORRISON, in BAD BOY.) But Grandma and I were anxious to see how I looked and acted. At least I was anxious—so much so that I had Grandma at the theater before it opened in the morning.

I didn't look the way I thought I looked at all. My dark red hair, worn now in long curls down my back, photographed patent-leather black. That didn't bother me, but my profile did. I hated my profile, and I hated my nose, and I thought to myself, oh, dear, what am I going to do about her?

I got through my first film, The Bad Boy, *by doing exactly what the director told me to do. You can see I'm keeping a weather-eye on him instead of looking at the camera.*

Her, of course, was me. Maybe that was the first thing I learned. To be objective about this creature on the screen. To think of her as her, not me.

First or not, it was the easiest thing I learned, because as far as I was concerned, not only then, but in all the years I was in Hollywood, she wasn't me. It wasn't that I didn't care about her. I cared very much. Maybe even more about her than about me. And she belonged to me. But she wasn't me, any more than—as I was to learn one day to my sorrow and my pain—I was her.

In any case, right then I was concerned with what could be done about the way she looked.

As the picture went on, I saw that she had good angles, and I saw that she had bad angles. I said to myself, now next time I must remember not to get into that particular position. It's a bad angle.

As leading lady to Bobby Harron in my second picture, An Old-Fashioned Young Man, *I had a new hair-do. It was a do-it-yourself job. I did it with rags and kid curlers.*

I saw something else. A couple of my positions in closeups in *Bad Boy* resulted in something even more distressing to me than a bad angle. Almost no angle at all. Unless you're crazy about ears.

I couldn't figure out how, even knowing as little as I did, I could have contrived to get myself into such an unfavorable position as to be almost totally hidden from the camera. It wasn't until I started working in my second picture, *An Old-Fashioned Young Man,* once again with Bobby Harron, but this time as his leading lady, that I found out.

One day, after we had finished shooting, an old character actor beckoned to me, saying, "Come here, girl, I want to talk to you."

He took me off into a corner and said, "Do you know what Bobby and the rest of them are doing to you?"

I shook my head.

"They're upstaging you, that's what they're doing." He frowned at my obviously perplexed face. "You know what upstaging means?"

I shook my head again.

"Well, now, look here. Suppose you and me are in a double shot— you know what that means, don't you?"

"Yes," I said. "Both of us in the camera together."

"Okay. Now. Suppose while we're talking, I move back like this." He moved a step back. "Now in order to keep looking at me while we're in this conversation, you have to turn your head toward me and away from the camera. You've already turned it, see?"

I nodded.

"Okay. Now, while the screen will show my full face, what will it show of you?"

I got the picture. "My ear."

"That," he said, "is upstaging, and if you keep letting them get away with it, you're never going to see much of your face in the movies. Here. Let me show you a little trick." He took me by the shoulders. "Now when a person stands to your left, like I'm doing, you angle your left shoulder a little toward the camera, and then put your right foot behind your left foot. That'll swing your body around, and you'll have a three-quarter view. And then if he starts moving back, you just move back, too, to keep even with him. Get the idea?"

I got it, and thanks to an old man's kindness to a know-nothing beginner, nobody ever upstaged me again. I would have thought, in fact, nobody would try, once they realized I was onto them. But actors are a determined lot.

Some years later, when I was in a featured-player film as it was known in those days—that is, a film in which no one is starred, but three or four people share equal billing at the top—I was doing a scene which called for a triple shot with Milton Sills and Conway Tearle.

Now Milton was a fine and very knowledgeable actor, and Conway was a fine and very knowledgeable actor, and there standing in the center between them was little me, who, by that time, was pretty knowledgeable, too.

The three of us got into position, the lights were turned on and adjusted, the camera got us in focus, and then a crewman came over and put chalk marks around our shoes, as was customary, so we could see where to stand and not move out of focus.

Everything set, the scene started rolling. Pretty soon, Milton began edging back. Well, I thought, he's not going to get away with this, I know what he's doing. So I edged back. Then Conway saw what we were up to, and not wanting his ear to the camera, he moved back, too.

The director stopped the scene, saying, "Now, now, now, you're all out of focus. Stay in your chalk marks."

Once again the scene began. Once again the same thing happened. Desperate now, the director had a stagehand nail a board behind our feet. The scene started again. Pretty soon I saw Milton Sills step over the board, so I stepped over the board, and Conway did the same. The director gave up. He shot the scene by using three individual closeups.

I suppose, thinking back on it, there isn't an actor anywhere who won't upstage another actor if he can get away with it. Including little me.

Upstaging and favoring the good angles of my face were the first technical things I learned. Something else I learned in my second film I would have learned just as well in Tampa, Florida, though not at fifteen.

Because I was a leading lady in this film I had to wear high heels. They were nearly my undoing, and they served to make the picture even shorter than it was intended to be. I wobbled so, all the long shots had to be cut out.

I learned, too, to put on make-up. I had to. We all did. Griffith Studio, as well as the others, was strictly do-it-yourself. That included fixing our own hair—washing it, drying it (by hand—hair driers hadn't been invented yet), and putting it up in curlers and rags to make those beautiful long curls that were the current style.

Hairdressing at home and at the studio was arduous enough. On location it was a trial. You had to round up a washtub from somewhere, get a pitcher for rinsing (many, many rinsings to get the bar-soap out of your hair and the shine back in—shampoo hadn't been invented yet, either) and, if you were lucky, someone to help you. Also plenty of towels. And, of course, on the dusty desert it was not only a trial but an oft-repeated one.

The desert did have one advantage. It was dry. Mary Pickford used to tell about the problem she had once when she was making a picture on location in a humid climate. Her hair, which was as straight as mine was naturally, would start to droop after a while, so shooting would stop, Mary would put her hair up in curlers and rags, and then the whole company would just sit there for an hour while it dried, so she could go before the camera once again in those famous curls.

But I loved it all, do-it-yourself and all, because I was doing, as my mother had said that fateful night in Tampa, the only thing I had ever wanted to do.

More important, I was learning how to do it better all the time—partly because I watched what other actors did and asked them questions and listened to them discuss technical problems with each other and with the director and cameraman, and partly because everything we did in the making of silent pictures was done not just once or twice but over and over and over again. I don't mean, in this instance, retakes or even rehearsals, though they would eventually account for doing the same bit of a scene so many times that sometimes you couldn't keep count. I mean the fact that so many silent movies followed a formula, so that I did the same kind of scene with the same kind of action and improvised dialogue over and over again, playing, for the most part, the same kind of character.

There was a stage melodrama of many years before my time in Hollywood in which an innocent young thing turned to her father to ask in wonderment, "Papa, what is beer?" The line carried over into vaudeville sketches and into the lingo of silent film directors. The director would say to the girl playing the young, pure, innocent heroine, "Get that 'Papa, what is beer?' look on your face."

That look was on my face through a great many movies—too many movies—too many made long after I knew full well what beer was, and a number of other things as well, until there came a day when "Get that 'Papa, what is beer?' look on your face" was enough to curdle my insides.

But not yet. I hadn't made that many movies yet. And if I knew what beer was, I knew precious little else. One day I overheard an older actress talking to a friend about a girl who'd been given a star part by a well-known director. "Of course," she added maliciously, "she paid the price." I wondered how big the price was and if my father could afford to buy a part like that for me.

Most fifteen-year-olds today, I suppose, know the so-called facts of life. I and my girl friends at the studio didn't know them and wouldn't have dreamed of asking anyone. Sex, if it was spoken of at all, was something whispered. The gossip I heard about famous stars

My third movie was a profound drama entitled Hands Up! *I didn't know the facts of life at the time and wasn't sure what was going on. After that one I got fired.*

and producers and directors was heard in fragments, because as soon as I or any of the other young girls joined the circle where the talk was going on, the talk stopped. I doubt that we would have understood it anyhow.

We were fully as innocent as the heroines we portrayed on the screen, though any resemblance between us and them stopped right there. At least, it did for most of us.

Two of the girls I had met on that courtyard at the studio my first day in Hollywood soon found out that life really was the way it was in movies. Within a year Mildred Harris had married Charlie Chaplin, and Winifred Westover had married the big Western star, William S. Hart.

Myself, I wasn't anywhere near being a bride or a sweetheart. I didn't even go out on dates. I don't suppose I would have had time to if anybody asked me, which nobody did. I was at the studio most of the day, I had my school lessons every night with my tutor, and a piano lesson every Sunday, which meant hours of practicing in between.

I didn't care. The only future I was interested in for me right then was my future as a star in Hollywood.

By the end of my third picture I wasn't just interested. I was downright concerned.

On payday I lined up with the other players to collect my weekly salary of fifty dollars. When I got to the window, I noticed that my pay envelope was blue instead of the usual yellow. I opened it and saw inside what I thought was a beautiful letter. It started out, "*We regret to have to dispense with your artistic services.*" I was on top of the world. There it was in print. Artistic services. I was an artist.

Then it hit me. I was fired.

*I got $100 a week for playing the lead in
Little Orphant Annie. I asked for it but
when they gave it to me, I nearly fainted.
I am third from the left on the floor.*

CHAPTER 3

A GOOD HORSE ANY DAY IS HARD TO FIND

I wasn't the only one fired. We all were. According to the rumors, Mr. Griffith had gone broke, and the studio was closing. But it wasn't my pride I was worried about salvaging. It was my career.

I could see Grandma starting to pack at once, relieved that this whole episode was over in little more than a month, and she could get out of this den of iniquity and go home.

It was all I could do to drag my feet back to our bungalow, but I finally got there. I didn't say anything to her when I went in. I just handed her the letter.

Grandma took one look at it and stretched her hand out like a policeman stopping traffic. "Now, my dear, not a word of this to the family. I have some money—enough to take care of us until we see this thing through."

I stared at her open-mouthed.

"Well," she said, "you certainly can't quit now when you've hardly more than started." She beamed at me. "Besides, I like it here in California."

I thought there was no one in the world like my grandma.

As it turned out, we didn't have to dip into her savings.

Mr. Griffith had not gone broke at all. He had simply decided to stop making all those program films such as I had appeared in and devote the operation of his studio solely to the big pictures he himself would direct, keeping on staff only those key players and technical personnel who had been and would be working on his pictures with him.

Needless to say, that didn't include me. But there was the matter of my contract with him. Mr. Griffith's manager called me in to say that if I couldn't find work at any other studio, the contract would be honored until my six months were up. He did more. He sent me to a theatrical agent who, he said, would help me find work.

I soon learned that when it came to getting work at other studios the Griffith name was magic. The Griffith name and one other name.

The first studio I went to in search of a job was Selig, where, the agent told me, they were looking for a girl to play the lead in *Little Orphant Annie*, adapted from the James Whitcomb Riley poem. When I walked on the set, the director looked at me and said, "Do you have an aunt in Chicago named Liberty Howey?"

"Yes," I said.

He nodded. "The part's yours."

I nearly flipped. No questions about my experience. Not even so much as a request to see a still picture of me. Aunt Lib's "Give me Liberty, or give me death!" obviously packed more punch than even I had imagined. At least, men didn't forget her.

When I went over to the business office I decided if they were crazy enough to give me the part without a test, they might just be crazy enough to give me a bigger salary than the fifty dollars a week Griffith paid me. I asked for a hundred dollars a week. They gave it to me without batting an eyelash.

I rushed home to tell Grandma the good news. She didn't bat an eyelash either. She said, "You should have asked for two hundred."

She also said this should be a lesson for me, that with each new job I should ask for more money, even if it was only fifty cents more, because then I would know I was progressing.

I took Grandma's advice, and each time I did get more money, though never enough to suit Grandma. When the big day came in which I signed a contract with First National for ten thousand dollars a week, Grandma—not very much to my surprise—said, "You should have asked for twenty."

After I finished *Little Orphant Annie* for Selig, I got a job opposite

Charles Ray at Ince Studio in *The Busher,* a story about a bush-league ballplayer. Again without a test. Because of the magic of the Griffith name. Because people in Hollywood, who of all people should have known better, had accepted as literal truth Uncle Walter's absurd story about how I was a Griffith find.

So far Mr. Griffith had not so much as set eyes on me. Nor I on him.

Also playing in *The Busher* was a young man whose chief interest in the movies at that time was writing scenarios, though he did play the role of heavy in an occasional film. I had never met him before, but I saw a lot of him from then on. So, soon, did millions of other women. His name was John Gilbert.

In spite of my fears from time to time that free-lancing from one studio to another might be a precarious way to make a living, I had no trouble finding a new job as soon as I had finished the one before, and I ended up making four films in 1918. That doesn't sound like much compared to being in three films in only a little over a month in 1917, but then films were getting longer and taking longer to shoot, and my roles were getting bigger, too, taking up more shooting time.

I suppose I must have had crushes on some of the men I played opposite in my early movies, but it wasn't until I was given the role of leading lady in a Western called *The Wilderness Trail* when I was sixteen years old that I completely lost my heart to a thirty-nine-year-old cowboy turned actor, Tom Mix.

I had played in a Western once before—*Hands Up!* for the Griffith Studio. It had been a great experience for me. It had been an eye-opener as well.

The characters and situations in most silent Westerns were as unrealistic as those in most other films, but they were the only things that were. Everything else about Westerns was the genuine article.

The cowboys were real cowboys who found riding the range in Hollywood movies easier and better-paying than on the Lone Prairie. The Indians were real Indians—their costumes and headdresses not out of wardrobe but handed down to them from their ancestors.

The train we used in *Hands Up!* was a real train which hauled the entire company out into the desert for location shots and hauled us back again. The private car belonging to my railroad-magnate father in the picture was also real—and with such polish on its elegant wood paneling the walls had to be soaped down to kill the glare.

Most astonishing of all, the train robber was real. He was such a small, insignificant-looking man it was hard to believe at first he was none other than Al Jennings, the great train robber who had once been the scourge of the West. But he was, and now, having served his time behind prison walls, he was making a respectable living in Hollywood doing the one thing he knew so well how to do.

I don't know if he liked holding up trains for the movies or not. I do know he didn't like me. I was absolutely fascinated by him and followed him around between scenes staring at him. Finally I screwed up my courage and blurted out, "Show me your gun, please, will you?"

He scowled at me. "What for?"

"I want to see the notches for all the men you've killed."

He gave me a withering look. "I never killed anyone, and I am now a minister of the gospel."

What a letdown that was.

Before I was assigned to the picture the director asked me if I could ride a horse. I said I could, because I knew I wouldn't get the part otherwise, but I didn't know if I could or not. Still, I figured riding a horse couldn't be too difficult. Why I thought that I don't know. The only time in my life I'd ever been on anything even approaching a horse was when I was twelve years old and a friend let me ride her Shetland pony. It was a short ride. I fell off.

Almost the first scene we shot was one in which I was supposed to be riding hell for leather up the side of a mountain trying to escape the bandits who had kidnaped me. As I climbed into the saddle, the head bandit, Monte Blue, who later became a star and whose real name was Montgomery Bluefeather, said to me—no doubt from the look on my face—"Girl, have you ever been on a horse before?"

"No," I whispered to him, "but please don't tell. I want to play this part so badly."

"All right," he said. "Now. See that horn on the saddle? When I hit this horse on his rump, and the camera starts, you just hang onto that horn. I'll be right behind you, chasing you, and when we get to the top of the mountain, I'll get you off all right. Meanwhile you just try to stick in the saddle."

To the surprise of both of us, I made it to the top of the mountain. But I hadn't exactly stuck in the saddle. By the time Monte got to me I was sitting between the horse's ears.

When I was on location with Tom Mix *in* The Wilderness Trail, *he tried to teach me how to shoot. I had a crush on him but he never noticed it. He preferred my mother's company to mine.*

In addition to rescuing me, Monte suggested I take some riding lessons. I did, and when the opportunity came, early in 1919, to play opposite Tom Mix in *The Wilderness Trail*, I could say I knew how to ride a horse and mean it.

Many people think that men who are actors and wear grease paint aren't men. Some aren't. Tom Mix, who not only wore grease paint but some of the fanciest clothes I've ever seen, was about as real a he-man as they come. Not that he wasn't vain and proud of his looks. He was. But he was a little more proud of his horse's looks than his own. In fact, he loved his horse Tony more than he loved anyone, even, I'm afraid, his wife.

Tom was a tall, handsome man, part Indian—and proud of that, too —with a slim no-hips figure and a face tanned to leather by the sun. He had strong jaw lines, a large, slightly hooked nose, ebony black hair, and brown eyes so dark they were almost black. In my love scenes with him I nearly swooned away—though I must say I didn't forget to keep the best side of my face toward the camera.

The fact that Tom Mix considered me a little girl whose mother was more interesting to talk to than I was—Mother, who was about Tom's age, always came out West to be with me on long locations— didn't bother me in the least. I was absolutely enchanted by him and would sit for hours listening to him tell stories about his life.

As a young man he had joined the Marines and fought in the Boxer Rebellion in China. From there he went to Africa and saw service in the Boer War. At one time he was a sheriff in Oklahoma. Another time, as a U. S. Marshal, he captured a pair of cattle rustlers single-handed. He'd even faced a firing squad in Mexico after joining Francisco Madero's forces there, but talked his way to freedom. His own life was many times more exciting than anything he ever did on the screen.

Like all the other cowboys on the set, Tom was for real in that department, too.

The biggest event in a cowboy's life at that time was the Pendleton (Oregon) Roundup, with all the best cowboys from all over the West competing in it for the gold belt buckle that was top prize. To win it, a man had to outdo everyone else in roping, riding, bronco busting, bulldogging a steer—all of the traditional rodeo events.

Tom Mix wore one of those gold belt buckles. (So, too, did Hoot Gibson, another top cowboy who became a star and later married my friend Sally Eilers.)

All the wranglers, as the cowboys were called, took great pride in their appearance. No woman on the best-dressed list was ever as particular about the way her clothes fit her as they were about theirs, and Tom Mix, who had his clothes custom made at Porter's in Prescott, Arizona—as every cowboy did who could afford it—was the best-dressed of them all. He even had Western style evening clothes. One I remember was a purple dinner suit, worn over black boots and with a large black Stetson. But my favorite was his white tuxedo, so beautifully fitted to him he looked as if he'd been born wearing it.

Real class he was, as the cowboys used to say about him. They were right. A real sure-enough classy cowpuncher. The best.

Tom had a cattle ranch somewhere in the West—in Nevada, I think—the TM Bar ranch, with his brand the initials TM over a bar. Everything he owned had his brand on it—saddles, automobiles, guns, clothes. Even his handkerchiefs had his brand embroidered in the corner.

This was no more than might be expected of any wealthy cattle rancher with a brand of his own. But again Tom outdid them all.

After he married one of his first leading ladies, Victoria Ford, a beautiful, fragile girl who loved diamonds as much as he loved to shower her with them, he bought a huge Italian villa for her in Beverly Hills.

In her mind's eye Victoria had it all decked out with beautiful French antiques when, to her consternation, Tom told her it had to be furnished Western style.

He insisted. She wept. So a compromise was reached. The villa had two large adjoining drawing rooms. The first was hers, done with Aubusson rug, delicate Louis XVI furniture. Through double doors beyond was Tom's "settin' room," the walls covered with animal heads, Navajo rugs on the floor, mission-type furniture.

But there was no compromise to the villa's crowning touch. That was straight Tom Mix. On top of the roof was a huge sign displaying in electric lights his beloved TM Bar brand. Everybody for miles around knew where Tom Mix lived.

All of the cowboys in Hollywood were what we would call characters and what they themselves no doubt thought of as being individualists. They swaggered about the studios and up and down Hollywood Boulevard in their cowboy clothes. They did things to attract attention, like driving around in an automobile with a saddle slung over the hood, or having a specially made horn that blasted forth an Indian war whoop. Maybe it was just smart publicity, or maybe it was because they couldn't ride horseback down Hollywood Boulevard to a saloon on Saturday night, shooting off their guns and whooping it up.

I say that latter, because when we went to Flagstaff, Arizona, to shoot location scenes for *The Wilderness Trail*, and when the following year Tom asked me to do another film, *The Cyclone*, with him (after first making sure my mother would come along!) and we went on location to Prescott, whooping it up at the saloon on Saturday nights, guns and all, was exactly what the local cowboys did.

Even the towns looked like the towns you still see in the movies and on television. Flagstaff was only a few blocks of buildings along a dirt street, with another dirt street down beside the railroad lined with saloons. At night, especially Saturday nights, when the cowhands came to town to spend their week's wages, that street really hopped.

But the replicas we see today of Western towns and the re-creation of jumping Saturday night saloons aren't the only things that are authentic.

In Prescott, where we made *The Cyclone*, my mother and I stayed at a hotel that looked like something straight off a movie set—a balcony across the second-story front held up by posts and covering the sidewalk below it. One Saturday night Mother and I were standing on the balcony just outside our bedroom when we saw two cowboys walk in opposite directions down the street, turn, take aim, and fire. And saw one of them fall dead.

The most eerie thing about it—and the only thing not like the movies or television—was that nothing happened. No rushing of people out of the saloon. No sheriff and his posse saddling up to ride after the killer and hang him. Only the sound of honky-tonk music from the saloon as the man who was left got on his horse and rode away into the stillness of the night.

It may have been because cowboys and Indians in the early Westerns were real cowboys and Indians (nor was Al Jennings unique—two of the Daltons were still alive then and busy at the studios playing badmen in Westerns) that most of the movie stunts were real, too—that is, performed by the actors themselves, not by stuntmen doubles.

The cowboys were always doing stunts, even between scenes. They rode Cossack—the rider passing from one side of the horse under the horse's belly to the other side. They rode Roman—standing astride two horses going at a running pace. They also took some awful spills, which I suppose was why they'd never let me try either of those stunts. I would have if they'd let me. I'm afraid I didn't have much sense whenever I made a Western. I always wanted to do everything the cowboys did.

I did get to do my own stunts in the movies. We all did our own stunts. It was a matter of pride.

There was one exception. Tom Mix's horse Tony.

Tony had at least five different doubles to perform his stunts for him. Tom wouldn't let Tony do them, for fear he might break his leg. It was a matter of practicality, I guess, as well as love. The way Tom looked at it, there were plenty of stars around and plenty of leading ladies, but a good horse was hard to find.

In my first picture with Tom, *The Wilderness Trail*, I was supposed to have been kidnaped by dope runners, taken to Chinatown, and locked in an opium den (well, I told you the stories were pretty far-fetched).

The climax of the picture came when Tom, riding his faithful horse Tony (that is, one of the doubles of faithful horse Tony), galloped up four flights of stairs to rescue me, and we came crashing down, horse and all, through the ceilings of all four floors.

The crashing down was, of course, the big stunt. The opium den, which was built on the back lot of the studio, had floors which were made of chicken wire, covered and then lightly plastered, so that the weight of the horse and us on him would make the floors crash through, yet give enough support to break each fall for us.

It sounds scary. Looking back on it, I think it probably was scary, but I had such confidence in Tom I never even questioned doing the scene.

Everyone in the studio came out on the back lot to watch—maybe even to hold their breath watching.

We were a crashing, smashing success, and when we finally arrived down on the ground, a great round of applause went up.

To Tom it was all in a day's work. He was only pleased the horse hadn't been hurt.

In another scene the horse, with Tom and me astride, had to jump through a plate-glass window. At least, it looked like glass, but no glass ever smelled that delicious. It was actually a very thin pane of sugar candy—the theory being that candy was less dangerous than glass, though I must say that as we plunged through that brittle candy, the edges looked very sharp to me. But then, with Tom in the saddle, I would have jumped across the Grand Canyon if he had said it could be done. He was a hero to me off the screen as well as on.

The most frightening stunt in *The Wilderness Trail* took place on

Location was among the more primitive experiences of early Hollywood. This is the way we filmed The Desert Flower *in the Mojave Desert. The setting was too authentic for comfort.*

location in Flagstaff. In my first Western, *Hands Up!* I was kidnaped as part of the story. This time I was kidnaped for real.

An Indian on a nearby reservation took a fancy to me, sending a present to me every day at the hotel—an Indian doll, a silver bracelet, a turquoise ring—finally a note saying he wanted to marry me, that I'd look so pretty in a tepee cooking his food over a fire. Neither Mother nor I paid any attention to the note.

One day I wasn't scheduled to work until afternoon, so I spent the morning at the hotel (probably washing my hair—it would take that long to do it). After lunch one of the cowboys picked me up in a buckboard wagon to take me out to the location, an hour's drive from town.

About halfway there, an Indian rode up on horseback and came alongside the wagon saying I was his squaw. He'd come to take me home where I belonged. When the cowboy told him to ride on, he muttered something and came closer. The cowboy struck at him with his whip.

With that, the Indian moved right up against the wagon and grabbed me, lifting me off the seat and into his saddle. Off we rode, me kicking and screaming, the cowboy after us, whipping the horses to try to keep up with us.

We'd gone about the distance of four blocks when I maneuvered myself into a position where I could kick the horse. The horse reared up, and I fell off. (There is something to be said sometimes for falling off a horse.)

The Indian, to my relief, rode away. Apparently he found himself a more docile squaw. We never saw him again.

The head cowboy in my second Tom Mix picture, *The Cyclone*, was Buck Jones, who also became a well-known movie star. Buck taught me to rope. I became pretty good at it—not good enough to jump into the rope and twirl it over my head as he and the other cowboys could do, but good enough so that five years later, when I was starring in my own Western, *The Desert Flower*, I could spin a rope with ease.

Buck also taught me how to roll a cigarette with one hand. I became an expert at that, but unfortunately I was never called upon to do it in a movie. I did come across my dad one time, however, rolling one with both hands and doing a pretty sloppy job of it. With one hand behind my back—fingers crossed—and acting as if this was really nothing at all, I rolled him out a perfect cigarette. When he stared at me in disbelief, I winked at him and said, "It's what comes of going on roundups with cowpunchers."

Tom was highly respected by the ranchers, because he was one of their own. When most people made Westerns in which a herd of cattle had to be frightened into a stampede for a scene in the movie, the ranchers made them pay so much for each cow after the stampede was over, claiming usually a loss of about three pounds per head. For Tom there was no charge.

The Cyclone was a movie about cattle rustling, and a ranch-owner friend of Tom's let us use his entire spread for the location shots. He also, since it happened to be roundup time for him, let us go along while his cattle were being branded. We spent one entire day in the saddle—Mother, too—interspersing movie scenes with real-life action.

At the same time that a young bull was branded, it was castrated, making it a steer. Afterward the cowboys would fight to see who got the "fries," as they called them. They would roast these small glands over the branding fire and eat them, the word being that "fries" gave them great sexual powers.

The word couldn't have been too far off. Today, doctors use a hormone called Testosterone to increase fertility in childless men.

One day one of the cowboys told us of a deserted town a couple of hours' ride away. Since there was a road, we went by car. It was a weird—and ghostly—place. The village looked lived in, but there was no one there, not even a dog or cat. On the shelves in the general store were bolts of calico covered with dust. A dirt-covered display case contained threads and pins and other notions. There was a half-full barrel of beans and some very old strings of garlic. Some of the houses had furniture in them. It was as if someone had said, "All out!" and the townspeople had packed what they could carry and fled.

What had happened there was not the plague—not the classic kind, anyhow. The mine nearby had closed, and when a new strike was made in Colorado, everyone had rushed there to stake a claim.

Perhaps the most memorable experience I had in this, my discovery of the West when it was still really the old West, not long removed from pioneer days, was seeing my first desert sunset. In the desert there is no twilight. One moment the sky is brilliant with reds and purples, and almost the next totally black.

I remember sitting with Tom and some other cowboys around a dying fire watching the sunset. Suddenly, without warning, that flash flood of blackness came. I thought it frightening and said so. Tom said, "There's nothing about darkness to be frightened of. It's a covering that's saved many lives on the desert."

Having heard so much about his life, I supposed he knew whereof he spoke.

To me the West will always be a colorful and romantic place, and to have seen it with and through the eyes of Tom Mix was one of the high spots of my life. All I could think was where else would it be possible for a girl my age to have had such experiences except in the movies?

As a cowboy, Tom Mix had few rivals off screen. On screen he had a big one—William S. Hart.

The two were as totally unlike as you can possibly imagine. Hart was a tall, thin man with small, close-set blue eyes which, seen behind a gun, made him look like Sure-Shot Sam, the Western man.

Shortly after this still was made of the camera crew and me in The Desert Flower, *I fell off that hand car and broke my neck. But anything for my art!*

He was anything but. A Shakespearean actor, he came to the movies via the legitimate theater, hired by Ince Studio in 1914, after his performance as the original Messala in the stage production of *Ben-Hur*, to be their Western star.

Hart never did his own stunts. He couldn't. But the public didn't know. Maybe they wouldn't have cared if they did. He had a big following.

His following didn't include me, though I'm sorry I never had an opportunity to play opposite him. Being a William S. Hart leading lady would have helped my career, and my career always came before my emotions. Almost always anyhow.

For a long time Bill Hart lived with his maiden sister Mary in a big house in Hollywood. Norma Talmadge was said to be his big love, but he ended up marrying my friend Winifred Westover in 1918—he a man of forty-eight, Winifred no more than seventeen or eighteen.

When they returned from their honeymoon, the rest of our gang at Griffith thought it would be a great idea to dress up in cowboy clothes with cap pistols and go call on Winifred, bride of the big Western star, shooting off our guns as we arrived.

From our reception, it hadn't taken Winifred very many days to find out that life, after all, wasn't exactly the way it was in movies. She came running out of the house looking scared to death, with a "please go home" expression on her face.

We probably would have, but Bill came out behind her and asked us to come in. We sat down feeling awkward and silly. Bill pulled Winifred onto his lap, and we talked for a few minutes, wished them happiness, then beat it out of there.

Later, when they were divorced, Winifred told me her story. That day as she sat on his knee he kept pinching her—and they weren't love pinches either. He was cruel to her almost all of the time.

At dinner her first night in the house she took the chair at the foot of the table, whereupon her husband flew into a rage saying his sister would sit there, she was the head of the house.

The sister, in turn, treated her like a trespasser. Since Bill sided with his sister in all things, including her, Winifred finally gave up and went home to her mother.

I cannot fathom why Bill Hart married Winifred in the first place. If he had loved her, they might have overcome the age difference. But he finally admitted himself that the only person he ever truly loved was the woman who dominated him all his life—his sister.

After Winifred's baby was born, Bill made a great fuss in the press about how Winifred wouldn't let him see his darling son. She told me she once sent the little boy with a nurse to Hart's office, but the secretary sent them away. Hart refused to see him.

I have to say that William S. Hart's friends adored him. Many women loved him. My own feelings about him are colored, I'm afraid, by his shabby treatment of the young girl who was my friend. Whenever I think of him I still see him as he looked at us that day out of those tiny, hateful eyes—as if he would like us to vanish in thin air.

When I put that up against the kindness and generosity of Tom Mix, the contrast is such that no matter what rivals they might have been on the screen, there is no rivalry between them as far as I'm concerned. Tom Mix wins hands down.

But then Tom Mix was, as his cowboy friends put it, real class.

Mother came to nurse my broken neck. This was the only peaceful location I ever had. I was once kidnaped by an Indian, who carried me off, kicking and screaming, on his horse.

Among my first Hollywood friends were Bessie Love (left) and Corinne Griffith (center). In spite of the warm climate I bought my first fur coat.

CHAPTER 4

MAY I ASK WHO'S CALLING?

One day during those months when I was still under contract to Griffith but working at other studios—I was at Ince at the time making *The Busher* with Charles Ray and that occasional heavy, John Gilbert—a message arrived asking me to come over to the Griffith Studio that afternoon when I finished work. The great man who had "found" me wanted at last to meet me.

My knees wobbled so walking that familiar half block from our bungalow to the studio I wasn't sure I'd make it there. My throat was so dry I didn't think I'd be able to say anything to him if I did.

He was standing out in the courtyard in front of the studio talking to someone, probably about the movie he was making then— a movie about the First World War called *Hearts of the World*. He'd just returned from Europe, where he'd filmed location shots— some of them right in the trenches. Now he was here in Hollywood to shoot the interior scenes.

I suppose I expected him to be ten feet tall and to look the way I imagined God must look. Mr. Griffith was a kind of God to movie people—spoken of with reverence, looked upon as someone almost too legendary to be real.

Far from looking like God, he didn't even look like a director. Most directors in those days favored riding habits and boots. Mr. Griffith, who was somewhat under six feet tall, had on an ordinary brown business suit—a rumpled one, at that—and a big straw hat.

He wasn't at all handsome. He had an exceptionally full mouth, the lower lip hanging down, and his nose, a hooked nose, was enormous—way out of proportion to the rest of his face. I made some comment about it one time to Lillian Gish, and she said he was very proud of his nose, because it showed his Welsh ancestry (as did his full name, seldom used in full—David Lewelyn Wark Griffith). He was, in fact, supposed to be descended from a line of Welsh kings. I can believe it. No one I ever knew could look or be quite so imperial as Mr. Griffith. When I met him I had an impulse to curtsy.

In spite of my dry throat I managed to acknowledge the introduction, but whenever I get nervous, my Southern accent returns, and the voice I heard coming out of me was so thick with Georgia and Florida, I looked around to see who was speaking.

Mr. Griffith laughed and said, "I didn't know you were Southern."

He was Southern himself—from Kentucky. For a few minutes he talked to me about the South, putting me at ease. Then he asked me if I would like to play a bit part in *Hearts of the World.*

That nearly undid me all over again. Would I like to? To work in a Griffith picture was the dream of my life.

Besides, as I told him after I got my wits back, wasn't it about time I did, since he'd been the one to "discover" me?

He laughed with me about that. Then he told me to come to the studio the next morning and get a plain blue smock from wardrobe before coming on the set. I was to play the part of a French child in a household of people enduring an aerial bombing attack by the Germans.

If I had wobbled all the way over to the studio from our bungalow, I floated all the way back. I couldn't believe it. Working for Griffith at last. I had visions of being a star overnight. After all, wasn't it said that a bit part in a Griffith film was better than a featured part with anybody else? Wallace Reid had played only a bit as the blacksmith in *The Birth of a Nation.* When the picture was released, he became a star. Lightning could strike twice.

The set I reported to the next day was a room in a French

farmhouse which had been partially destroyed by the bombing. The actors assembled, the prop man threw some Fuller's earth over us to make us look as if we'd been splattered with dirt and plaster.

In one corner of the room was a broken Provincial dresser with an alarm clock on it. My bit was to be so terrified by the bombing that I ran to the clock, setting it ahead to make time pass and the bombing be over.

This was a pure Griffith touch. His pictures were filled with them.

I rehearsed the bit several times. Mr. Griffith was kind, but it was more than that. There was something about him that made me want to do even more than I was capable of doing just to please him.

The small scene, when it was finally shot, apparently did please him. I left at the end of the day thinking my golden hour had arrived.

When I saw the picture I wept. The sequence had been cut out.

After the release of *Hearts of the World*, Mr. Griffith closed his Hollywood studio and took his company to Mamaroneck, New York, just outside New York City, where he bought a large estate and built a studio on it. Out of that studio came some of his greatest financial and artistic successes, among them *Broken Blossoms*, *Way Down East*, *Orphans of the Storm*. Out of that same studio came the failures that drained away his fortune and brought him to ruin. No, not quite to ruin. It remained for Hollywood—the Hollywood he had created—to do that.

David Wark Griffith was—is today—the biggest name in Hollywood. All of the so-called new ideas are outgrowths of his ideas.

Film technique was virtually unknown until he came along. Most scenes were filmed as if the actors were performing on the stage of a theater, the camera stationed in the center, back far enough to take in all the action going on in front of it.

Griffith did not initiate the use of such devices as multiple camera set-ups—shifting the camera from one spot to another in mid-scene—flashbacks, long shots, closeups, fade-ins, fade-outs, cross cuts, and accelerated editing, but as a director for the old Biograph Company in New York he was the first to make use of all of these devices together and to evolve from his experimentation with them the basic technique of making motion pictures.

I can remember hearing the story about how horrified the heads of Biograph were when Griffith started using closeups. "Why," they said, "the public won't stand to see a chopped-off body on the screen or a face with no body showing at all. It won't make any sense to them."

It made sense to them right from the start. Everything Griffith did in the way of film technique made sense to them. Most important of all, what he did made motion pictures the exciting, creative art form that it is. The movies owe David Wark Griffith an enormous debt.

They repaid it by breaking his heart. By not letting him do the one thing he wanted to do, the very thing he had made it possible for everyone else in Hollywood to do—make motion pictures.

At the end, out of the many he had helped, he had only one true friend left—his great love, Lillian Gish.

Lillian Gish is one of the most wonderfully warm and generous women I have ever known, beautifully and unbelievably educated—self-educated, because she never went beyond the third grade in school—a dedicated actress, strongly career-minded, yet feminine to her very soul.

Lillian Gish was the real *femme fatale* in Hollywood. Not Jean Harlow or any of the other sex symbols on the screen. I think men were embarrassed when they went out with Harlow. I do know she never had any really big-time beaus.

None of the sex symbols did—the Theda Baras, the Clara Bows, the Barbara Lamarrs. They sat home on Saturday night while girls like Lillian Gish and Janet Gaynor and Bessie Love and Norma Shearer had dates with all the big producers and directors and the wealthy and social Easterners. They were the kind of girls men wanted to be with and be seen with.

The list of men whose hearts Lillian Gish captured is a long one. And an impressive one. Colonel Robert R. McCormick of the Chicago *Tribune* said she was the most fabulous woman he had ever known and asked her to marry him. George Jean Nathan spent an entire summer in Europe with Lillian begging her to marry him. Nathan's co-editor of the *American Mercury*, Henry L. Mencken, was mad about her. Joseph Hergesheimer's heroines were all Lillian Gish. He couldn't have her, so he mooned over her on paper. Read

We all knew each other in the picture business in those days. Here I am between Dorothy Mackaill (left) and Mary Astor (right). How do you like my hat?

Cytherea. The girl is Lillian. Jack Gilbert, when he was playing opposite her in *La Boheme,* said she was "the elusive dream girl." King Vidor, who directed the picture, said, "She represents the woman every man hopes to find." Joseph Medill Patterson, Colonel McCormick's cousin and owner of the New York *Daily News,* was enchanted with her. He said she was the most intelligent woman he ever knew, as well as the most romantic.

There were more. And she wouldn't marry any of them.

Because of David Wark Griffith? I don't know. I doubt that anyone ever will.

There was much speculation in Hollywood my first years there about Lillian and Mr. Griffith. People said this was one of the greatest love stories in movie history. Yet they were very formal with each other on the set. He always called her Miss Gish, and she

always addressed him as Mr. Griffith. Whenever they went on location, Lillian's mother and sister Dorothy went along. So nobody
really knew for sure how things stood between them.

They did have between them a dedication to work that has seldom
been equaled. Richard Barthelmess, who played opposite Lillian in
Way Down East, told me years later that in the scenes where Lillian
is floating on a piece of ice dangerously near the falls, Mr. Griffith
let her do the scene without using a double. In another scene she
insisted, in behalf of greater realism, on lying on the ice until her
lips were blue and her face frosted with snow.

Lillian told me once that Griffith asked her to marry him, but
she would not say why she refused him—whether it was because
she didn't love him or because she had made up her mind that
marriage and a career didn't mix.

Whatever happened between them, Griffith soon began courting
a young woman named Carol Dempster, who had played a bit part
in *Intolerance* and small parts in some of his other pictures. More
significant in the long run, he began giving Carol Dempster starring
roles—roles that should have gone to Lillian.

No one, least of all the formula-loving movie public, could understand his interest in this new girl. She was not at all the soft,
feminine, innocent-looking creature who was the Griffith type. She
was nice-enough looking, but she had an angular body and a thin,
sharp face. Her eyes were beautiful—big and brown—but not much
expression showed in them on the screen.

Griffith became infatuated with her, lost his head over her.

He lost his perspective as well.

When anyone in public life, from politics to pictures, begins to
believe his own press, his downfall is in the making. Griffith had
read so much about his ability to discover talent, he became convinced
he could make another Lillian Gish out of Carol Dempster. It was
a fatal error. She couldn't act, and he was unable to teach her to
do so.

Nor would the public accept her. In 1921 he starred her in a
picture called *Dream Street*. The picture flopped. Against all advice
he starred her in another picture the following year, *One Exciting
Night*. It, too, was a failure at the box office.

Meanwhile Lillian Gish, his greatest star—and a proven moneymaker—was ignored. Lillian, fed up with Griffith's treatment of her,

left his studio to sign with another at three times the amount Griffith had been paying her.

The profits Griffith had made from his Gish spectaculars were used to finance the Dempster pictures. As each picture he made with her lost money, he soon went broke. He borrowed money to finance more films. When they, too, failed, he became bankrupt. He now had no alternative but to return to Hollywood to look for work (without Carol Dempster, who retired from the screen and married somebody else).

There is an old saying still current in Hollywood that a director (or a star either, for that matter) is only as good as his last picture. No matter how many successes a director may have had, once he makes a bad film he's on shaky ground. Two in a row can wreck his career.

When Griffith arrived in Hollywood he found that the big companies were reluctant to hire him because of his recent failures. United Artists finally let him shoot a film about the Civil War era so dear to his heart—a film called *Abraham Lincoln,* for which he himself had written the script.

Abraham Lincoln was a talking picture. It cost a lot of money, and money is always king in Hollywood.

Critical reaction to *Abraham Lincoln* was mixed. Some critics said Griffith had surpassed himself, that he was reborn. Others said the parade had passed him by, that he couldn't handle the new medium of talk.

It was the reaction at the box office that really counted. The public wasn't interested in the picture, and it was a financial failure.

Griffith made another picture called *The Struggle.* After its release it was found to be so bad it was recalled.

Word got around that Griffith had lost his touch, that he was senile. The fact that he was drinking too much didn't help counteract the rumors.

He wandered around like a lost soul. His whole life lay in making motion pictures, and nobody would let him make any. Producers refused to see him. When he called them on the phone, they were too busy to talk to him. People who knew him went out of their way to avoid him. Other people laughed at him. Laughed at D. W. Griffith, the man who had made all their swimming pools and their race horses possible!

Eventually the rumors and stories about him stopped, to be supplanted by something far more destructive. He was just plain forgotten.

One day he was killing time walking down Hollywood Boulevard when he saw a crowd gathered in the forecourt of Grauman's Chinese Theater. A young star was putting her hand- and footprints in the cement for posterity and the tourist trade.

Mr. Griffith walked over to watch the ceremony. As the news cameras began rolling, he came closer and smiled at the girl. A policeman tapped him on the shoulder, saying, "Move on, buddy. No loitering." Griffith, the man who was the father of it all, moved on.

There was one who stayed faithful. Lillian Gish. Incensed at the treatment given Griffith, she stormed the studios trying to shame them into giving Griffith a picture to direct. She never got anywhere, but she never stopped trying.

Was it love for him—a making up on her part for the love she had once denied him? Or was it simply the unswerving loyalty of an old friend who believed in his genius as firmly now as she had in the bygone golden years?

No one could say. No one knew.

I don't know that it matters. Whichever it was, it came to the same thing.

One night during this time Lillian asked me and a few other friends to dinner at her house. Griffith was to be there.

I wanted to weep when I saw him. He was old. Not body old so much as soul old—old and empty, as if he had been beaten with discouragement until he had become devoid of any emotion whatever.

Lillian must have seen him as the rest of us did, but she put on a great performance. She led him into conversation, getting him to reminisce until the light returned to his eyes, and for a brief time he became once again the strong, vibrant, imperial man he had been.

Mr. Griffith died in Hollywood in 1948 at the age of seventy-three. In the years since his death, he has been acclaimed everywhere as the Master. Honors are paid him. His films are shown in art museums around the world, where he is acknowledged to be the greatest film director who ever lived. In Hollywood there is talk of erecting a statue of him.

Hollywood started acclaiming—and reclaiming—David Lewelyn Wark Griffith almost at once. Great crowds of people attended his funeral. All the big names in Hollywood were there.

They were anxious to pay tribute to him.

They could afford to. He was dead now. Safely dead.

A scene from Look Your Best (*1921*).
The man in the overcoat is Antonio
Moreno. I'm the one without wings.

CHAPTER 5

THE EGG-CRATE WALLOP

Shortly after making my first picture with Tom Mix in 1919, I made a second picture with Charles Ray at Ince Studio called *The Egg-Crate Wallop*, a story about a prize fighter whose previous experience as a drayman handling heavy egg crates had given him a wow of a punch. In one of the scenes I was supposed to go through a door, be hit on the backside by the door, fall down, and come up with a reaction that would get a laugh.

The director worked on the scene with me one entire afternoon, but—in comedy lingo—I just didn't know how to "take it."

I knew then I needed comedy training, but I didn't do anything about it until the following year when I read an article in *Photoplay* in which Cecil B. De Mille said that no girl could be a great dramatic actress unless she had comedy training. This was why he was looking to the slapstick comedy studios for his future stars.

That decided me.

At that time the two great comedy studios in Hollywood were Mack Sennett and Christie Brothers, and I didn't know which to apply to for a job.

Grandma decided that one.

I knew if I went to Sennett's (where De Mille said he had found Gloria Swanson and had just now found a Spanish beauty with great dark eyes and split-second timing named Bebe Daniels, who had not only had Sennett training but had also been Harold Lloyd's leading lady) I would have to start out as a bathing beauty.

I was standing before the long mirror in my bedroom to see if I could make the grade, when Grandma came in wanting to know what I was doing in a bathing suit with no beach in sight.

I explained.

Grandma said, "You will not be a bathing beauty as long as I am with you. If you have to parade around with only half your clothes on to be an actress, I'm taking you home tomorrow."

I went to Christie Brothers.

After I explained to Mr. Charlie, the business-manager brother, and Mr. Al, the director brother, why I was there, we made a verbal deal, sealed with a handshake. I was to be paid two hundred dollars a week for one year, with the privilege of making outside films. Mr. Charlie further suggested that any money an outside studio might pay for my services over my two hundred weekly would be mine to keep.

Mr. Al was as good to me as his brother. While I was with Christie Brothers I made two two-reelers and two five-reelers under his direction, and under his direction I learned the comedy technique I needed so badly for my career.

It was during this time that Hollywood itself was given an egg-crate wallop. It reacted about the same way I had when the door hit my backside, knocking me flat on my face. It didn't get a laugh either.

Grandma was so shocked when she read the story in the paper, she was on the point of packing our belongings and taking me back to Tampa. Roscoe (Fatty) Arbuckle, a top star at Paramount, was accused of murder.

Murder of about the worst possible kind.

A girl named Virginia Rappe, who played bit parts at Paramount, had attended a party in a suite of rooms engaged by Fatty Arbuckle and some fun-loving friends at the St. Francis Hotel in San Francisco over the Labor Day weekend of 1921. On Monday afternoon, hearing screams of anguish from the suite, house detectives burst in to find the girl lying on the bed in Fatty's bedroom almost nude and hemor-

In two-reelers like The Roman Scandal, *made by Christie Brothers, I got my comedy training. Grandma wouldn't let me apply to Mack Sennett for a job as a bathing beauty. She threatened to take me home.*

rhaging badly, a drunken Arbuckle trying to help her.

The hotel doctor was sent for. He diagnosed her condition—a punctured bladder—and she was taken to the Wakefield Sanitarium, where she died a few days later. When the story broke, Fatty's name was broadcast to the world as a lecherous beast who had raped an innocent girl.

This was no image for a funnyman idolized by the children as well as the adults of a nation. (To give you an idea of Fatty's hold on the affection of children and the impact this story had on them: because the girl's name happened to be Virginia Rappe, a great many children thought the word rape was coined from this awful happening.) Newspapers across the country screamed their shock and

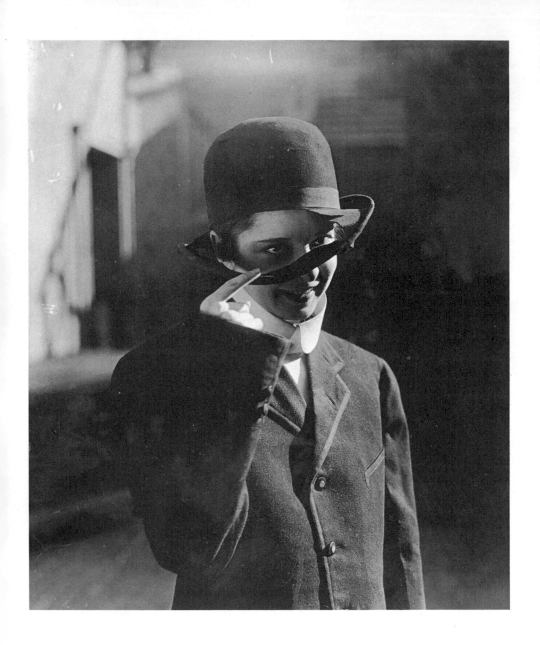

Her Bridal Nightmare *was the name of
the film in which I played this waif. I
hesitate to remember the plot!*

indignation in banner headlines and front-page stories. Paramount canceled Fatty's contract.

Fatty was tried for murder and acquitted, the evidence proving he had had nothing to do with the girl's death. She had a history of serious bladder trouble, had, in fact, consulted the hotel doctor about pain in her bladder only the day before. Additional evidence proved that Virginia Rappe was no innocent girl, but quite the contrary. This wasn't the first time she had lent her obliging presence to men on drunken weekends.

In spite of this evidence, newspapers kept the story alive, playing up Fatty's debauchery and the girl's "innocence." My Uncle Walter in Chicago helped by printing some of the biggest and juiciest headlines. The public as well as the press demanded Fatty's hide and got it. He was dispatched—and speedily—to oblivion. (And not left in peace even there. For years afterward the Fatty Arbuckle story was hashed and rehashed as one of the greatest sensations of its kind in an era not yet used to that particular kind of sensation.)

On the strength of this episode studios inserted a so-called morality clause in all new contracts to the effect that if an actor became involved in a scandal his contract would be canceled then and there.

But Hollywood's troubles were not yet over.

After I had been working at Christie Brothers for some months (we had made both two-reelers, *A Roman Scandal* and *Her Bridal Nightmare,* and one five-reeler, *So Long Letty,* adapted from the Broadway musical), my agent sent me over to the Neilan Studio to see about a part in *Dinty* with the child star Wesley Barry.

I knew what Marshall Neilan looked like before I met him at his studio. Before becoming a director he had been an actor. I'd seen him in films playing opposite Mary Pickford at the Bijou back in Tampa.

As befitting one chosen to guide America's Sweetheart along the untrod path of love right up to the threshold of bliss, he was a good-looking man with curly dark hair, big blue eyes, and clean-cut features. I liked him the minute I met him. I also hoped he would like me. As one of Hollywood's big-shot directors he was in a position to help my career.

He liked me. At least, he hired me—at $750 a week, no less!—and when *Dinty* was finished, he offered me a one-year contract at the same grand salary.

The Christie brothers were as pleased as I was. In spite of the fact that I still had six months to go on my verbal agreement with them (and would make one more five-reeler for them, *His Nibs*, starring Chic Sale), they insisted I take Neilan's offer, convinced this was my big chance, anxious for me to make good, content to be able to say one day that Colleen Moore had once been a Christie girl.

The Christie brothers, as my cowboy friends would say, were real class, too.

Maybe I was luckier than most people in my dealings in Hollywood, but I don't think so. Hollywood had its share of skunks, the same as any other town or industry, but it had many more good, decent people, in spite of the public's conviction that we were living in a veritable Sodom and Gomorrah.

The only skunk I'd ever come up against was a man named Magee. After I made *Little Orphant Annie* for Selig, the New York office arranged a contract for me to make another picture, *A Hoosier Romance*, at a salary of $150 a week. Mr. Magee, Selig's Hollywood manager, handed me the contract to sign, saying, "Here it is—a very good contract for a little girl just turned sixteen."

I looked at the contract, and it said $125 a week. When I protested, Mr. Magee said I had misunderstood.

Being under age, I had to mail all my contracts to Mother to sign. Since I didn't know what else to do at that moment, I went ahead and mailed it. I found out later that he had cheated me.

I was so angry I used to dream of the day when I would become a star and would somehow be given a chance to get even with him.

The day came. I was a star, and some minor executive job was being filled at the studio. Mr. Magee was pointed out to me as the candidate for it, and I was asked if I knew him. I said yes, I'd known him years before at Selig Studio (and had since made a picture whose title expressed my feelings about him exactly—*Slippy McGee*). I thought to myself, here's your chance, girl. Then I looked at him again. He looked so old and so frail and so in need of a job I couldn't do it. I just said he was excellent at Selig and I was sure he'd be excellent in this job. They gave him the job.

The Christie brothers were right about Neilan being my big chance, though stardom was still three years away. Marshall Neilan, or Mickey, as his friends called him, was to be responsible for a number of important and exciting things that would happen to me—some of them also two and three years away. Some, but not all. It was because of Mickey Neilan that I at least nibbled at the edges of the big excite-

Marshall Neilan, better known as Mickey, hired me to play in Dinty
*at $750 per week. He became a lifelong friend and a big influence in
my life. We're both Irish.*

ment that happened in Hollywood on the first day of February in
1922.

Excitement? If the Fatty Arbuckle case had rocked people in Hollywood, this one left them reeling.

One night about a year before that time Mickey called to invite
me on a double date for an evening of dinner and dancing at the
Cocoanut Grove. My date was a young man he knew from Pasadena.
Mickey's date was Mary Miles Minter.

Mary Miles Minter was a very beautiful blonde with long curls
who was a big star at—again—Paramount, where studio executives
were trying to make her into another Mary Pickford.

According to studio gossip, Mary's mother, Mrs. Shelby (Mary
Miles Minter's real name was Juliet Shelby) was so particular about
her darling daughter she never let her out of her sight. She was with

her every minute on the set (my mother never came near a set except for location trips, nor my grandma either), and she wouldn't permit Mary to have a date or go anywhere unless she or Mary's sister Marguerite Shelby was along.

This eagle-eyed surveillance, according to the same gossip, didn't exactly stem from mother love.

Mrs. Shelby was one of those well-born Southern women who never let anyone, including the fan magazines, forget it. As a girl she was of the genteel poor. Having wangled a million-dollar movie contract for her daughter, she was now of the Hollywood rich. And determined to stay there.

Mary had reached an age where she wanted romance and a little freedom. The thought of losing this gold-mine daughter to a husband filled Mama with such terror she became almost insanely jealous.

That night when we picked Mary up, she had a boy with her named Thomas Dixon, of the Eastern pencil-making family. Mickey was a bit startled when Mary introduced the boy as her escort, but she explained later that her mother only agreed to let her go, and go unchaperoned, because she was under the impression Mary had been invited to a large party being given by Marshall Neilan, and that many girls our age besides me would be there. Since the Dixon boy was known to her mother through friends, Mary figured her chances of going were better if he was along.

Playing all the angles at once, Mary had also met her mother's initial objections by threatening to stop making movies.

I'd never met Mary Miles Minter before, but I began to get an idea of what the studio gossips were talking about.

She asked me how old I was. When I said eighteen, she said she was seventeen, almost eighteen, and tired of being treated as if she were six years old.

We had a gay evening. Mary, in fact, seemed almost too gay. She was like a bird released from a cage—laughing, chattering, dancing, her face flushed with excitement. She never stopped. Mickey was amused, the Dixon boy enchanted.

The moviegoing public was somewhat less enchanted when it read in the morning papers on February 3, 1922, that Mary Miles Minter's director, William Desmond Taylor, aged forty-five, had been found murdered in his bungalow the previous morning—shot once through the small of his back by a .38-calibre revolver—and that in the closet of his bedroom hung a little pink silk nightgown with the initials MMM embroidered in the center of the yoke.

Further investigation uncovered, in the toe of one of Taylor's riding boots, a package of passionate love letters written to him by Mary Miles Minter.

Informed by a neighbor of Taylor's death soon after Taylor's houseman discovered the body when he arrived for work, Mary arrived on the scene, clawing her way through police lines, sobbing and screaming out her love for Taylor. Interrogated later by the police, Mary said she and Taylor were to have been married as soon as she was of age and could get away from her mother.

That dear lady, who had been openly antagonistic to Taylor, found herself regarded as a first-class suspect. One of Taylor's neighbors, Faith MacLean, wife of the prominent actor Douglas MacLean, had heard what sounded like a shot ring out from the direction of Taylor's house at eight o'clock the evening before. Going to the window to investigate, she saw a man come out of Taylor's house, stand there a minute to look both ways, then hasten down the alley. But there was something about the man's appearance that didn't sit right. A cap was pulled well down over his face, a muffler hiding the lower half. The suit on his short body looked bunchy. Under oath at the preliminary hearing, Faith MacLean testified that the man looked more like a woman dressed as a man.

The fleeing murderer, if such it was, was not the only person trying to disguise his or her identity.

William Desmond Taylor, it soon developed, was not William Desmond Taylor at all, but one William Cunningham Deane-Tanner, an Irishman from County Cork as well born, if not so vocal about it, as Mrs. Shelby herself. Well born, well educated, and, in his previous life as an antique dealer in New York, where he was married to a wealthy and social ex-Florodora girl and the father of a daughter, well established.

One day he went out to lunch and didn't come back. Nor did he go home. The following day he phoned his office and asked to have $600 brought to him at the Broadway Central Hotel. The employee who brought the money found his usually impeccably dressed employer disheveled, red-eyed, and haggard, and with his mustache shaved off. Tanner took $100 and instructed the man to take the balance to his wife. He then vanished, to be heard from no more.

His adventures during the next few years gradually came to light. He went to Alaska three times in search of gold. He was shanghaied onto a sailing vessel and taken around Cape Horn. He worked as a clerk for a Western railroad, as a bookkeeper in a mine, played in stock companies in Boston and Chicago, and toured Hawaii with another troupe. Finally he landed in Hollywood.

He now became William Desmond Taylor, beginning as an actor, winding up as a director—and as a director, made Mary Miles Minter the big star she was.

A brother, Dennis Deane-Tanner, had followed William to New York, went to work, married, fathered two children. He was continually broke and borrowing money from his brother. Shortly after William's disappearance, Dennis also disappeared.

William Desmond Taylor had a valet named Edward P. Sands, who seemed to have Taylor completely in his power. Sands forged checks in Taylor's name, stole clothes and valuables from him and pawned them, yet was neither fired nor punished. Sands also knew Taylor's true identity. Pawn tickets found after the murder were in the name William Deane-Tanner and were for items Taylor told friends Sands had stolen from him.

Was Sands Taylor's missing brother? If so, he was missing again. He disappeared two weeks before the murder.

A year and a half before his murder, Taylor had appealed to an assistant U.S. attorney for help in breaking up the traffic in drugs, mentioning that a friend of his, a well-known actress, was being taken by the dope peddlers for more than two thousand dollars a month. The attorney was under the impression that Taylor was more interested in saving his friend than in wiping out the drug traffic. Taylor had, however, spent over $50,000 of his own money toward that end.

Now Sands, brother or not, was suspected of being connected with the dope ring.

Speculation, in fact, was endless. Had Taylor's murder been ordered by the dope ring? Was Sands the murderer? Had Sands been murdered, too? Or had Sands been paid by the real murderer to disappear, so that guilt would be shifted to him?

Each day the story became bigger and bigger in the papers. It was more exciting to us than any picture being made at any studio, especially since we knew all the characters. Only real life, which regularly gets away with murder, could have produced it.

The last person (at least the last of any consequence) known to have seen Taylor alive was his good friend Mabel Normand, the most popular comedienne on the screen. On her way home that evening, she stopped at Taylor's house to return a book she had borrowed. As she was about to walk into his house (the front door was open—Taylor never bothered to lock a door) she heard Taylor talking to someone, apparently on the phone. Not wishing to eavesdrop, she walked out onto the courtyard which Taylor's house and seven like it formed a U shape around, waited a few minutes and came back.

Hearing no voices this time she knocked. Taylor came to greet her, asking her in for a cocktail. Taylor's houseman, who worked by the day, going home each night, served them. Taylor seemed harassed. He pointed to his desk, which was littered with canceled checks, saying, "Sands has disappeared, but before he went he forged my name to thousands of dollars worth of checks. His signature is so good I can't tell it from my own."

Taylor asked Mabel to stay for dinner, but she begged off, saying she had to report on location early the next morning. It was then about 7:30 in the evening.

Walking with Mabel to her car, Taylor said, "I have the strangest and most ghastly feeling that something is going to happen to me."

A half hour later he was dead.

Had the murderer been there all along—talking to Taylor before Mabel arrived, going to the back porch to wait until she and the houseman left? Three half-burned cigarettes were found at the back door.

Was blackmail involved? When Taylor's body was discovered near his desk, arranged to look as if he had had a heart attack, his check book lay open with a pen alongside, as if he had started to write a check and then thought better of it. He was known to have had a large sum of cash on him that day—$2300—telling friends he intended to deposit it the next day. Instead, he had deposited it that same afternoon.

More speculation in the papers. And implication by insinuation. Insinuation, too, by intimation.

And nothing ever came of it.

Well, not nothing. Not by a long shot. But no solution. No photograph of Dennis Deane-Tanner could ever be found to see if he was Sands. Sands himself was never located, although a worldwide, lengthy search was made for him.

No clue of any consequence was ever turned up. It seemed to us almost as if the police didn't want the case solved, as if they were marking time until the furor would die down. The district attorney who handled the Taylor case was later sent to prison for taking bribes in another case.

Marguerite Shelby sued her mother for $133,000 for "protection" during the investigation. After the investigation ended, Mrs. Shelby went to Europe, to return seven years later asking to be cleared of any suspicion in the Taylor murder. Mary Miles Minter sued her mother for an accounting of the million dollars paid by Paramount for Mary's services—money which Mary had never seen. Much of it was missing, but she retrieved enough to live on comfortably.

She needed it. Her career as the portrayer on the silver screen of sweet American girlhood was finished. As one wag put it, "Let this be a lesson to all rising young actresses—never have your nightgowns monogrammed."

In Hollywood, where the William Desmond Taylor murder continued to be a lively topic of discussion for many years, I heard one opinion, and on good authority, as they say, that Mary Miles Minter didn't have her nightgowns monogrammed—at least, not that particular one—but that some of the top brass at Paramount, deciding she wasn't going to become another Mary Pickford, after all, and wanting to be rid of her, planted the nightgown in Taylor's bedroom. So far as I know, Mary never denied that it was hers, but then I don't suppose, considering her passionate declaration of love for Taylor, and the letters in the toe of his boot, a denial would have done her any good.

But the most tragic victim of the William Desmond Taylor murder was Mabel Normand. I didn't meet Mabel until the following year, but the trick fate—and circumstances—played on her made me shiver, and I never saw her afterward but that I didn't think of the horror of her experience—and wonder about the public, on whose whims the careers of all of us depended.

Mabel Normand made her start in motion pictures, as so many of us

I met practically everybody who was a celebrity in those days—people like Babe Ruth (left) and Bill Tilden (right)—but what I really wanted was a date to go dancing at Sunset Inn.

did, with D. W. Griffith, but in the early days at Biograph in New York along with Mary Pickford and Lillian Gish.

She was a beautiful girl, a petite brown-eyed brunette, and a marvelously funny one. Mary Pickford told me that one Sunday she and her mother were having lunch when in popped Mabel looking so dejected Mrs. Pickford said to her, "What's the matter? Why the long face?"

"I've just come from confession," Mabel said, "and the priest gave me an awful penance."

"Then," said Mrs. Pickford, "you must have been a very bad girl."

"That's the trouble," Mabel answered. "I can't remember what I did last night, because I had too much wine, so I just told him everything I could think of that I might have done." She shrugged. "I figure it's better not to take any chances with the hereafter."

Also working with Griffith at that time was a young actor named Mack Sennett, a bashful, rough sort of man with ambitions to be a director. He fell in love with Mabel, finally managed to bring himself to tell her so, and proposed to her. They became engaged.

Sennett soon found two backers and went to California to set up his own studio. When he became established, he sent for Mabel.

The engagement drifted on for several years. No one knew who kept changing the date. Finally in 1915 Mack said there had been enough postponing and announced that he and Mabel were to be married in two weeks.

Meanwhile a close friend of Mabel's had come to Hollywood looking for a job. Through Mabel's influence she was given one at the Sennett studio. Mabel even advanced money to her. Soon Mabel heard rumors that Mack and the girl had been seeing each other, had, indeed, been seen having dinner together only two days after Mack had announced their wedding date. Mabel went to the girl's house to have it out with her.

The house was dark when she arrived, but victrola music was coming from an upstairs window. The kitchen door was open, so she went in. When she went upstairs she heard Mack's voice coming from the bedroom. She opened the door and when she saw them together —and saw Mack's stricken look—she fled from the house.

As a very young girl Mabel had contracted tuberculosis. Though the disease was thought to have been checked, it had left her in a weakened physical condition. She collapsed now and had to be put to bed.

Mack tried everything from flowers to gags to make amends. Finally a reconciliation was effected between them, but it was short lived. Two nights later, still suspicious of Mack and her friend, Mabel drove to the beach area where the girl lived and found Mack and the girl together in a restaurant booth. Mack later explained that he was telling the girl it was all over between them because he loved Mabel, but Mabel had had enough. So had her frail physique.

Only that day the doctors had told her the tuberculosis was active once more, that she would have to have her lungs drained periodically and spend more time in bed. She collapsed again—such a total collapse it was feared for a while she might never be able to work again.

Mack was crushed. In his attempt to win Mabel back he had a story written for her—not the usual two-reel Keystone Comedy, but a six-reel feature film called *Mickey*. The picture, released in 1918, made a fortune. It also made Mabel Normand the screen's leading comedienne. But it didn't bring Mabel back to Mack. When her contract with him expired, she left to sign with Samuel Goldwyn for $175,000 a year.

With the change in studios came what seemed to be a change in personality. Always conscientious about her work before, she now became undependable, showing up late or not at all. In the middle of a picture she took off for Paris on a wild spending spree. One dress, according to newspaper accounts, was made of real gold cloth and cost $10,000. She drank champagne, bought jewels, became the toast of Paris. Altogether she spent $250,000.

One morning, hung over and filled with remorse, she packed her trunks and left. When she arrived in New York a phone call was waiting for her from Mack Sennett. He told her to come home and go to work, that he needed her. He had found another *Mickey* for her, would persuade Goldwyn to release her from her contract. When she hesitated, he said, "If it were like the old days, I would make you come home."

"If it were like the old days," she replied, "I would never have left." She hung up.

But she did return to Hollywood, and Sennett finally persuaded her to make the film—*Molly O. Molly O* had just been released when the Taylor murder broke in the headlines.

After Taylor had made his unsettling remark to her on that fateful evening, "I have the strangest and most ghastly feeling that something is going to happen to me," Mabel Normand got in her car and went home, ate dinner, read for a while, and went to bed.

Early the next morning a friend called to tell her Taylor had been murdered. She had no more than put the phone down when she heard a wild clamor outside her door. She was later to relate of that harrowing morning: "When the door opened, the wildest mob I ever saw tumbled into my living room—detectives, newspapermen, photographers shooting off flashlights. They eddied around me asking a million questions I couldn't understand. Most left after I told them all I could remember, and I sat there crying, some still staying and asking questions. Finally it dawned on me, hours after they had raided

My mother, Agnes Kelly Morrison, and my father, Charles Morrison (I'm in the middle), always gave me their love and confidence and I always gave them mine.

my apartment, that it might be in some of their minds that I had murdered my friend. That ghastly possibility made me frantic, and I can well imagine the more I talked, the less sense I made. It was a perfectly innocent coincidence that I happened to have been the last person to see Bill Taylor alive."

Not so coincidental in the minds of the public was the fact that Taylor had an actress friend being taken by dope peddlers and the fact that Mabel Normand was taking medication of some kind—perhaps narcotics—for her constant lung trouble. Might not a drug addict kill to avoid exposure or to put an end to blackmail perhaps being demanded to prevent exposure?

At the preliminary hearing proof was presented that Mabel Normand could not possibly have killed Taylor. Her chauffeur and a man named Arto who was in no way connected with her testified to the fact that she had left William Desmond Taylor very much alive. Arto further testified that after she left, Taylor returned to his house alone. Her maid testified to Mabel's arrival at home some distance away soon thereafter—and to the fact that she had not gone out again that evening.

The public, caught up in all the implications, refused to be swayed by the facts. Women's clubs all over the country stormed the theaters demanding that Mabel Normand's films be banned.

Mabel, bewildered and crushed at the stories implicating her in the Taylor murder, turned to the only man she had ever loved in her life—Mack Sennett.

He stood by her, tried to shield her, encouraged her. When he was forced to withdraw *Molly O* from circulation he didn't blink an eye. Or say a word about the half-million dollar loss he took. Instead, he told Mabel he had another story for her, that what she needed was to get to work right away.

When she replied that she was nothing but a liability to him now, he said, "They can't crucify an innocent girl."

But they did.

Mabel made two more pictures for Mack Sennett—*Susanna* and *The Extra Girl*—and she made some short comedies for Hal Roach, but the films were given only a few bookings, so she finally had to give up.

Lost, disillusioned, her physical condition further weakened by the strain and heartbreak she had endured, she hung onto life a few more years. She married a childhood friend, the actor Lew Cody, and seemed in her life with him to have recaptured some of the gaiety and excitement of the pre-Taylor years. But the tuberculosis which had haunted her throughout all those years finally destroyed her lungs, and Mabel Normand died on February 21, 1930. She was thirty-five.

There was, of course, another victim of Hollywood's scandals. Hollywood itself.

From the very beginning the public had influenced what came out of Hollywood by the simple expedient of staying away from those movies it did not like or approve. Now, stunned by the realization that their beloved screen images were not, as they had beguiled themselves into believing, the images of life itself, people lost faith in their ability to participate with intelligence and taste in what had seemed to them an exciting and wonderful dream come true but which, on closer scrutiny, looked more like a shell game.

If the public's reaction to Hollywood's scandals was not quite the tear-stained "Say it ain't so, Joe," it was disillusionment of a kind—box-office kind—sufficient to make Hollywood look to the same salvation Judge Kenesaw Mountain Landis had brought to major-league baseball.

In 1922 Will Hays—eminent, respectable, a recognized public servant—was engaged at a salary of $100,000 a year to try to save the motion picture industry from collapse. From then on every film made had to be passed on by the Motion Picture Producers and Distributors of America—or, as everyone called it, the Hays Office.

The public, relieved of its moral responsibility, could now devote all its energies to enjoying—and believing once again—the new product a revamped Hollywood began turning out for it—Hays Office-approved make-believe.

In Dinty, *directed by Mickey Neilan, I
made my first bid for stardom. Here I
am in costume for the title role.*

King Vidor (left) was my director in a picture called The Sky Pilot, *made on location in Truckee, California. We ran into a spell of unusual weather.*

CHAPTER 6

BOY MEETS GIRL

Charlie Chaplin could be—and often was—as funny off the screen as on it. There was, too, in his life that underlying pathos which made his little tramp the master characterization it was.

Charlie's older brother Sydney, who was also a great comedian —in my estimation as great as Charlie himself—played with me in *The Perfect Flapper* in 1924—one of his last pictures, I think, before he gave up acting to become Charlie's business manager.

Sitting with me on the set between scenes, Sydney told me stories about his and Charlie's childhood in England when they— his mother, Charlie, and himself—were so destitute they had to live in the workhouse, or poorhouse as we would call it.

At fifteen Sydney took a job as cabin boy on a ship going to Australia and began dreaming of making enough money to bail his little brother and his mother out. When he returned to England, he found that his mother had become mentally unbalanced and had been put away. From that time on, the two brothers were inseparable.

In 1910 Charlie, then twenty-one, toured America with Fred Karno's pantomime troupe, which he had joined some years before after getting his start in show business in the London music halls. His skill at pantomime attracted the attention of Mack Sennett, who was by that time making his famous Keystone comedies. It was in such films as *Kid Auto Races at Venice* and *Tillie's Punctured Romance* that Charlie's little tramp with his trick derby, his tiny mustache, baggy pants, oversized shoes, bamboo cane, and awkward gait first became known.

As soon as Charlie and Sydney had established themselves in Hollywood, they tried to bring their mother to California, but even though they guaranteed she would not become a ward of the state, United States law forbade the entrance into this country of insane persons.

Finally, through influence in Washington, and I suppose because of pity for the mother, Congress passed a special law enabling the Chaplins to bring their mother in. Charlie and Sydney bought a house for her in Santa Monica and engaged round-the-clock nursing care.

The pitiful part of it, Sydney said, was that their mother knew nothing of what went on around her. When he and Charlie would go to her house to have dinner with her, she would look at them and then turn to the nurse and say, "Who are these two big men? Where are my little boys?" At dinner she would take rolls from the table and put them in her purse, apologizing, "For the little boys."

Charlie himself once gave a photograph to Carey Wilson, the screenwriter, inscribing it, *"from that little waif Charlie Chaplin."* I've often wondered if he didn't indeed think of himself as that, and if maybe that explained his predilection for child brides.

My friend Mildred Harris was the first of them. His next wife Lita Grey, the mother of his two older boys, was only sixteen when he married her. Paulette Goddard was the one exception, but in spite of her sophistication, Paulette had a childlike quality about her that made her look and seem a teenager. His present wife Oona was in her teens when they were married. Over the years Charlie paid court to many women his own age—Edna Purviance, Pola Negri, Claire Windsor—but he always ended up wheeling a perambulator with some child bride by his side.

(Another teenager, Joan Barry, didn't make bride status and sued him. According to the gossips, Joan wasn't the first, but this scandal hit the papers, forcing Charlie to flee the country.)

Charlie was deathly afraid he would become mentally unbalanced. He couldn't sleep nights. His great friend Sid Grauman, who owned many theaters in addition to Grauman's Chinese, also suffered from insomnia, and he and Charlie became night prowlers. Often Marshall Neilan would go along, and the three of them would dream up gags to play on their friends, calling them up in the middle of the night and scaring the wits out of them with some hair-raising story. Then at dawn they'd go home and go to bed, their night frights gone with the sunrise.

The first time I ever saw Charlie in person was in 1918 or 1919 when Pavlova was making a tour of the United States, and some "private" people in Los Angeles gave a party in her honor one night after the ballet. Why I was even at the party I don't know, since I was very young. Most likely, since my mother's friends were all non-theater people, she was invited, and I went with her.

In any case, I was there, and so was Charlie. To the delight of all of us, Charlie put on a performance that rivaled the one the partygoers had just come from. He did an imitation of the great Nijinsky (then retired and living in a sanitarium in Switzerland), with leaps and *entrechats* that were sensational, yet he'd never had a ballet lesson in his life.

I have seen him imitate a bullfighter, and Manolete in all his glory was never as graceful. Nor his kill as funny. One time at Marion Davies', Charlie imitated Lord Duveen. He even *looked* like Duveen as he went from painting to painting, commenting on each one.

He could imitate the sounds of any language, making you think he was actually speaking it. Many a foreigner subjected to Charlie's performances strained his ears in bewilderment at hearing his own language, yet not understanding a word of it. Double talk in twenty languages!

But of all the performances Charlie ever gave, the one I cherish most was one given to five select—you might even say five overwhelmed—people.

As the motion picture industry developed and prospered, releasing organizations were formed to distribute films to theaters. One of these releasing organizations was First National, whose board of directors was made up of the owners, or in the case of partnerships, one owner-representative, of twenty-six of the most powerful theater chains across the United States—Balaban & Katz in the Chicago area,

Ruben & Finkelstein around Minneapolis, Sanger Amusement Corporation in New Orleans, Moe Mark in New York, Robert Leiber in Indiana, the Skouras Brothers in St. Louis, etc.

In 1922 these twenty-six men, anxious to get more and better films for their theaters and wanting to develop their own box-office stars, decided to make First National into a producing organization as well. Richard Rowland, production head at Metro who had made Valentino's great picture, *The Four Horsemen of the Apocalypse* in 1921, was brought in to head the new producing company—his office in New York. A publicity man from the legitimate theater named Earl Hudson was appointed head of the studio in Hollywood, where the films were to be made.

The producing company had been in business less than a year when the twenty-six owners gathered together in Hollywood for a board meeting, the number one topic on the agenda their purchase of 1923's sensational bestseller, Giovanni Papini's *Life of Christ*. The movie adapted from it was to be the big picture of the coming season, with Mr. Rowland himself supervising the production of it.

Since 1917, when Charlie Chaplin had gone into independent production, writing and directing his films as well as acting in them, he had been releasing his films through First National and had been one of their most valuable properties.

This was no longer so. As a founding member, along with Mary Pickford, Douglas Fairbanks, and D. W. Griffith, of a new releasing organization, United Artists, Charlie had left First National when his contract with them expired in September of 1922.

Nevertheless, he invited Mr. Rowland and three of First National's owners to lunch at his studio while they were in Hollywood—I suppose they thought just for old times' sake—and since Charlie's former bosses were now my bosses—I had signed with First National in 1922—they invited me to go with them.

When we arrived, Charlie ushered us into his studio living room. On one wall was a large bay window, the bright California sunshine streaming through. It was a beautiful day.

We were all sitting there chatting, waiting for lunch to be served, when Charlie stood up and, turning to Robert Leiber, the president of First National, said, "I hear you've bought Papini's *Life of Christ*."

Mr. Leiber nodded.

Charlie nodded, too. "I want to play the role of Jesus."

If Charlie had bopped Mr. Leiber over the head with a baseball bat, he couldn't have received a more stunned reaction. Not just from Mr. Leiber. From all four of them. They sat there like figures in a waxworks. Even their faces had turned sort of waxy yellow.

"I'm a logical choice," Charlie went on. "I look the part. I'm a Jew. And I'm a comedian."

The bosses looked more stunned, if possible, than before.

Charlie explained to them that good comedy was only a hairline away from good tragedy, which we all knew to be true. "And I'm an atheist," he added, "so I'd be able to look at the character objectively. Who else could do that?"

They had no answer for him.

He stretched his arms high over his head, his fists clenched, and in a blood-curdling tone of voice screamed, "There is no God! If there is one, I dare Him to strike me dead!"

The five of us sat there chilled and tense, holding our breath, but nothing happened, not even one small clap of thunder. The California sun shone outside, the chirp of birds came through the window, and I suppose God was in His heaven, and all was right with the world—all but for five very shaken people in the Chaplin studio.

There was silence in the car going back until Richard Rowland said, "He's the greatest actor alive, and he'd give an historical performance, but who of you would have the nerve to put in lights on a theater marquee: Charlie Chaplin in *The Life of Christ?*"

Mr. Leiber said wistfully, "It would be the greatest religious picture ever made, but I'd be run out of Indianapolis."

Mary Pickford later told me that one time she and Douglas Fairbanks and Charlie were all sitting around the swimming pool at Pickfair when Charlie, who couldn't swim, got up and jumped into the pool with all his clothes on, screaming, "I am an atheist! If there is a God, let Him save me!"

He was gurgling and going down for the third time when Douglas, also fully dressed, jumped in and pulled him out. Mary, meanwhile, was running around the pool shouting, "Let the heathen drown!"

Maybe it isn't as difficult for a comedian to display in his own life some aspects, at least, of the character he portrays on the screen as it is for the so-called dramatic actor, especially one who is known to movie audiences as a great lover. For one great lover, at least—

in his day the greatest of them all—it wasn't just difficult. It was hopeless.

To most young actresses in Hollywood, including me, Rudolph Valentino had about as much sex appeal off the screen as a lemon. But that wasn't the half of it. The matinee idol of millions of adoring women (even my grandma's heart beat a little faster over him), the personification of male mastery in love, Rudolph Valentino was in his own married life so far from being masterful as to be that most pitiful of all males, the henpecked husband.

A weak man, and a bit on the stupid side as well, Rudy married strong-minded women who soon discovered, if they didn't know it already, that he was a pushover for them. His first wife, Jean Acker, bossed him around until she became bored doing it. His second wife nearly ruined his career—though not intentionally.

At the time, Rudy and I were working on adjoining sets. The Valentino set, as usual, was closed to visitors, so to satisfy the girls in our office who were dying for a close-up look at the screen's great lover, we cut holes in our side of the set, charging a penny a peek.

I couldn't resist taking a few peeks myself, not because of Rudy, but because of the incredible happenings going on next door.

Rudy's second wife was Natasha Rambova, whose real name was Winifred Hudnut—of the Hudnut perfume and cosmetics family. Natasha was an exotic, Oriental-looking girl with a tall, slim figure who painted her eyes slanted and wore turbans—even, it was said, to bed. She had been a dancer, but she decided she wanted to be a writer and do Rudy's scenario for this picture. Submissive as always to wifely demands, Rudy let her do it. The result was quite literally something out of this world.

Every night Natasha would hold a seance, calling forth help from the spirit world in her creative undertaking. Then, pencil and paper in hand, she would go into a trance and start writing. After her out-pourings were typed up, they were brought onto the set the next day and given to the director.

Now even the best scenarios in those days were not the detailed and finished products they are today. Although we had progressed from the sketchy outlines of those earliest years, writers would often leave whole pages blank except for the notation, "Love scene here," or "Comedy routine here," relying on the director's imagination and ability to carry the story along.

The problem for Rudy's director, however, was not what to do with the blank pages, if there were any, but what to do with the others. The script made no sense at all, inspiring one comment that Natasha's "control" must be the now-deceased Laura Jean Libbey bent on proving she wasn't the world's worst writer, after all. (A writer of potboilers about the working girl, such as *When His Love Grew Cold* and *Miss Middleton's Lover,* people used to say of her that Laura Jean Libbey was to literature what the Cherry Sisters were to vaudeville. The Cherry Sisters were so bad, people in the audience threw vegetables at them—and derived such pleasure out of doing it that the Cherry Sisters became a great attraction, but had to perform behind a net to ensure continuing this attraction.)

Word finally reached Valentino's New York financers that the only thing Natasha's efforts were adding up to was a mounting production cost, so Natasha was ordered off the set and a screenwriter brought in to straighten out the tangle.

After Natasha moved out of Valentino's life, Pola Negri moved in, weeping and carrying on at his funeral about how she was his great love. Maybe she was, though Hollywood tended to regard her performance as a publicity stunt designed to bolster a faltering career.

If so, she had ample time in which to perfect her performance. Valentino must surely have had one of the lengthiest memorials in history. He died in New York City on August 23, 1926. A funeral was held there August 30, and on September 2 the body was taken to Grand Central Station to be shipped to Hollywood. A second funeral was held in Hollywood, where he was finally interred on September 7, fifteen days after his death.

By that time public interest—or newspaper interest, at least—had waned, but in the few days after his death, people in New York lined up for blocks outside Campbell's Funeral Parlor waiting to file by his coffin for one last look at their hero.

They didn't come any closer to seeing the real Valentino then than they had in the movies. Adela Rogers St. Johns, covering the story for the Hearst papers, learned on her arrival in New York that the undertakers were so afraid of violence, they had removed Rudy's body to another room, substituting a wax likeness in the coffin.

Though Valentino was the biggest washout of the screen lovers, very few of the others measured up to their image either as far as the girls who dated them were concerned. In fact, in my years in Hollywood, the most sought-after beaus were not actors at all, but writers and directors and producers—men like Victor Fleming, Tay Garnett, King Vidor, Carey Wilson, Winfield Sheehan, Irving Thalberg, William Seiter.

Marshall—Mickey—Neilan was the greatest beau of them all.

His good looks and his Irish humor were irresistible, though the latter was not always so to the studio owners he worked for—the great untouchables he delighted in cutting down to size. One time when he was under contract to M-G-M, and a new contract was brewing, he said to a group of people at the studio, "An empty taxicab drove up this morning, and out stepped Louis B. Mayer."

His relationship with Mr. Mayer was not further enhanced when, at a big M-G-M preview one night, attended by all the brass, the great trademark of Leo the lion came on the screen, blinked, and then gave forth not the familiar growl but a tiny kitten's mew. The audience roared, but Mr. Mayer took it as a personal insult.

On another occasion, during the investigation of the William Desmond Taylor murder, Mickey was eating dinner at the Brown Derby restaurant when he was summoned to a booth occupied by Adolph Zukor, majority shareholder and chairman of the board of Paramount Studio. In plain hearing of the diners nearby, Mr. Zukor shook his finger at Mickey and said, "They're investigating everyone, so you'd better be a good boy."

Mickey nodded. "Yes, I hear they're going through the whole motion picture industry from A"—he paused and pointed a finger at Mr. Zukor—"to Z."

The laugh Mr. Zukor got was not the one he'd intended, but considering that both of Hollywood's big scandals had come out of his own studio, I think he deserved it.

(A third was yet to come, and again from Paramount—the announcement in December of 1922 by Wallace Reid's family that his collapse on the set one month before was due not to nervous exhaustion, as had previously been stated, but to excessive use of drugs.

In my opinion Wally Reid was the best-looking man ever to be in the movies. The pride of Paramount Studio, he received more fan mail than all their other stars put together.

According to his wife Dorothy, Wally had been struck on the head with a rock some months before, and he had been given narcotics to ease the pain. Returning to work too soon, the pain persisting, Wally began taking a small shot each afternoon to see him through the rest of the day's shooting schedule. Before long he was hooked.

Adela Rogers St. Johns was a great friend of Wallace Reid and his wife Dorothy, just as she was a great friend of mine. Adela was also a top newspaper reporter and in a position to influence the press in Wally's behalf after the story broke.

The press was sympathetic this time, but the public, informed of the truth in order—according to the family announcement—to arouse sentiment to the necessity of suppressing the traffic in narcotics, was instead shocked, and Wally's career, as well as his life, hung in the balance.

Adela and Dorothy had persuaded Wally to enter a hospital and take a cure. One day Adela came to our house in tears. When I asked her what was the matter, she told me she had just come from seeing Wally at the hospital. He was completely off drugs now but in very bad shape physically as well as emotionally.

While she and Dorothy were there with him, the doctors told him if he wanted to go back on a half grain a day, he could get enough strength to work.

"Did he?" I asked.

"No," she answered, so choked up she could hardly speak. Wally knew it wouldn't work, she told me, that he wouldn't be able to limit himself to that minimal shot, but would end up hooked again. "He said he would rather be dead."

He died on January 18, 1923. (He was only thirty years old.)

I sometimes think Mickey Neilan preferred making a witticism that was repeated all over town to making a great motion picture. His producers undoubtedly thought so, too, and not without reason. He was always late in arriving on the set, and whenever he had a mob scene scheduled, he wouldn't show up at all, but would let hundreds of extras sit around sometimes for as long as two days doing nothing but draw their pay checks. Yet he had a great talent, and the films he made had an unbeatable combination of humor, heart, and box office.

He drank too much and too often, and when he had too much to drink he could be sharp-tongued and mean. Yet for all his wisecracks he was a kind, warmhearted person. When he went broke and lost Neilan Studio, he wouldn't sign the big contract Goldwyn offered him until he had found jobs for everyone who worked for him.

He made a million dollars and ended up without a dime. He didn't lose it on the stock market as many people did. He spent it—spent it on a great big glorious time. I saw him do it.

He was a charming, crazy, obstinate Irishman who lived a full and exciting life—a complex man and a maddening one sometimes, but never a dull one. And there is something—quite a lot, I think—to be said for that.

I don't know how many romances other than his own Mickey played a part in, but there were at least two, and I remember both of them, one because it was so funny, the other because it was mine.

One afternoon Mickey invited me to go with him to the Chaplin Studio. He was bringing the famous *Ziegfeld Follies* beauty, Peggy Hopkins Joyce, to meet Charlie.

Peggy Hopkins Joyce made her first million dollars as a very young girl in Chicago when her much older husband Stanley Joyce divorced her. From Chicago she went to New York where she worked as a show girl for Flo Ziegfeld and for a hobby collected diamonds, inspiring the coining of the word golddigger.

Her appetite for diamonds momentarily sated, Peggy had persuaded her current admirer to finance a movie in which she would be the star. Since Mickey was a friend from somewhere in both their pasts, he was chosen to direct it.

There were two problems. Though Peggy photographed like an angel, she couldn't act. Mickey was going out of his mind trying to get a performance out of her. The second problem threatened more than the state of his mind. Peggy's boy friend was getting jealous.

Mickey's whole motive in taking Peggy to meet Charlie was in the hope that Charlie would fall for Peggy and take her off his neck.

At least I thought that was his whole motive. I should have known Mickey was as incurable a gag man as he was a romantic.

I couldn't understand why, on the way over, Mickey kept telling Peggy how terribly rich Charlie was. But he did. I supposed he thought adding the world's most famous comedian to her collection might not be enough for her, and to help his plan along he threw in the part about the money.

Anyhow, from the moment Peggy was introduced to Charlie, the success of Mickey's plan seemed assured. Among her other assets— and by this time they were considerable (Harold Grieve, who did the sets for Peggy's film, told me years later that Peggy carried an old shoe box around with her wherever she went, never letting it out of her sight. When his curiosity finally led him to ask her what could be so precious about an old shoe box, she took off the lid and showed him. Inside was five million dollars' worth of diamonds)—Peggy had the most famous legs in America.

She perched on a table in the center of the room, crossed her famous legs, showing just enough thigh to whet a man's appetite, and gave Charlie one of her dazzling smiles. Mickey and I left soon afterward with no Peggy.

In the car going back, Mickey could hardly contain himself. "I knew it would work," he said, shaking with laughter. "How I'd love to see the look on her face when she finds out there won't be any diamonds coming forth from him."

Neither of us were there to see the look on her face, but the newspapers recorded in nice, big headlines what Peggy had to say about Charlie's courtship of her.

Mickey hadn't lied when he told Peggy how rich Charlie was. Charlie was one of the richest men in Hollywood. What Mickey neglected to add was that Charlie was also one of the biggest tightwads. He even cut his own hair.

The big romance in Mickey's own life was more than big. It was spectacular.

At the time, Mickey was engaged to Blanche Sweet, another of the actresses who started at Biograph and who was now stuck in the young married rut on the screen. Before she had a chance to get more than a glimpse into its real-life counterpart, she was displaced.

Like the basketball team that gets knocked out early in the tournament by the ultimate champion and takes what satisfaction it can in saying it took the best to beat it, Blanche, whether she took any satisfaction from it or not, was displaced by a woman who didn't just represent glamour. She invented the word. Gloria Swanson.

In his book *The Founding Father*, Richard J. Whalen expressed the magic of Gloria Swanson so aptly, I can do no better than to quote him: "To the movie audiences of the twenties, Gloria Swanson was the embodiment of the American dream of beauty, wealth, and sophistication. Petite chic, her teeth dazzling white, her coiffure flawless and gleaming like patent leather, she was the queen of Hollywood. Her appeal to men was obvious, yet women, too, were attracted. As they watched her sweep through luxurious settings in sumptuous costumes, she reflected their daydreams. This was what it was like to be rich and beautiful. They studied every detail and imitated what they could. If she dabbed perfume behind her ear, and the label was visible on the screen, sales of that brand leaped . . . The queen of the films exerted an attraction that went beyond commonplace physical beauty. There were more beautiful women in the movies, but none possessed her silken grace and regal self assurance."

Gloria did more than represent all that to her movie audiences. She represented it to everybody in Hollywood as well. And when you add to her glamour a very good mind, a sparkling wit, a talent for conversation, and a childlike quality of mischief and laughter, you get a combination that is devastating. You get Gloria Swanson.

I'll never forget the entrance she made at the birthday party she gave soon after she and Mickey started going together. Her guests had arrived—the guest list a veritable Who's Who in Hollywood and all of us dressed in our dressiest best—cocktails had been served, and all without any sign as yet of the hostess. Suddenly Gloria appeared at the top of the stairs.

There was no spotlight, no flare of drums, but there might as well have been. A hush went over the room as she stood there in a red ruffled dress smiling down at us, looking like a painting by Velázquez.

The room was filled with beauties—Corinne Griffith, Billie Dove, the Talmadges, the Bennetts—but nobody was looking at them. All eyes were on Gloria, drawn to her as if by a magnet.

At the foot of the stairs Mickey stood enchanted, his adoration of her plain to see, an electric wave passing between them that could be felt by everybody present.

After a moment Gloria came down the stairs to greet everyone, smiling, excited, apologizing for being late, saying she had been looking at the surprise Mickey had given her for her birthday—a theater projection room he'd had built in her basement. (The projection room, or at the very least a portable machine, was *de rigueur* in Hollywood, where the established form of entertaining was a small dinner party followed by the viewing of some just-finished movie—borrowed, usually, from the friend who'd just finished it.)

The projection room wasn't Mickey's only present. He had bought every American Beauty rose in Los Angeles and Santa Barbara and all points in between and had them put on a truck and dumped on her front lawn that day, turning it into a rosy red half acre.

Along about that same time he wrote a song for her which, with words added, became a hit of 1922 and has since become one of our great standards—"Wonderful One."

The next we heard of Mickey and Gloria, they were in Europe. In London they had a great and spectacular fight. In a rage, Gloria popped a champagne bottle over Mickey's head. As Mickey said afterward, "Only Gloria would use a magnum—and filled, at that."

Mickey went to Paris, where a two-page cable awaited him from Gloria. In it she told him the only answer was for him to forget her. He cabled her back, FORGOTTEN. MICKEY.

A couple of days later a large, heavy box was delivered to Gloria from Cartier's, the jewelers in Paris. Gloria, thinking how dear it was of Mickey to send a peace offering, hastened to open it. Inside the box was a common garden rock with a note saying, *"This is the load you've taken off my mind."*

Gloria's sense of humor was as highly developed as Mickey's, and she burst out laughing.

With laughter came forgiveness, and they soon made up. But a romance crackling with the high voltage theirs was couldn't last, and it didn't. Mickey went back to Blanche Sweet, and this time he married her. Late in 1924 Gloria went to France to make a picture, *Madame Sans Gene,* and brought back to Hollywood the first of what would eventually become if not commonplace, at least of little more than passing interest—a title. In France she had met and married Henri Marquis de la Falaise de la Courdray.

The pictures in the newspapers showed him to be very handsome, and we were all anxious to get a look at him. We soon got the chance. A gala preview of *Madame Sans Gene* was held in Grauman's million-dollar theater in downtown Los Angeles. I was there. So was almost everybody else in Hollywood. The theater was jammed with the young and the beautiful, all in glittering formal attire.

Just before show time the lights dimmed, and the orchestra struck up "The Marseillaise." A spotlight was turned to the rear of the theater. There was Gloria in a shimmering white gown coming down the aisle on the arm of her handsome, titled husband. They looked like a king and queen from some mythical Balkan kingdom.

The audience, in a gesture of complete spontaneity, stood up and cheered. I have never seen anything like it before or since. But then, as Mr. Whalen pointed out in his book, Gloria was a queen. The queen of Hollywood.

My own romance, when it finally came in 1921, was pretty spectacular itself.

I was ready for it. Ready? I'd just about come to the conclusion that I was another of those Hollywood rarities—the real-life image of one film anyhow, a film I made along about that time, *The Wallflower.*

During my first couple of years in Hollywood, the fact that my social life was barren to the point of being almost non-existent didn't bother me. I was so absorbed in movie-making and so busy with all my various lessons—school work, piano, ballet, horseback riding—I hardly had time to think about, let alone do, all the fun things a normal teenage girl does. But when I reached seventeen—a seventeen made almost unbelievably innocent by my isolation—the natural longings for love and attention—for a beau—began to stir in me.

At the studio I heard a lot of talk about romances between different stars and their directors. So far not one single director had ever said anything to me that couldn't have been said in front of my grandma. No one, director or otherwise, had ever even tried to sneak a kiss.

The older girls at the studio carried on constantly about the big times they had with their dates at the Sunset Inn down at the beach or at the Vernon Country Club, which wasn't a country club at all, but a night spot where there was a dance band and where the prize for the Saturday-night dancing contest was a big gold cup.

According to them, the Sunset Inn was by far the better place. Abe Lyman, who played there, had the best dance band in town, and besides, the gold cups there were bigger.

I was in no position to judge. I'd never been within shouting distance of either one.

Wallace Reid, they said, was at the Sunset Inn with his wife every Saturday night dancing, and he was very good. But, they added, the best dancers of all were Bebe Daniels and Harold Lloyd, who had shelves filled with gold cups.

They said Bebe was awfully young to be at Vernon and the Sunset Inn, but then Harold Lloyd was the nicest young man in town, and

Bebe's family adored him. Besides, they only came to dance, not drink.

(An accident at Roach Studio, where Harold Lloyd made his films, nearly put an end not only to his dancing and acting, but to him. He was posing for a publicity still in which he was to hold a papier-mâché bomb, the flame sputtering along the fuse, next to his wondering face. Papier-mâché bombs were a standard prop in comedy studios. So were bombs filled with powder, and somebody had grabbed a bomb from the wrong bin. Harold lighted the fuse, but the photographer took so long getting ready, he got tired of holding the bomb up and let his hand drop to his side. At that moment it exploded. If he'd still had it up to his face, his head would have been blown off. As it was, he was knocked to the floor, his face torn and bleeding, and half his hand blown off. He was rushed to Methodist Hospital, where the doctors were able not only to save his eyesight but to patch his face so that eventually it healed without scars.)

One time when I was standing on the corner of Sunset and Fountain in the rain waiting for a bus, I saw Harold and Bebe drive by in his stripped-down flivver. The car had no top, and Bebe was huddled close to Harold holding newspapers over their heads.

I had a car of my own by that time—a Hudson the family had bought for me when I was making *Little Orphant Annie*—and a chauffeur to drive it, since I wasn't old enough, but I would have traded it in right then, top and all, and chauffeur and all, for a ride in Harold Lloyd's flivver.

Everything in me longed to get to the Sunset Inn, but I didn't know how I'd ever manage it. Almost the only men I knew were those at the studio, and they were all too old for me except maybe some young third assistant director who couldn't possibly afford the price of an evening at the Sunset Inn. Anyhow, nobody had asked me. I was beginning to wonder if anyone ever would, if maybe I wasn't so unattractive no man would ever want to marry me or even pay me the compliment of making a pass at me.

In all my life thus far I'd had a grand total of two dates—neither of them anything to write home about. One, a friend of my piano teacher, took me to a movie and afterward to an ice cream parlor for a soda. The other, a boy whose family was known to one of my aunts, took me to a dance in Pasadena. Everybody there was my age, but the things they talked about were things I didn't know anything about, and they weren't interested in the movies and what I was doing, so except for the dancing it wasn't any more exciting than going to the movies with Grandma.

My first big moment, romantically speaking, came when I was almost eighteen and was making *So Long Letty* for Christie Brothers. Between scenes I started playing jacks on a packing box near the set. The next thing I knew, who was playing with me? None other than Mr. Al himself, who had already asked me to please stop calling him Mr. Al, because it made him feel so old, and just call him Al the way everybody else at the studio did.

I hadn't been able to bring myself to do it. He was old. To me anyhow. He was actually about thirty-five, but I thought he was at least ten years older than that, probably because although he was tall and nice-looking, he was partly bald.

I thought I noticed the stage hands and other people in the company smiling at us and at each other, but I was too naïve to understand why. They, of course, knew what he had in mind. I was the only one who thought he liked jacks, in spite of the fact that he couldn't seem to get past the twosies.

One day soon after this (he had now progressed to foursies without a mistake) he came to my dressing room to talk about a scene. At least I thought that was why he was there, until he came over and, putting one arm around me, lifted my chin with his other hand, saying, "Colleen, you're a very nice girl."

I stared at him, my heart nearly stopped with excitement. Could this be it? If so, what was supposed to happen next?

Would he ask me to his house to see his etchings? I'd read that this was one approach to make to a girl. Then a more delightful thought crossed my mind. Maybe he'd ask me to go dancing at the Sunset Inn.

One thought after another raced through my mind. Maybe he was going to make a pass at me. How did men make a pass? What did they do? What did they say? How could I say no without making him angry?

I decided I liked him. And, after all, he was a widower, so it would be quite proper for me to date him.

Then I took another look at him, and I could hear my grandma saying when he came to call, "Is it Colleen or me you want to take dancing?"

I blurted out to him, "You've been so good to me, Mr. Al, if you were my own father I couldn't like you more."

He took his arm away and, giving me a kind of cross-eyed look, said, "I feel like your father. Especially right now. What I was saying was you're a very nice girl, and I hope you always stay that way."

I expect what he really felt like was a fool. If he did, he wasn't alone. I felt like one, too.

Mr. Al wasn't the only man I mistered. It was, after all, the way I'd been brought up. The first time I met Mickey Neilan, when he hired me to play in *Dinty*, I addressed him as Mr. Neilan. Then, as I was leaving the set, he called out, "Hey, Irish!"

I looked back, and he grinned at me. "My name is Mickey Neilan. Mickey, remember, and don't ever call me Mr. Neilan again."

I didn't. Mickey, of course, wasn't as ancient as Mr. Al. He was only an elderly twenty-nine. But he had more than a few years on his side. Mickey had, as the Irish say, a way with him.

Although I had graduated from leading lady to featured player two films before I made *Dinty* for Mickey (the pecking order in Hollywood at that time was extra, bit player, leading lady or man, featured player, star), and although I had managed to price myself up to $500 a week for the outside pictures I made while I was with Christie Brothers, still Mickey and *Dinty* were my first real boost toward stardom—first because with Grandma's advice firmly in mind, I asked Mickey for the $750 a week he paid me, and second because on the strength of my death scene in *Dinty*, he decided I was a budding Sarah Bernhardt and hired me to play opposite John Barrymore in *The Lotus Eater*, at the same time signing me to a one-year contract.

When you have a $750-a-week property on your hands, you don't let her sit around doing nothing, and Barrymore not being immediately available—he was playing Hamlet on Broadway—Mickey loaned me out to another studio, where I met another of Hollywood's big beaus. King Vidor.

King looked so nearly my age when I bumped into him my first day there, I took him for an assistant director. A mighty handsome assistant director. He had the whitest teeth and the bluest eyes I'd ever seen, eyes that turned up at the corners, giving him a Tartar look. His hair was black and very straight and brushed back from a high forehead. All in all he was, as my grandma would say, a fine figure of a man.

I found out soon enough that the young man was King Vidor himself, the owner of this great, block-long studio, and that, in spite of his appearance, he wasn't so young, after all. He was all of twenty-six.

All of twenty-six. I have to laugh today at how absurdly young so many of those "elderly" fellows were when they became the owners or the heads of motion picture studios. Irving Thalberg of M-G-M was twenty-seven. Bernie Fineman of Robinson-Cole was thirty. Junior Laemmle, who ran Universal, was barely twenty-five. Ben Schulberg of Paramount, whom we thought of as an old man, was only thirty-two.

But then we were all young—even the motion picture industry itself.

The picture I made for King was *The Sky Pilot.* Since the action was laid in the snow country, we went on location to Truckee in northern California, where we stayed in a hotel over the Southern Pacific Railroad Station out in the middle of nowhere, the village we used in the picture was one the studio built across the tracks.

Another location we used was up in the mountains, about an hour's ride from the hotel. Horse-drawn sleighs took us there in the morning and brought us back at night, the coming back at night the fun part—racing along through pine forests in the moonlight, the snow crunching under the runners in the frosty air, the bells on the horses jingling, all of us singing.

If my life in Hollywood at the studios was an isolated one, it was even more so on those long location trips. At Truckee there wasn't even anybody else around, and nothing to do at night except sit in the waiting room of the station. The nearest movie was in the real village a sleigh ride away. So we made our own fun. We decided to put on a show and asked everyone in the company to prepare an act.

King and I worked all week on a mind-reading act, learning an elaborate code. I was Madam Zaza, he Professor LaTour. We were a big success, but the real thrill out of that performance came over forty years later when I bumped into King one afternoon in Paris. The first thing he said to me was, "Please tell me, Madam Zaza, what it is I have in my hand." Without hesitation I said, "A dime, Professor, a thin dime." We had both remembered.

By the time we returned to Hollywood, Barrymore was concluding his Broadway run, so the rest of my scenes in *The Sky Pilot* were shot quickly, and Mickey and my mother and I headed for New York.

We'd no sooner gotten there than we were whisked off to Florida for the exterior shots. The story of *The Lotus Eater* concerned a millionaire who sailed to the South Seas in search of happiness and was wrecked on an island that was something out of paradise. Mickey had chartered a beautiful black sailboat about a hundred feet long to use in the picture and to ferry us back and forth from Miami to an island off the Florida coast where we shot our scenes.

All of us in the picture wore Grecian robes, Barrymore a short Grecian tunic with high gold-laced boots. He was without doubt the handsomest man I'd ever seen. Every evening after work he'd put on swimming trunks, climb to the highest mast of the boat and dive off, his bronze body silhouetted against the sun. I would catch my breath at the sheer beauty of it.

Barrymore was also as incurable a gag man as Mickey himself. One day when we were working on the island, a group of Mennonites, dressed in their somber black clothes, came trudging along a path between the palm trees. Barrymore spied them coming, hid behind a tree, and as they came up jumped out at them in his Grecian tunic and make-up, screeching at the top of his lungs.

The Mennonites must have thought he was Satan himself. The women grabbed up their skirts and ran off screaming, while the men grabbed their hats and flew right behind them.

The very first scene I played with Barrymore was a love scene in which he held me in his arms while I begged him to stay with me on the island. I was so overwhelmed at playing opposite the great Barrymore (had even gratefully descended a rung back down to leading lady to play with him) I just froze.

Mickey took me aside and kidded with me until I relaxed. But I was never really comfortable working with Barrymore. I was too much in awe of him.

I was so sure he thought I was a complete ninny, I was absolutely bowled over when he asked me to play the ingenue in *Claire de Lune*, which he was going to do on Broadway that season with his sister Ethel.

I didn't get to do it. Mickey wouldn't let me. But I took what comfort I could in the fact that I'd been asked.

We did the interiors for *The Lotus Eater* in New York. I was

The legends about John Barrymore are founded on truth. He was almost unbearably handsome. In my first love scene with him in The Lotus Eaters, *I was so overwhelmed I froze.*

thrilled to be working right where the movies had started, but I was more thrilled about something else. For the first time in my life I became practically a social butterfly. Mickey took me to one party after another—parties filled with celebrities from the theater and other arts, and filled, too, with men of all ages paying attention to me. Mickey even let me go out on dates with a couple of them. I was in seventh heaven.

Then we returned to Hollywood, and it was back to the movies with Grandma again.

One nice thing did happen. A group of press agents from the different studios got together and picked thirteen girls, including me, whom they predicted would be the future stars. A ball was given at the Ambassador Hotel, where we were introduced as the Wampas Baby Stars (Wampas meaning Western Association of Motion Picture Advertisers Society).

Being elected by this group of men who had access to all the news media in Hollywood—foreign news agencies as well as American, because movies and the people in them were now of interest to the whole world—was a big boost up the ladder for me, resulting in worldwide publicity.

But whatever it did for my career, it did absolutely nothing for my social life.

Along about this time a group of us girls formed a club—Our Club, we called it, thinking the name terribly chic. Mary Pickford agreed to become our honorary president, and why not, when our purpose was such a lofty one—to help new actresses get jobs. Too lofty, as it turned out. What we ended up doing was to help each other get jobs. When anyone went to be interviewed for a part and didn't get it, she'd quick call up all the other girls in the club so one of them could.

But Our Club also filled a gap in our lives, providing us with an opportunity to do what eighteen-year-olds everywhere were doing. We met at each other's houses and sat on the floor drinking hot chocolate and eating cookies and talking by the hour. Our favorite poet was Edna St. Vincent Millay. We were always quoting "My candle burns at both ends, It will not last the night; But ah, my foes, and oh, my friends, it gives a lovely light." We felt it would be the height of existence to burn a candle at both ends. Even at one end.

The cartoons of John Held, Jr. we thought fabulous. Our author was F. Scott Fitzgerald—we loved everything he wrote. We dreamed of someday owning a Marie Laurencin painting. We talked about the Russian revolution, which was called the great experiment. And, of course, always and endlessly, we talked about the movies.

One by one the girls became engaged—Mildred Davis to Harold Lloyd (Mildred had taken over as his leading lady, too), Virginia Fox to Darryl F. Zanuck, Helen Ferguson to the Western star William Russell, Patsy Ruth Miller to Tay Garnett.

Finally my turn came.

It was August 18, 1921, the day before my nineteenth birthday. My parents and my brother Cleeve had moved to California earlier that year. Dad was tired of having a separated family, and since he'd become interested in asbestos mines in Arizona, he gave up the business in Tampa.

The phone rang. It was Mickey Neilan calling to ask my mother if I could join him and his fiancée Blanche Sweet (pre-Gloria) that night at the Sunset Inn for dinner. He had an attractive young man for me to meet named John McCormick.

Mother said yes, and my heart leaped. I was going to the Sunset Inn at last!

By the time we arrived there I was too busy staring at John McCormick to even notice the Sunset Inn (which turned out to be a strictly ordinary restaurant, its only claim to fame the music of Abe Lyman).

John was tall—six feet two—long-legged and slim, with a handsome figure and a handsome face—blue eyes and dark hair, a wide mouth, a nose that turned up just a bit. I was absolutely taken with him.

He asked me to dance, and we hadn't gone twice around the floor before he looked down at me and said, "I'm in love with you. When are you going to marry me?"

I was dumfounded.

I was also now almost nineteen. Not a sophisticated nineteen, but, after all, I'd seen a lot of movies. "Call me up in the cold gray dawn," I said, "and tell me that."

"I will," he answered.

When he told me he'd had his twenty-seventh birthday the day before (funny, he didn't seem a bit elderly to me), and I told him my birthday was the next day, he said it was fate, that I must marry him a

My girl friends in Hollywood were all acting in the movies, as I was, and like girls everywhere we organized a club. We called it Our Club and the stated purpose of the organization was to help each other get jobs. I don't remember how effective we were, but I do remember that we had a lot of parties where refreshments were served. Here is a typical meeting of Our Club: Back row, left to right, Anita Stewart, Patsy Ruth Miller, Helen Ferguson, Billie Dove, Carmel Meyers, Virginia Fox, Gertrude Olmsted, Julanne Johnston; Center row, left to right: Kay Hammond, Ruby Keeler, Ona Munson, Clara Horton, Lillian Rich, Loretta Young; First row, left to right, Aline Mac-Mahon, Ruth Roland, Carmelita Geraghty, Mary Pickford, Colleen Moore, Pauline Garan, Ann Harding.

year from this very day. Then all our lives we'd have three days in a row to celebrate.

He also told me a little about himself. A university graduate, he'd worked for a while on a newspaper in San Francisco, where his parents lived—he was an only child—and now he was a press agent for First National.

He'd been in love with me before he met me! *The Lotus Eater* had been released through First National, and John had handled the publicity, sending out pictures of me along with the others. He'd also voted for me as one of the Wampas Baby Stars.

It began to seem like fate to me, too.

At five o'clock the next morning, the phone rang. The voice on the other end said, "It's the cold gray dawn, and I love you. When are you going to marry me?"

This time I had no answer at all.

He asked me to have dinner with him that night. When I said I'd promised to have dinner with Grandma, he said, "Fine. We'll take Grandma with us. See you at seven." He hung up.

At nine o'clock that morning the doorbell rang. Outside stood a man with an enormous bouquet of balloons—about fifty of them, all colors—and a card saying "*Happy Birthday*."

At nine-thirty a telegram arrived, the first of nineteen I was to receive that day. When put together, they told a fairytale, the last one arriving at six-thirty that evening, ending, of course, AND THEY LIVED HAPPILY EVER AFTER.

In between telegrams I received candy, American Beauty roses, a visit from an organ grinder with a monkey who handed me a happy birthday note, and, to top everything, an entire carton of chewing gum (I had told him I liked gum) with a funny jingle on every stick inside.

I was overwhelmed. Grandma said only an Irishman could have such imagination, and she definitely wasn't going to dinner with us.

She should have. That way somebody would have eaten. Neither John nor I took so much as a bite of anything. We just sat and looked at each other, he doing all the talking, me getting more starry-eyed by the minute.

I couldn't understand why, as the days and weeks and months went by, my mother didn't want me to get engaged to him, why she kept saying I should go slowly and not get serious until I was sure.

I was as sure as I could be. I was hopelessly in love with him. And it wasn't as if my mother didn't like him. She did. The whole family did.

Liked him and gave in to him finally, making him change his plans only in the matter of time. On August 18, 1922, we became engaged—my ring from my imaginative John a three-carat diamond held up at the sides by an emerald cut in the shape of a shamrock. We planned to be married a year from that day.

Outside of the fact that we were so much in love, we had the biggest thing in either of our lives in common—motion pictures. And with me being an actress and John a press agent, no conflict. On the contrary, he was a big help to my career, sending out twice as much press coverage on me as before.

I needed his help. I was in trouble.

The trouble started out looking like another of those boosts toward stardom. When Mickey Neilan lost his studio and went to Goldwyn, he was still so convinced I was a budding Bernhardt he sold Rupert Hughes, one of America's best-known writers who was now doing scenarios for Goldwyn, on casting me in *The Wallflower*.

Although I was still a featured player, and billed that way, my role in the picture was a starring one. *The Wallflower* was a big success. It should have made me a star, but it didn't. I couldn't figure out why.

I made another Rupert Hughes picture—an Irish story Rupert wrote especially for me, *Come On Over*. It, too, was a success. Still I remained a featured player.

A third Rupert Hughes picture, *Look Your Best*, was the story of a ballet dancer—and contained, incidentally, a dance sequence that was way ahead of its time. I was to dance into a pool, then the rest of the ballet would be shot underwater. My costume was a skin-tight net covered with fish scales made of dime-size gelatin sequins. The music started, and I danced in. Since the pool was heated, and the air was not, I stayed in the water while the cameramen adjusted lights and lenses for a closeup. The closeup was never made. By the time they got to it, the sequins had melted, leaving me practically in my birthday suit. Since the sequins couldn't be duplicated (and I'm not sure we would have dared try it again anyhow), the number was cut out.

During the filming of *Look Your Best*, right after John and I became engaged, Rupert Hughes (he was also the uncle of a shy,

gangling teenager who used to visit me on the set—Howard Hughes)
gave a big party at the Cocoanut Grove. I knew that all the Hollywood brass would be there, including Mr. Goldwyn himself, and I
wanted something really elegant to wear.

The best friend of the working girl at Goldwyn Studio was Miss
Sophie Wachner, head of wardrobe and designer of all the clothes worn
in Goldwyn pictures. Whenever any of the girls had an important
date, she'd go to Miss Wachner with a long face, saying she had
nothing to wear to impress her beau. Miss Wachner always came
through—but under pain of banishment if any of us ever told anyone.
We didn't even let on to each other. If I was out dancing and saw a
girl wearing a gown I was wearing in a picture, I'd pretend I'd never
seen it before. And vice versa.

I went to Miss Wachner now and begged to be allowed to wear
the beautiful beaded dress to the party that I was wearing in *Look
Your Best*. She said, "Yes, if you watch out for the catsup and don't
wiggle around in your chair. The beads can't be duplicated."

During the party Mr. Goldwyn asked me to dance. He said, "That's
a beautiful gown you're wearing. And expensive looking."

I thanked him and thought, "It is expensive. It cost you five hundred
dollars. And if you knew I was wearing a gown being photographed
in the middle of a picture, you'd flip."

Rightly so. Had I torn that dress, thousands and thousands of
dollars of retakes would have had to be made of me in another gown.
But, like all her other borrowers, I didn't let Miss Wachner down.

I wished I could have said the same for Mr. Goldwyn. When *Look
Your Best* was released, it, too, was a big success. Me? I still wasn't
a star, and I still couldn't figure out why.

I made some more pictures for Goldwyn and some for other studios,
finally reaching the point where I was getting $1000 a week. But as
far as my future was concerned, I wasn't getting anywhere. That
was what counted.

I couldn't go on being a featured player forever. Either I became
a star, or I would fall back and become a leading lady again. I
decided to make a last-ditch stand. Either somebody—anybody—gave
me a starring role and star billing, or at the least a featured role with a
firm commitment that I would be groomed for eventual stardom, or
I wouldn't take the job.

It became pretty lonely in that ditch. And pretty scary. For three months I didn't take a job (or get any salary either, since I was only under contract by the picture).

Out of desperation I bought a mink coat to make me look prosperous and devil-may-care. Maybe also to hide the trembling.

Far from being upset about my burning ambition to become a star, John understood. He even shared my ambition.

More than sharing it, he did something about it.

One night he came to the house looking ready to burst. Mother tried to get him to tell us what the big secret was, but he said no, it was for me alone to hear first.

We got in his car, and he drove around the block and parked, of all places, in my own back alley. There he told me the big news that First National was entering the production end of the business, and that the board of directors was going to sign up eight young people who had star possibilities. He was going to try to get them to take me as one of the eight.

He began his campaign the next day. Each morning with the aid of the bell captain he pasted a picture of me on each director's mirror—a new one every morning with a new legend underneath in the short, pithy paragraphs he wrote so well.

The twenty-six bosses thought him very funny and finally told him to stop, they were intending to sign me anyway. The Rupert Hughes pictures I'd made at Goldwyn had been especially well received in their theaters. They thought I had great box-office potential.

They signed me to a contract for four pictures at $1000 a week, week in and week out. They gave John a new job, too—made him the assistant to the Hollywood production head, Earl Hudson, at $750 a week. Everything looked perfect.

Then John disappeared.

My first knowledge of it came when his secretary called our house to say she couldn't find him anywhere. Terrified he'd been in an accident, I called a friend of his, George Landy, and asked him if we should call the police.

George said, "No, Colleen. Do absolutely nothing. I know where he is, and he's okay."

This sounded odd to me, but since George wouldn't say anything more, there was nothing for me to do but hang up and wait for some word from John.

Two days later he showed up at our house with a three days' beard, bloodshot eyes, and shaking as if he'd just come in out of a blizzard.

I was bewildered. Mother wasn't. She sent John to the Athletic Club, where he lived, and then she sat me down for a mother and daughter talk. She said she'd heard rumors that John was a periodic drinker. Well, now we had proof of it. She advised me to break my engagement before I ruined my life.

I stared at her in disbelief, every bit of love I had for John welling up in my heart, making me want to protect and defend him. I felt it simply could not be true that he was an alcoholic of any kind. He wasn't just gay and witty and charming. He had a brilliant mind—too brilliant a mind, too promising a future to destroy himself by becoming an alcoholic. There had been some reason for his getting drunk for those three days. Some good reason. After all, shouldn't a man be allowed to get drunk once in a blue moon if he had a good enough reason to?

I didn't drink. Not because I had anything against it. It had something against me. It made me ill. But I knew plenty of people who did drink without it bothering them.

At eight o'clock that evening John came back, shaved and looking his usual handsome self. He asked Mother if he could speak to me alone. She said yes and went upstairs.

"What happened to you?" I asked.

He looked away from me without answering.

I frowned at him. "Mother thinks we should break off our engagement."

Because autumn nights in California are chilly, there was a fire burning in the grate. John took my hand, and we sat on the floor in front of the fire. He told me that the only reason he drank was because he wasn't sure I really loved him, that August 18, 1923 was so far away he was afraid I might back out, and our August dream would never come true.

I was more bewildered than before. "But I do love you," I protested, looking into his eyes with all the love that was in me.

While John had been talking, he put the poker in the fire, holding it there until it became red hot. Now, before I knew what he was doing, he pulled back his sleeve and laid the end of the poker against his arm, searing the flesh.

I screamed.

He put the poker down and turned to me. "This is to remind me," he said in a low voice, "every time I look at the scar, how close I came to losing the only thing that matters in my life—you."

I threw my arms around him, crying my love for him, reassuring him that he belonged to me, and I to him, and nothing—nothing—could change that.

I believed it. I think, for a little while anyhow, he believed it, too.

My first picture under my new contract with First National was a Western called *The Huntress*, in which I played the role of an Indian girl. Since I loved making Westerns, I was pleased.

I was also excited almost beyond words. It was to be a starring role, billed as such.

After shooting the interiors we went on location high in the Sierra Nevada Mountains above Bishop, California. It was the middle of winter and cold. Not cold. Freezing.

When I think of the comfort most movie people today enjoy—and expect—on location, the hardships we endured in those silent film years seem fantastic. The company stayed in the log cabins of a summer camp. Mother, of course, went with me, sharing my cabin. Every morning before we got up, the prop man came in and lighted the small pot-bellied stove. He also put water on to heat, not only so we could wash, but so I could put my grease paint in hot water to unfreeze it.

There were no bathrooms, of course—just an old-fashioned outhouse reached through a path in the snow, which was over five feet high. For baths, the prop man brought in a large tin washtub and filled it with hot water.

The proprietor of the camp made a fortune on us. The food he served was inedible, consisting entirely of tough meat and boiled potatoes. I ended up living on raw eggs, canned milk, and crackers, and I lost five pounds. When the film was put together, a very thin little Indian crawled in under the tent, while inside a nice round little Indian stood up.

The Indians we used in the picture were Paiutes. We shot our scenes on their reservation. In one scene I was supposed to bathe an Indian baby in a small tin tub outside my tent. No squaw would let us have one. They said it was too cold.

One baby was adorable and the right size and age. The director kept offering more and more money, and finally the mother gave in. She then told us her main reason for refusing was that she'd sewn the child up for the winter. She actually had. We unstitched the baby, who was a bit high by then, and gave him the bath. After the scene the mother sewed him up again—all but the bottom, where she left room to change him. But no water would touch him until spring.

Other than the difficulty over the baby, the Paiutes were very cooperative. It was the critics who scalped us.

They should have. Except for a few uproarious scenes, *The Huntress* was a bad movie. Worse still, it was a flop at the box office.

Worst of all, the twenty-six bosses decided I couldn't carry a picture, and I was bumped back down to featured player.

I would have liked to blame my failure on the fact that *The Huntress* was so bad. But I couldn't. I'd been in some very good pictures. In three of the best of them I'd had what amounted to starring roles. I hadn't made the grade even then.

Since my contract with First National called for three more films, I had three more chances to become a star, but those chances wouldn't be worth any more than my chances in *The Wallflower, Come On Over*, and *Look Your Best* if I couldn't figure out what was wrong with me. Because it had to be me.

If I could only think what.

It was through my brother Cleeve that I finally found out.

CHAPTER 7

BOY GETS GIRL

Marriage was one problem people in the motion picture industry were never able to work out to everyone's satisfaction—more often than not, the two people most intimately involved weren't able to work it out to their own satisfaction. In the earliest years, press agents tried to keep the off-screen marriages of on-screen lovers a secret, the theory being a sort of where there's life there's hope, its natural sequitur where there's hope there's box office.

The undoing of this theory lay in the very zeal of the press agents who had spawned it. The more the public was told about the movies and the people who made them, the more it wanted to know. As Hollywood and its citizens became more and more publicized—and glamorized and idolized—the public developed an insatiable appetite for information—information of the most minute and intimate detail.

With fan magazine writers and gossip columnists everywhere, and everywhere bent on whetting the appetite even as they satisfied it, keeping something so un-minute as a spouse and family forever hidden became difficult if not impossible.

The press agents handled the thing as best they could—and wherever they could, they capitalized on it. When, for instance,

Seventh Heaven became a great hit, Charles Farrell and Janet Gaynor obliged the studio publicity department by being seen together a few times in public, so that some mileage could be made out of an off-screen romance said to rival the heart throbber created on the screen. Neither of the two was willing, however, to go so far as to get married just to make a few headlines—Charlie marrying Virginia Valli, Janet marrying first a "private" person and then the famous M-G-M designer, Adrian.

What could have been a press agent's wildest dream come true, and to an ardent public no doubt the most thrilling marriage of the decade, was the wedding of Jeanette MacDonald. Unfortunately, however, Jeanette didn't marry Nelson Eddy. She married Gene Raymond.

Her disappointed fans accepted her choice with as much grace as they could muster. Not so, her future mother-in-law. In a fit of jealousy—and demonstrating a pioneer spirit—she picketed the wedding.

One wedding that didn't create nearly as much furor in Hollywood at the time it took place as it did some thirty-two years later, when movie people read about it in a book written by Irving Shulman, was Jean Harlow's wedding to Paul Bern.

Jean and Paul Bern, who was head of the story department at M-G-M, were married in the evening of July 2, 1932. Their wedding reception was held the next morning in Paul's garden. According to Mr. Shulman, Paul beat Jean so brutally on their wedding night that covering make-up had to be applied before the reception to the many black and blue marks on her body.

To a lot of people in Hollywood, that remark alone made it apparent that not only did Mr. Shulman not know Jean Harlow or Paul Bern, he must not have spoken to anyone who did. If he had said that athletic, tennis-player, good swimmer Jean had beaten up Paul, the story might have had some credence. Paul was smaller than Jean, and had it been possible for a man of his nature—he was one of the kindest, gentlest men I've ever known—to even try to harm her, he couldn't have hit her more than once before Jean would have floored him.

But my rebuttal of Mr. Shulman in this instance is based on more than a long-time friendship with both Jean and Paul. I was at the reception.

*One of the exciting weddings in Holly-
wood was that of Jean Harlow to Paul
Bern. The reception was held in the gardens of Paul Bern's beautiful house. Here
I am with (left to right) Cedric Gibbons,
Carmelita Geraghty, Lois Wilson, Wins-
low B. Felix, Marion Nixon, Colleen,
Carey Wilson, and Dolores del Rio. Ma-
rino Bello, Jean's stepfather, is standing
behind me. Jean and Paul were both dear
friends.*

My friend Marion Nixon, the Fox star, and I went there together. Through a misunderstanding on our part we arrived an hour early. After wandering around the garden a few minutes, we went up to the house to talk to Jean, who was dressed, as usual, in slacks. A short time later her mother came in saying, "Baby, you'd better get dressed before the other guests start arriving."

Harlow never wore underclothes. She hated them. I guess if I'd had her beautiful figure (yes, beautiful, but not the voluptuous Jayne Mansfield figure Shulman suggests—Jean was a size thirty-four), I wouldn't have wanted to bind it up with girdles and bras either. Anyhow, she took off her slacks and blouse, standing there as the good Lord made her (and what a job He did!), while we helped her into her long garden dress.

Now if she'd been covered with black and blue marks or had marks covered with make-up, we would have known it. You can't fool an actress about covering make-up. Jean had no marks, no make-up. If she was anything other than her usual self, she was happier.

In his book, Mr. Shulman also led people to believe that Jean and Paul were married only a few days. They were married almost a year, and they were happy.

A few months after the wedding I gave a party for them. At one point during the evening when Jean and I were upstairs together, she said to me, "All I want out of life is to be able to sit at Paul's feet and have him read to me and educate me."

It was an understandable remark. An erudite man, Paul was a teacher by instinct. He used to give me books to read, just as he did to Joan Crawford and a number of other people.

After dinner that night, the party broke up into three groups. One group went into the living room to play charades, another into the library to play poker, and the third into the sun room to play our favorite "Murder." ("Murder" required two teams—one to plot the crime, the other to solve it. I think we enjoyed it so much because it gave us the opportunity to polish off certain friends and situations—of which known triangles were our pets—in spectacular ways. If the murder happened to be a particularly ingenious one, the writers, I noticed, left rather abruptly.)

One of the guests that night was Prince Ferdinand Liechtenstein, and both he and Jean were playing poker. Paul, who was German and a stickler for protocol, had told Jean she must be sure to address the prince as "Your Serene Highness." During the evening I went to look in on the poker game and heard Jean, who'd had a few glasses of champagne, saying, "I raise you two, Your Serene Highness."

The prince laughed and said, "I'll call that and raise you two."

The others at the table had already folded.

Jean looked at her hand and nodded. "Okay. I'll call that and raise you—uh—five—uh—Your Serene Highness."

The prince looked from her to his hand, a smile tugging at the corners of his mouth. "Very well. I call."

He was so confident of winning he didn't even wait for her to show her hand, but laid his own down—three sixes and two nines.

"Well—uh—Your Serene Highness—"

He held up a hand. "Please, Jean. No formalities. We're friends, aren't we?" He gave her an indulgent smile. "Now, what do you have?"

She grinned at him as she laid down her cards. "Four queens, Tootsie-boy Prince." And she swept in the pot.

When Jean and Paul left, I helped him on with his coat. It was so heavy, I said to him, "What's in your pocket—all my silver?"

He said, "We live up a lonely canyon, and someone might try to hurt my darling."

The irony, of course, was that it was Paul himself who finally did hurt her—by using the gun to kill himself. Yet I've always thought he did it to protect Jean. Before he came to Hollywood, Paul had a common-law wife who became unbalanced. He saw that she was taken care of in a private sanitarium, continuing to pay for her treatment even after he came to Hollywood. But then some shyster lawyers got hold of her, and she threatened to make a big scandal in the newspapers claiming she was the legal wife, not Jean.

In any case, Paul provoked a fight with Jean—such a fight that she went to spend the night with her mother. Then he wrote a note of apology to her and killed himself.

Mr. Shulman made quite a point in his book of asking where Paul's money went, insinuating that something sinister might have been going on. There are any number of people in Hollywood who could have told him where it went. There used to be a saying there whenever questions arose regarding money: Mickey Neilan spent it, Harold Lloyd saved it, Paul Bern gave it away.

Paul Bern no doubt had his faults, the same as anybody else, but a kinder, more generous, more truly Christian man never lived. We all mourned his death. When Jean Harlow married again, her new husband, a cameraman named Hal Rossen, looked so much like Paul they could have been twins. It was as if Jean was trying to replace Paul as nearly as she could.

Perhaps the most unusual wedding in Hollywood, if you don't count Gene Raymond's mother, was that of Ruth Roland, the serial queen, who spent her salary buying up miles of real estate along both sides of Wilshire Boulevard. Since she was a member of Our Club, we were all invited to her wedding at the Beverly Wilshire Hotel.

Ruth, who loved to sing—and would yodel at the drop of a request—said she didn't want a wedding with somber songs. She wanted something bright and gay. So as Hollywood's richest movie star and her bridegroom, a handsome but not exactly well-heeled actor named Ben Bard, left the altar, the orchestra played "I Can't Give You Anything But Love."

My own wedding took place as scheduled, on August 18, 1923.

Pre-wedding jitters are a common enough thing, even to the most starry-eyed, most absolutely certain-of-themselves lovers. John and I had our share.

I had more than my share. If I was jittery about John, I was even more jittery about my career. In August of 1923 the so-called moment of truth was approaching for both.

As far as my career was concerned, I had taken what amounted to another last-ditch stand. Only this time I didn't sit around waiting for somebody to come up with the right role for me. I found it myself.

I don't know now why it took me so long to figure out what was wrong with me as an actress. I'd had my finger on it the night of that telephone call way back in Tampa.

The moviegoing public of those years was as formula-minded about its heroines as it was about the stories they played in. "Papa, what is beer?" expression notwithstanding, I just wasn't the accepted—and acceptable—model for a sweet young thing in the throes of her first love. The necessary curls I could manage, the same way Mary Pickford and the others did, with time and effort. But no amount of either could make my five-foot-five boyish figure into a curvy, petite five-foot-two or transform the sauciness of my freckled face with its turned-up nose into the demure perfection of a Mary Pickford.

Not only did I not look the part I didn't feel it either. That was where my brother Cleeve came in. Cleeve, and a man named Warner Fabian.

Cleeve was now attending Santa Clara College in northern California. When he came home for weekends, the girls he brought with him didn't look any more like the sweet young things I was playing in the movies than I did. They were smart and sophisticated, with an air of independence about them, and so casual about their looks and clothes and manners as to be almost slapdash.

I don't know if I realized as soon as I began seeing them that they represented the wave of the future, but I do know I was drawn to them. I shared their restlessness, understood their determination to free themselves of the Victorian shackles of the pre-World War I era and find out for themselves what life was all about.

Then I read Warner Fabian's sensational best-seller, *Flaming Youth*, and when First National bought it, I knew that here was my chance for stardom. Sweet young thing I was not. Pat, the heroine of *Flaming Youth*, I was.

I begged for the role, but the New York office said I wasn't the type. I was a dramatic actress, better in costume parts. Frantic for fear they'd give the part to somebody else, I said to John, "Get that part for me for a wedding present, or else." Apparently I spoke more sharply than I meant to, because he gave me a strange look and said he'd do his best.

But it was my mother who came up with the answer. She said, "Why don't we cut your hair and then make Hudson give you a test for the part?"

I was elated.

She picked up the scissors and, whack, off came the long curls. I felt as if I'd been emancipated. Then she trimmed my hair around with bangs like a Japanese girl's haircut—or, as most people call it, a Dutch bob.

It was becoming. More important, it worked. Hudson made a test, and we sent it off to Mr. Rowland in New York.

Five days later I had the part.

We started shooting at once. Never had I been so happy in a movie role before. I loved every scene. After six years of treacle, it was heaven to be given a little spice.

John was so excited over the early rushes, he sent them to New York. Mr. Rowland was just as excited, predicting that First National would have a new star when the picture was released. He and John both said I had a new personality. They were wrong. I didn't have a new personality. I was just growing up.

Although the public—and only the public—would determine the accuracy of Mr. Rowland's prediction, I was absolutely convinced that the role of Pat in *Flaming Youth* was my key to stardom, just as I was absolutely convinced that marriage to John was my key to happiness. What jitters I had about either one I kept to myself. Or tried to, anyhow.

So did John.

One night after work, shortly before our wedding, John and I drove down to what is now Malibu Beach. We parked the car and walked down to the shoreline, admiring the water and the white sands of the beach glistening in the moonlight.

While we were standing there, John took my hand and said, "I've thought of a name for you—a private name. Irish like Colleen, but a name that doesn't belong to the public. Only to me." He smiled down at me. "Alanna. Little one." He took me in his arms. "Please always stay my Alanna. My little one."

I was enchanted. As I looked at him there in the moonlight, he seemed so strong and brave and dependable, I said a small prayer of thanks to the Blessed Mother for such happiness as was mine now and would be mine forever.

The next night he disappeared again.

This time I didn't call his friend George Landy. I told my family John had gone to visit his parents in San Francisco. I prayed he had. When I heard nothing from him, I knew that he hadn't.

He finally called me three days later to say he'd gone to San Pedro with some friends to take some publicity stills on a yacht. He'd fallen asleep on deck, and as a joke his friends had put out to sea.

I knew he wasn't telling me the truth. The story was full of holes. But I didn't say anything. I figured that had been his way of getting rid of the jitters. At least now they were rid of.

We were in the middle of *Flaming Youth* when we were married, which meant that we couldn't go away on a honeymoon or even celebrate our three days in a row. We couldn't even take one day off after the wedding. But neither of us wanted to change that magic date. John said we'd go to Europe as soon as the picture was finished. As for the three days, we'd have them to celebrate the rest of our lives.

Here I am with my bridegroom, John McCormick, photographed aboard our yacht shortly after our marriage. This was a happy moment but the sailing was not always so smooth.

We had a quiet, late-afternoon wedding at the Catholic Church in Beverly Hills—in the sacristy, because John was an Episcopalian. Only our families and a very few friends were there. Carmelita Geraghty, an actress who was my best friend, was my maid of honor. My great friend Adela Rogers St. Johns and her husband Ivan, who was head of *Photoplay* and an old friend of John's, were there. Earl Hudson, was John's best man. With John's parents and my parents and Cleve and Grandma, it made twelve of us in all.

At the wedding supper afterward John proposed a toast to my dad and mother for having given me to him—a funny, sentimental, beautiful toast. Then he downed his champagne in one gulp. Downed a second glass the same way. I remember watching him and thinking what bad table manners.

We went from the supper to John's car, which Cleve had decorated with white ribbons and tin cans, and drove the half mile to our new house. Mother had rented it for us. Because of a superstition on John's part, I didn't set eyes on it until he carried me across the threshold. It was a dear little house, the same house Norma Shearer and Irving Thalberg later lived in when they were first married.

That night it was filled with flowers, and when we came in, a cook-housekeeper whom my mother had engaged greeted us with a bottle of champagne and two glasses.

I took only a sip or two, afraid it would make me sick. John drained the entire bottle. His voice got louder. He became glassy-eyed. His mouth hung loose. He no longer looked like himself, but like some caricature of him.

Seeing the bewilderment on my face, he said to me, "It's our wedding night, Alanna, and I am drunk."

Then he started to cry—a sloppy, maudlin, drunken berating of self. I stared at him, shocked beyond words at this unknown creature groveling there.

The groveling stopped as abruptly as it had begun, and he became braggadocio.

I didn't know which was worse. Where was my poet, my witty guy, my brave, strong, handsome John? Who was this stranger?

I burst into tears and ran upstairs to our room. Sitting there crying, I wondered if I should go home. I shook my head. How could I face running home to my mother on my wedding night?

I didn't go home. I just went on sitting there, crying, torn between my own anger and hurt and feeling sorry for John, wondering, finally, if I should go down and help him upstairs.

I went out in the hall to the top of the stairs and, looking down, saw that the living room was dark. A light shone from the guest room. I went down the hall to it and looked in. There was John in his pajamas sprawled on the rug with a nearly empty bottle of Scotch beside him, a large stain on the rug where some of the liquor had run out of the bottle.

I stood there for a moment staring at him. Then I ran back to our room and locked the door and crawled into the big double bed and buried my face in the pillow, sobbing my heart out.

CHAPTER 8

FLAMING YOUTH

The next morning before I left for the studio, I looked in the guest room. John was gone. I wondered when I would see him again and what excuse I could give at the studio for his not being with me. I had to cover up somehow. If I didn't, it would be in all the columns.

I remembered my mother's warning to me about a husband who drank. I knew I could have the marriage annulled, since it hadn't been consummated. Once again tears started down my cheeks. I didn't want the marriage annulled. I loved John. I wanted to be Mrs. John McCormick, and not in name only.

I dried my tears. My cover story wouldn't be very convincing with eyes red and swollen from weeping.

At the studio the company crowded around me offering congratulations. The press agent brought over the morning papers showing pictures of John and me leaving the church the day before, radiant, smiling. It seemed light-years away to me.

Playing the happy bride for all it was worth, I acknowledged the congratulations and laughed at the jokes, telling everyone John had gone to the train to see his parents off. I was doing a great job, I thought, but I didn't know how long I could keep it up. I asked the director if we couldn't get started.

The scene I had to play that morning was the one in which Pat comes downstairs in her pajamas the morning after a drunken brawl given by her parents. Looking around in bewilderment at the wreckage, she sees her still-drunk father sitting at the organ struggling through a tune, and she sinks to the floor, weeping bitterly. When the picture was released, the critics said I gave great realism to the scene.

Shortly before noon I heard a new flurry of congratulations and glanced up to see John standing on the set surrounded by well-wishers, looking happy, handsome, mischievous. I found out later that with what must have been superhuman effort, he'd pulled himself together and gone to the Athletic Club for a steam bath.

After asking the director to shoot around me, we got in the car, and he drove me home. He said nothing. Neither did I. When we pulled into the driveway he told me to go into the house while he put the car away. Inside, a balloon was tied to every chair and table, each painted with a different slogan—"*John is sorry*," "*John loves Colleen*," "*John is on the wagon*," etc.

I started to laugh. He came in from the dining room, where he'd been hiding, and took me in his arms. "I almost shot myself this morning when I realized what I'd done to you." He pulled a gun out of his pocket and showed it to me.

I grabbed it and screamed, throwing it across the room.

He reached in his pocket again and handed me a flat gold charm in the shape of a heart, the words "*Love never dies*" engraved on it.

He held me close, saying, "This is my religion, Alanna, and those three words are my prayer. My love for you will be forever."

I believed him. I told myself he would never drink again, that it was just the excitement of the wedding that had started him off, and once he got started, apparently he couldn't stop.

By the time *Flaming Youth* was finished, I was very tired. It had been a hard, if exciting, part. At one point in the filming it had also been almost the finish of me. A scene was to show me jumping from a yacht in mid-ocean, going down, coming up to yell "Help!" and going down again, the scene then fading out.

We built a corner of the boat in the big tank at the studio. The director told me we couldn't rehearse the scene because of getting my clothes wet, so he gave me my instructions and shouted, "Camera!"

Although I knew how to swim, I'd never jumped over a yacht railing before. I got a noseful of water. I choked and went down again, taking in more water. I came up yelling for help and went down a third time. Richard Arlen, who was just starting his career and was working as an extra in the movie, jumped in and pulled me out.

The director, who'd been sitting there thinking what a great actress I was, yelled at him that he'd spoiled the scene. That he may have, but he also saved me from drowning.

I was glad when the picture was finished. About all John and I had had time to discuss were rushes and retakes and magazine interviews. I longed to sit down and visit with my new husband as a wife. I was tired of talking about Colleen Moore. I wanted to talk about the McCormicks.

Yet I couldn't blame John. Nor would I have wanted anything less than the intense concentration he was putting into this effort to achieve stardom for Colleen Moore. I'd put in six years of intense concentration myself working and training toward this moment.

It paid off. *Flaming Youth* played to packed houses everywhere it was shown. In most places it was held over for a second week, which in those days was really something. It even achieved to the *crème de la crème* of critical acclaim—it was banned in Boston.

With *Flaming Youth*, a new word entered the American vocabulary —flapper. She was the new American girl, Colleen Moore her prototype.

As a recent article in *Playboy* put it, "First of the new breed was Colleen Moore, who was about as sexy as a Shirley Temple doll, and her own fault, too, because she had as beautiful a body as any of the sex stars who came after her. It was her acting alone that made her popular—that and the creation of the film flapper, a liberated young lady of vast appeal to the movie millions. The flapper got her name because of her peculiar habit of wearing unbuckled galoshes. This slapdash disregard for convention symbolized the kind of girl whose spirit was free and who was willing to kick up her spiked heels in the uninhibited pursuit of pleasure. Colleen Moore helped give a name to a new generation in 1923. She made *Flaming Youth*. Overnight she was a flaming star."

College girls everywhere cut their hair in Dutch bobs. They copied my clothes. No longer did a girl have to be beautiful to be sought after. Any plain Jane could become a flapper. No wonder

One of my good friends was Harold Lloyd, the great comedian, who had the most magnificent house and gardens in Hollywood. Here we are at a masquerade party.

they grabbed me to their hearts and made me their movie idol.

John and I left for our honeymoon abroad, visiting on the way the twenty-six key cities of the First National owners so I could shake hands with the salesmen, make personal appearances at the theaters where *Flaming Youth* was playing, and be interviewed by the press. It wasn't until we were on board ship on our way to Europe that we had time for fun. We danced, we made friends, we read about all the exciting places we would be seeing for the first time in either of our lives.

John said, "Alanna, I'm going to take you to the Tower of London to see the spot where the little princes were murdered, and I'll hold you tight so the ghosts won't get you. And," he added, "we'll run across London Bridge to see if it really is falling down."

I laughed and held his hand tight as we walked around the deck. This was what I'd dreamed a honeymoon should be.

I never saw a thing in London except the Ritz Hotel. I spent the whole time there being interviewed and photographed, seeing theater owners, and attending a banquet given for me by London exhibitors.

The flapper, this new breed of American girl, was becoming international.

No, I take it back. I did see a bit of London—a street where we shot some exteriors for a future flapper film called *We Moderns*.

Because I was half Irish—purebred Irish, thanks to Uncle Walter—we went to Dublin, where *Flaming Youth* opened a new theater. (At this time new theaters were being built all over Europe on the order of the great movie palaces in America.) Newspapers splashed pictures of me all over the front page as "Ireland's own Colleen." It was Old Home Week in Dublin.

The theater opening there was a gala. I wore a divine salmon dress with a green taffeta cape—a very handsome cape covered with tiny plumes in a lighter shade of green. When the picture ended, I made a speech from the stage and then returned to our box, where the theater manager said that crowds had gathered in such force outside, the police had been sent for. He suggested I go out on the balcony and wave, and maybe they'd go home.

John and I went out. Looking down, I stared into a sea of faces. The papers the next day said there were ten thousand people there. It seemed even more. John was elated. He waved to the crowds, too, as exhilarated as if he were the star.

Against the advice of the manager, John said we must go out through the crowds. The police formed a cordon, but the crowds broke through it and surrounded me, grabbing at the feathers on my cape. Finally John lifted me up and carried me to the car, where I arrived looking like a picked chicken.

I had been tired enough when we finished making the picture. Now I became exhausted. I lost weight which I couldn't afford to lose, as I was over five feet five and weighed only a little over a hundred pounds. John said we would go to Switzerland, where I would have a rest. We'd go swimming in the Lake of Lucerne and see if the water was as blue as it was on the post cards. Instead, we went to Zurich, where I opened another theater.

The mayor of Zurich had arranged a dinner in my honor before the opening—I suppose at the urging of the theater owner. It was a large dinner at a horseshoe table filled with dignitaries. I was placed between the mayor and the American consul.

We'd no sooner sat down than the mayor, with a small bow to me, signaled the orchestra, who started playing "My Country, 'Tis of Thee." We all got up and stood very silent. When we sat down again, I said to the mayor, "That was the English national anthem, 'God Save the King.'"

I should have kept my big mouth shut. The mayor sent for the orchestra leader, spoke a few words to him in German, and no sooner had we started the soup course than the orchestra struck up again, this time with John Philip Sousa's "Stars and Stripes Forever." The mayor stood up, beckoning to all of us, saying excitedly, "*Stehen sie auf, bitte*—everybody please stand up."

We all stood, the orchestra finished, we sat down, and the American consul and I burst out laughing. When the mayor asked what we were laughing about, like an idiot I said, "That wasn't our national anthem. That's a march."

The mayor, red in the face, sent for the orchestra leader, spluttering German at him. The leader turned to me and asked the name of our national anthem. I said, "The Star-Spangled Banner."

He returned to the bandstand, the mayor watching him with an eagle eye. A few moments later the orchestra struck up "Yes, We Have No Bananas," the mayor rose, saying, "*Stehen sie auf, bitte*," and a tableful of by-now bewildered guests stood at attention once again. When we sat down, I smiled at the mayor and said, "That was lovely."

The theater in Zurich was enormous, patterned after the Balaban & Katz theater in Chicago, but with a large glass roof that rolled back in the summertime. In the pit was a one-hundred-piece orchestra—the mark in those days of a really first-class movie theater. Every seat in the house was filled.

I arrived in a blaze of glory—flashlight powder popping, fans cheering, a ceremonial red carpet laid down for me to walk on. The lights dimmed, the orchestra started to play, and the picture—*Flaming Youth*, of course—started to roll.

The musicians knew the score for the film perfectly, but the man in the projection room evidently didn't understand the instructions on the reels. He got them all mixed up. In the scene where my mother is dying, the orchestra was playing "The Charleston."

I didn't think things could possibly get any worse, but they did. The theater began getting so hot and stuffy, several people fainted. The manager sent workmen to open the new glass roof, but the machinery was stuck, and the roof wouldn't budge. The place became hotter and hotter. Soon we heard hammering. Suddenly there was a great crash as the roof shattered and glass cascaded down on us. The audience screamed and fled.

In Paris John and I managed to get in some shopping and sight-seeing between press interviews. We went to the Eiffel Tower, sat in the Tuileries Gardens, and visited Fontaine-bleau, where we pretended we were Napoleon and Josephine and where, in a Napoleon-like mood, he grabbed my hand as we were standing at the lake feeding the giant carp and said, "I'm going to make you the biggest movie star in America. Just watch me."

So great was my love and my admiration for him I didn't doubt him. Nor did I rebel openly at the fact that we spent most of our honeymoon talking about how Colleen Moore must be built up in Europe. She was, after all, important to both of us. But I longed to hear some of his opinions on marriage and religion and life. Almost all I knew was how he felt about the movies. The more he planned and schemed for Colleen Moore, the more I felt that as a wife I was becoming less important every day.

The return to the studio was gala. All twenty-six bosses were there for a board meeting, so happy over the money they'd made on *Flaming Youth*, they tore up my old contract and gave me a new one for $50,000 a picture for the next four pictures, all of them to be made in a year. I didn't get excited until I broke it down and saw that it came to almost $4000 a week. I was never able to count by the year.

Shortly after that, John and I were invited to a party given by Norma Talmadge and her husband Joseph M. Schenck, who had just moved to Hollywood from the East, where they had been making all their films. It was a thrill for me. Norma was the biggest star releasing films through First National. I'd never missed one of her pictures, but I had never met her. John, of course, knew her and her sisters Constance and Natalie, and Joe as well, because he'd handled publicity for their pictures.

The party was a Sunday-night buffet supper, though from the way the champagne flowed, I should say champagne supper. John, to my relief, drank ginger ale.

When I went upstairs to one of the bedrooms to leave my coat, I found Norma there reclining on a chaise and drinking champagne, surrounded by a group of women. She beckoned me over and, putting her arms around me, said, "So this is John's bride."

After she introduced me to the other women—I remember Mabel Normand was one of them—she smiled at me and said, a bit tiddly from the champagne, "I'm going to give you a little advice. Counsel for your old age. Just because you're married, don't pass up a big romance. Have something to remember when you're wearing carpet slippers."

Everyone laughed, including Norma. I wondered if the stories I'd heard about her were true.

Norma was a rare beauty, with large brown eyes and perfect features. She was years younger than her husband, who was one of the homeliest men I ever saw. Everybody said Joe Schenck had a heart of gold. He also had a lot in his teeth.

According to the stories, the only thing Joe wanted to do at night was play poker—the kind of poker where the stakes ran into the thousands—so he let Norma's leading man, Eugene O'Brien, take Norma dancing and to the theater. Didn't just let. Insisted on it.

Norma wasn't so tiddly that night that she didn't mean what she said. Later, when she made *Camille* with Gilbert Roland, and Joe sent them out dancing and theatergoing, they fell in love.

It was one of Hollywood's big romances. Norma and Gilbert went to Joe and asked him for a divorce—the way I heard it, on their knees. Joe refused, telling Norma she'd get over it and come back to him as she always did.

Norma, hoping to embarrass Joe into a divorce, rode down Hollywood Boulevard in an open car with her arms around Gilbert. They were seen by dozens of people, including columnists. Still Joe wouldn't budge.

Joe was so popular with his poker-playing cronies, who were all big-shot producers and studio and theater owners, that for a time Gilbert was barred from working. This made Norma furious and more determined than ever to divorce Joe.

People took sides—the women with Norma and about half the men with Joe. One story that spread like wildfire was that Joe had engaged thugs who had not only beat up Gilbert Roland but castrated him as well. When the story reached Gilbert, he went down to the Hollywood Athletic Club on a day when the pool was filled with men—all of them naked, as the custom there was. Gilbert came out, stood around a while, and dived in.

Norma finally got her divorce. Then, to everybody's consternation, she ran away to New York—alone. Hearing that I was going there on business, Gilbert came over to the house and begged me to see Norma for him, to tell her he loved her and wanted her to come home.

When I arrived in New York, I went to Norma's hotel room and gave her the message. She started crying, saying she loved Gilbert, but she wouldn't marry him because she was older than he was. She didn't. I suppose maybe she was afraid that someday he'd turn to someone younger, just as she had done.

Another party John and I went to after returning from our honeymoon was a big costume party Sam Goldwyn gave in honor of Norma and her sister Constance. We were all dancing after dinner when in from the street came two young characters on all fours, barking like dogs. In the doorway they sat up on their haunches begging, saying, "Please, can we come to your party? We're strangers and don't know anyone."

They were F. Scott Fitzgerald and his wife Zelda.

Everyone was delighted to meet them. I most especially, not only because he was my favorite author, but because *This Side of Paradise* was the novel which had first called attention to the new generation of young people, causing a sensation in literary circles— and scandalizing parents. (Or, as Fitzgerald himself wrote in a tiny version of *This Side of Paradise* for my doll house, "I was the spark that lit up Flaming Youth, Colleen Moore was the torch. What little things we are to have caused all that trouble. My author's name is F. Scott Fitzgerald.")

Since I had to be on the set early the next morning, I went upstairs to get my coat as Zelda went up to leave hers. Instead of taking off her coat, she took off all her clothes and went into the bathroom, where I heard water pouring into the tub. I couldn't leave then. I had to see what she'd do next.

In a few minutes she came out again, rubbed her hair dry, put on her clothes, and went downstairs, as if this was what everybody did when they went to a party. Even in Hollywood the Fitzgeralds were unique.

Toward the end of the year the bosses came out for another

At this masquerade party, given by Samuel Goldwyn for **Norma and
Constance Talmadge,** Zelda and Scott Fitzgerald crashed the gate.
Zelda took a bath. (*1*) Frank Borzage (director); (*2*) Betty Blythe
(actress); (*3*) Lou Tellegan (actor); (*4*) Marilyn Miller (famous
stage star); (*5*) Norma Talmadge; (*6*) Constance Talmadge; (*7*)
Joseph Schenck; (*8*) Eugene O'Brien; (*9*) Marion Davies; (*10*) Lady
Thelma Furness; (*11*) Mrs. Frank Borzage; (*12*) Mrs. Harold Lloyd;
(*13*) Colleen Moore; (*14*) John McCormick; (*15*) Buster Collier;

(*16*) Edwin Earle (actor); (*17*) George Fitzmaurice (director); (*18*)
Phyllis Haver (Sennett beauty); (*19*) Ronald Colman; (*20*) Natalie
Talmadge; (*21*) Lefty Flynn; (*22*) Viola Dana; (*23*) Mae Murray;
(*24*) Robert Leonard (director); (*25*) Sam Goldwyn; (*26*) Irving
Thalberg; (*27*) Fred Thompson (famous cowboy star); (*28*) Frances
Marion (writer); (*29*) Harold Lloyd; (*30*) Earl Williams (star);
(*31*) Jack Pickford; (*32*) Dolores del Rio; (*33*) King Vidor.

board meeting. John, who had developed a burning ambition to become head of the studio, went to work on them, using all the charm—and politics—at his command. Before the meeting had ended, Earl Hudson was out, and John was in—at a new salary of $50,000 a year.

Since we were both doing so well now, we bought a house out in the new Wilshire district—an eight-room Italian style house with a large garden in back.

John hated antiques. He liked nice Grand Rapids department-store furniture. That's what we bought. Mother positively shivered at my dining room with its expensive inlaid bastard Spanish-English-French dining table, iron gates, and floor-length red velvet drapes under gold valances. John and I thought it was grand.

Just before we moved in, Mother engaged a Japanese couple for us—Ben Fukeshima, a forty-five-year-old former restaurant owner, who was to be our butler, and his twenty-one-year-old mail-order bride Tsuiko, who had stayed at a mission house in Seattle for a while after coming over from Japan, so she could learn American cooking.

Ben and Tsuiko arrived the morning after John and I moved in. Since we'd already gone to the studio, Mother came over to welcome them and get them started.

Brides and fools are not to be trusted. John called me on the set that afternoon to say he was bringing some important English exhibitors and their wives down to watch me work. When they arrived, they were so charming I blithely asked them if they wouldn't like to dine with us and see a movie we were running that night. They accepted, and I called home. Introducing myself to Ben on the phone, I said, "There will be eight of us for dinner."

There was a short intake of breath, a pause, then, "Okay."

I didn't know much about these things. I'd always been able to ask as many people to dinner as I wanted, simply calling home and telling my mother how many were coming.

We arrived home, very proud to show off our new house. John mixed the drinks, giving me a ginger ale. Smiling tenderly at me, he pointed to his own glass and whispered, "Same as yours."

I smiled back, and as we looked into each other's eyes for a moment, love seemed to go between us like a beam of light. I knew our marriage was right and would succeed.

Ben came in to announce dinner. We walked proudly through the iron gates, sat down at our expensive inlaid table, and I rang the bell, feeling a very proper matron.

The soup went all right. I thought the silver seemed placed in an odd manner, but I was too excited at having my first dinner party to bother. It was the salad course, which in California precedes the main course, that brought the first hint of disaster.

I looked up as the pantry door swung open, and I gasped. In came Ben, that former hash-house restaurant owner, with a towel slung over one arm, and on the other, four big dinner plates, each containing a half head of lettuce, sliced tomatoes, and cucumbers— all evenly arranged and filling the entire plate. Oblivious to my shock, Ben served them and disappeared, returning with another armful.

The main course was beyond belief. Why Japanese Ben picked Virginia ham, I will never know. It seemed to me one needed a long line of Southern ancestors, preferably chefs, to be able to prepare one of those hams, which in those days had to be boiled for hours, usually after being soaked overnight, before baking. The meat was so hard it couldn't be cut. John looked at me bug-eyed as he sawed away. Getting more nervous by the minute, I said flippantly, "In America we always serve pemmican to our guests." They looked blank. I said, "Dried buffalo meat."

They took me seriously.

The dessert was ice cream and store cookies. I prayed for the dinner to be over. I was chattering like a magpie from sheer nervousness. The three English ladies were also nervous—I suppose from hunger.

One of them said, "I adore America but for this dreadful habit of chewing gum."

Ben heard. My mother had told him I liked to chew gum, and he had bought every brand on the market. Now he appeared with my best wedding-present silver platter beautifully arrayed with sticks of chewing gum.

He passed the platter to me first. Not knowing what else to do, I took a stick, peeled it, and popped it into my mouth.

The three English ladies, looking as if they were trapped in some kind of topsy-turvy world, followed suit. Almost choking with laughter, John suggested we go into the drawing room and see the movie.

The moment the lights went out, I ran into the kitchen and said to Ben, "Do you realize you came into the dining room with *four* plates on your arm?"

Ben smiled, showing his gold teeth. "Yes, but that not all. Can carry seven."

I burst into tears and ran into the library to call my mother. "Don't you know one never asks guests to dinner," she said, "until after at least a week when breaking in new servants?"

"I thought they were already broken in," I blubbered.

She said, "Stop crying. I'll come over in the morning and straighten it all out for you."

The next morning Mother sent for an experienced waiter who spent the day teaching Ben how to set the table and serve. Ben had refused to let Tsuiko do any of the cooking the night before. Mother straightened that out, too, explaining to Ben that the kitchen belonged to Tsuiko. His job was to watch the bills and take care of John and me.

Ben became very popular with the Japanese servants of our friends. Whenever I wanted to ask Charlie Chaplin to a party, I'd ask Ben to phone Charlie's manservant Kono. That way the message got through the Chaplin curtain.

At the time I thought it funny that Ben always addressed him as Mr. Kono, giving him the polite intake of breath the Japanese reserved for special people. Then when Pearl Harbor came, Mr. Kono disappeared. It was alleged—the way it was about almost every Japanese in California—that he was an admiral in the Japanese navy and had been head of a spy ring in California. If so, he couldn't have picked a better place to work. The world's great were always coming to see Charlie, and he usually entertained them in his home.

By the time Christmas arrived, I had made two more pictures, *The Perfect Flapper* and *Painted People*. In the latter one, Clara Bow, who was soon to become my biggest box-office competition, played a mean rich girl, attired in a lace dress with long, dark brown curls hanging down her back. She hadn't yet become the flaming redhead. I played the poor little heroine—a tomboy dressed in a baseball suit.

Here is a scene from The Painted People, *interesting because the girl at the left with the long curls is Clara Bow, before they found out she had "it."*

Two days was all Clara could take. She said to me, "I don't like my part. I want to play yours." With that, she went back to Paramount, where she was under contract, and demanded to be taken out of the picture.

The only time I ever met Clara socially was at a party given by Adela Rogers St. Johns in her English country house at Whittier, California. Clara was very bright but flighty, with a sketchy education. Adela and Hope Leighton, a writer at Paramount, were trying to remake her, as it were—to interest her in reading and taking some courses of study.

As I remember it, the party was being given in honor of William Randolph Hearst. In any case, Mr. Hearst was there, along with a number of other dignified and important people. After dinner we gathered around the fire to listen to them talk. The conversation was a fairly intellectual one, and Clara finally became bored, I guess, and decided the time had come to liven up the party.

She livened it up considerably. She stood up and, after getting everyone's attention, proceeded to tell the dirtiest story imaginable, with such perfect pantomime nothing was left to the imagination.

I was as shocked as everybody else, but I had to laugh inside, she did such a first-rate job. As for Adela, she took one last look as her Galatea was winding up this graphic performance and fled.

On Christmas Eve, John and I trimmed our tree and went to bed happy and excited over our first Christmas together. When I woke up the next morning he was gone.

I rushed downstairs. He was nowhere to be found. Neither Ben nor Tsuiko had seen him leave, but his car wasn't in the garage. I was filled with dread that he had gone off on another drunken spree, and angry and resentful that he had left me to open our presents alone. But I decided to wait a while on the chance that he might just have gone out for some present he'd forgotten.

Suddenly I heard a commotion outside. Around the front porch of our house was a wide cement terrace. There, behind the wheel of a Rolls-Royce touring car, its front end smashed against the porch, sat John. He gave me a happy, drunken smile. "Merry Christmas, baby. Here's your present."

As angry as I was, I couldn't help laughing, it was such a funny sight.

I knew by this time that eating could break a drinking cycle. To my relief, he got out of the car and came in and ate breakfast with me.

After breakfast when we opened our presents, he was every bit as gay and charming as I could have wished, topping off our presents with another surprise for me that he brought in from the kitchen— a little Irish terrier puppy from his father, who bred them.

John said we must go to the Desert Inn in Palm Springs for New Year's. Since the inn didn't serve liquor, he wouldn't be tempted. He took my hands and kissed the palms of them, saying, "I'm trying hard, so help me God."

"I know you are," I answered, "and I'm with you every step of the way."

And I was.

CHAPTER 9

IMAGINE YOU, GLADYS SMITH

After I became a star, the bosses built a bungalow for me at the studio. Spanish in architecture, it was built around a small patio containing a fountain and a large oak tree. Inside were, quite literally, all the comforts of home. I had a living room with a high beamed ceiling and a fireplace, a kitchen and back porch, and a very large bedroom which also served as a dressing room and which contained, in addition to the bed and chests, a dressing table with lights all around the mirror (we still put on our own make-up) and a small piano so I could practice if I wanted to. Off the bedroom were a wardrobe room and a bathroom with a sunken tub.

I felt I had arrived, yet the bungalow was a great convenience to me. I lived more of my life there than in my own home.

When I was working on a picture, I got up at six-thirty in the morning. This meant most mornings. My schedule called for four pictures a year, with no such thing as a vacation, and the only travel business or location trips.

I usually just put a polo coat on over my pajamas and was driven to the studio bungalow, where Katherine, my maid, had a bath drawn and breakfast ready to start when I walked in the door.

I felt I had really arrived when my bosses built me a Spanish bungalow on the studio lot. Here I am with my Packard town car, also a gift, in front of it. Some punkins, eh?

After breakfast I made up. Lucille, my hairdresser, arrived about this time, but since I wore my hair straight, all she had to do was keep it trimmed and the bangs even. She also gave me a manicure when I needed one.

While I was waiting to go to the set, the director would often come over to discuss problems—a retake of a scene shot the day before or a new gag sequence. The studio press agent was always there discussing angles for a magazine story or making arrangements for publicity pictures or telling me what newsmen from what part of America or what foreign countries would be visiting the set that day.

At nine o'clock I was on the set and ready to go to work. We broke for lunch around noon, then worked again until five-thirty or six, after which we went to the projection room to see the previous day's work—the rushes, as they were called. The director and I would divide the takes into "A" takes and "B" takes—the "A" negatives for domestic prints, the "B" negatives for foreign prints (the foreign prints were made abroad, because it was cheaper). If we were satisfied with the work so far, we went home. Otherwise we stayed on to discuss scenes we would retake the following day.

A picture took about eight weeks now to shoot. While it was being shot, John and the writers worked on the scenario for the next picture. The writers would often come home with John and me for dinner, and we would talk story until I had to excuse myself because it was time for me to go to bed.

When a picture was finished and a rough cut made of it, John and the director and the cutter and I and anybody else involved would look at it to see what should be added or cut or redone. When we thought the picture was ready to be seen, we took it to a theater in an outlying district for a sneak preview. During the showing we made notes, discussing afterward audience reaction and where the picture should be cut or lengthened.

This interval between the finish of one picture and the start of the next was a so-called rest period for me, but there was precious little rest to it. I spent days having fittings for the next film and then having tests made to see how the clothes photographed and if they were suitable to the character I was to portray.

At least one week was used up taking publicity shots. Since each magazine wanted an exclusive picture, the studio photographer would dream up all sorts of costumes and situations for me to pose in. I was photographed as a Chinese coolie, a pirate, a newsboy, a Dutch girl, a sailor. We'd spend three or four days at the house taking stills of me cooking, sewing, playing tennis, swimming, gardening. (I didn't have the vaguest idea of how to cook or sew or garden, and had no time to learn, but such pictures of cozy domesticity went over big with the fans, who were always looking for some link between their lives and the lives of their favorite movie stars.)

The interviews the press agent had been arranging were also held during this time—each of them with a different angle, since interviews also had to be exclusive.

The new picture started before I had time to breathe.

Not that I would have changed one minute of my schedule. I loved the work, the atmosphere, the camaraderie of studio life. Even when I had a day off, I went to the studio. In the first place, all my friends were there (most of them men, not by design, but because the only people with whom I had a continuing relationship were my director and crew, and they were men), and working together in any creative endeavor is the biggest binder of people to people that I know of. In the second place, so great was my absorption in movies, I wouldn't have known what else to do with myself.

We were all absorbed in movies, to the exclusion of almost all other things and all other people. The movies we made benefitted from it. I'm not so sure as individuals we did.

When Ben Schulberg came out to Hollywood as executive producer at Famous Players-Lasky, which later became Paramount, his wife Ad, with the help of Sol Lesser, the producer, began a series of Sunday night discussion groups on the Greek classics. Since the bulk of my high-school education had been obtained from private lessons with my tutor, I found these discussions stimulating, but the group soon disintegrated as one after another dropped out, preferring to talk movies.

Even our public social gatherings were industry affairs. Just as theater people in New York had their Sixty Club, which sponsored dances at the Ritz-Carlton Hotel, so we had our Mayfair subscription dances.

I've often thought that whoever dubbed us the movie colony hit

The versatility demanded of its stars by early Hollywood was remarkable. In Twinkletoes *I had to be a ballerina. Theodore Kosloff, the local dancing teacher, finally got me up on my toes.*

on an apt term. Hollywood is far different now, but in my years there it was a tight, provincial little world enjoying the society of its own people, wanting no other. Although we were part of the city of Los Angeles, homeowners in one or another of its suburbs, I think we never mentally unpacked our trunks. With a few notable exceptions, we took no part in civic or charitable endeavors, weren't interested in politics.

Almost the only "private" people we came in contact with were those who married into the industry. Generally they were women— the wives of producers and studio heads, who adapted, as good wives do everywhere, to their husbands' way of life. If, on the other hand, it was the husband who was a "private" person, his wife an actress, the marriage was sometimes hardly off the ground before it was on the rocks.

Part of the difficulty lay in the usual marriage-career conflict. A further part lay in the hours we kept—not only in the long number of hours which making movies required and which left little time to give to a husband and home, just as it left little time for any of us to take part in outside activities even had we been so motivated, but in the arrangement of those hours—an arrangement that also dictated in part our isolation from the world around us. When you have to get up at six-thirty every morning and report to the set clear-eyed and fresh-looking, you can't stay out late too many night befores.

One such marriage was that of Marion Nixon and Eddie Hillman. Eddie not only didn't work in the motion picture industry, he didn't work at all. As heir to a Chicago department store fortune, he didn't have to. He had a string of polo ponies, and when he wasn't occupied with them, he and a group of congenial friends lazed around the swimming pool of the house where he and Marion lived.

Almost every night he threw a party. The Firestone boys, Ray and Leonard, were often there, and Laddie Sanford and other visiting polo players. Morton Downey was a frequent guest, and a singing one, just as Vincent Youmans would oblige by playing the piano. Many picture people who weren't working would show up, and everybody would have a great time. There was only one drawback. Eddie could sleep till noon. Marion, who was starring in the Fox remake of *Rebecca of Sunnybrook Farm*, couldn't.

Finally Marion said to him, "Eddie, you get a job and start going to work mornings. I don't care if it's digging a ditch. I'm tired of seeing you and your friends hang around here all day long."

Scared that Marion might leave him, Eddie went to see his good friend Al Rogell, the director, and was given a job as Al's third assistant, scheduled to start work the next morning at Long Beach doing some exteriors.

That afternoon Long Beach had an earthquake (Eddie always said it was the shock of his going to work), but rather than delay the shooting or change location, the director had the story altered to incorporate the earthquake and its aftermath of shattered buildings.

The next morning Eddie's cook packed a delicious gourmet lunch and put two bottles of champagne in a portable icebox. Then Eddie rode off to work in his chauffeur-driven specially built town car.

A third assistant director doesn't have much to do, so after a while Eddie became bored and wandered away from the location to see what other damage the earthquake had done. One apartment house had its entire front blown off, leaving rooms exposed. While Eddie was standing there staring at it, two nuns drove up in a truck. Thinking him the owner, they asked the price of three bathtubs. Eddie said, "Why, nothing at all, Sisters. Just help yourselves." Delighted, the nuns had their workmen take four bathtubs, and Eddie went back to the location pleased at having been of some use to somebody.

A short time later a police wagon drove up. Out stepped two policemen and an irate man who was screaming, "One of these movie people stole my bathtubs!"

Eddie explained he hadn't stolen them, he'd just given them away to some dear little nuns. Money finally settled the argument, but the effort it entailed, plus the champagne at lunch, was too much for Eddie. When the company returned to the studio that afternoon for interior scenes in the conservatory of the hero's home, Eddie saw a nice wicker chair under a potted palm, sank into its roomy seat, and fell asleep.

The rushes next day showed Eddie snoring peacefully. The whole afternoon's work had to be retaken, and Eddie was fired from the only job he'd ever had in his life.

But if wealthy heirs like Eddie Hillman and his polo-playing friends were brought up living the good life, it didn't take the rest of us long, once we came into the possession of money, to figure out how to achieve to it ourselves. As more and more of us in Hollywood began earning bigger and bigger salaries, some of them pretty fantastic even by today's standards—and without today's tax bites—we splurged on homes and cars and clothes and swimming pools, partly, I suppose, because our intensive work schedules didn't permit such luxuries as travel, partly because what started out as necessities or conveniences became status symbols, and partly because most of us had more money than sense.

New houses were being built all the time and in all sorts of styles—English manors, Spanish haciendas, Italian villas, to say nothing of Hollywood French Provincial. Cecil B. De Mille built two houses side by side on the ridge of a hill. One housed his

It was an established custom for celebrities to "visit the set" and be photographed with the star. Left to right in this picture are William Morris, Jr., then a vaudeville entrepreneur, a Mr. Gillespie, Colleen, Robert Unger and Paul Whiteman, "The King of Jazz." I am in costume for Twinkletoes. *How do you like my blond curls?*

family, the other was his office and retreat. He also had a ranch where outside everything was very Western, while inside it was pure Cecil B. De Mille.

Even Charlie Chaplin built a house.

Although Charlie was noted for his stinginess, his loyalty to those working for him was so great, he kept his studio crew on the payroll year round, whether there was any work to be done or not, kept many of his early funnymen from the Keystone Comedies under contract, and paid Edna Purviance, his leading lady in his early films, her full salary until the day she died—which was in 1958.

One day, seeing all the unemployed carpenters at his studio, he decided to put them to work building a house for him on acreage he had bought next to Pickfair.

It was pennywise economy. Studio carpenters are not used to building for posterity. The sets they build are made to be torn down. Like Pickfair, Charlie's house had a name, too. Behind his back his friends called it Breakaway House, because a little at a time pieces of it began falling off—a bit of roof here, a windowsill there, until people began wondering when the whole house—or what was left of it—would break away entirely and go rolling down the hill to land in Benedict Canyon.

One afternoon as I was driving past Charlie's house, I saw his two boys, Sydney and Charles, Jr., out front with a lemonade stand. They were doing a thriving business serving workmen from the adjoining lot, where another new house was going up. It wasn't a hot day, and I wondered why the long line. I soon found out. I parked the car and joined the line. When my turn came, Charles, Jr. filled a glass for me from the pitcher, saying, "Five cents, please." It was pure Scotch.

Someone must have phoned Charlie, because I heard afterward he came rushing home from the studio to retrieve what was left of his stock of liquor. I also heard he cut off the boys' allowances until all the "lemonade" had been paid for.

During my starring years in Hollywood, I learned three lessons of my own about money. The first, demonstrated to me about as forcefully as Charlie's lesson to his sons, was that my capacity to continue earning money depended as much, if not more, on the whim of the public as it did on hard work or ability.

I had made four comedies in a row, starting with *Flaming Youth*, and I longed to play a dramatic part for a change. My big chance came when First National bought Edna Ferber's best-selling novel *So Big*. The role of Selina, who ages in the story from sixteen to sixty, was a challenge, and I wanted to prove I could play it. I was a big enough star now to demand the story I wanted, and it was given to me.

So Big received the best critical acclaim for me yet. (It also received a howl of anguish from Edna Ferber over the way the story was distorted to give the picture a typical Hollywood happy ending. She thought—and said—that since I was the star, I must have demanded the change. I hadn't. I didn't yet have the power to do that. If I had, I would have sided with her. In any case, many, many years later I was out at Elizabeth Arden's fat farm,

My favorite of all the roles I every played was Selina, in So Big, *from the Pulitzer Prize winning novel by Edna Ferber. I was typed as a comedienne, had to fight for the part.*

Main Chance, getting the regulation treatment when whom should I spy sitting a few feet away from me at the pool but Edna Ferber. I thought, oh, dear, it can't be, but yes it is, and I wonder what she'll—and then I thought, oh, well, the most she can do is throw me in the swimming pool, so I went over and said, "Miss Ferber, I'm Colleen Moore, and I just wanted to say hello." To my astonishment, she grabbed my hands and, pressing them to her, said, "Oh, my dear, how nice to see you. Of all the women who've played Selina in *So Big*, you're the only one who gave a true performance.")

In spite of the critical acclaim, *So Big* made only a few hundred thousand dollars profit instead of the usual million. Mr. Rowland and John both said to me, "All right, you've had your fun. Now, will you go back and give the public what it wants from you?"

The second lesson I learned about money came in 1926, when the bosses gave me a Packard town car. I thought they were spoiling me dreadfully until John said to me, "Spoiling you, hell. They're making a fortune on your pictures, and they want to keep you buttered up. Remember this about bosses, baby. They'll love you and think you're cute and sweet just as long as you keep piling up money for them the way you're doing." He shook his finger at me. "Don't ever forget this, baby. It's true. It's life."

The third lesson I learned was the most valuable of all.

Charles Brabin, who had directed me in *So Big*, also directed me in *Twinkletoes* late in 1926. (Charlie was married to and madly in love with Theda Bara, who in the early days, with her heavily blackened eyes and long hanging hair, was considered the *femme fatale* of the world. Theda, who was a great hostess, was also a very funny woman. At her parties she used to have us doubled up with laughter over her imitations of herself as the screen vamp.)

One day we were shooting a London street scene for *Twinkletoes* on the back lot. I didn't have to report to work that day until afternoon, but as usual, I couldn't keep away from the studio, so I drove over in the morning to watch the shooting.

I'd just been given the Packard town car. I'd also just spent four thousand dollars on a new mink coat. When I arrived on the set, I rushed over to Charlie saying, "Look at my new car!" I pirouetted in front of him. "And how do you like my new mink coat?"

Charlie took me by the hand saying, "Come here, Colleen. I want to show you something."

The London street was filled with extras dressed in poor Cockney clothes, sitting around on anything they could find, waiting for the sun to come out from behind some clouds so the long shots could be filmed. I sat on the arm of Charlie's chair, and he pointed to one of the extras. "I want you to look at that woman sitting over there on the curb. The one with the very straight back. She's now an old woman, but in her youth she was the toast of New York. Men drank champagne from her slipper. Her name is Frankie Bailey, and she made a thousand dollars a week. We pay her seven dollars and fifty cents a day to work as an extra.

I looked at the woman, who still had traces of her former beauty, and a small tremor ran up my spine.

"Now," Charlie said, "look at the woman behind the pushcart."

I did and saw a small, thin old lady with a very sweet face.

"As a lad in London," Charlie said, "I saved my pennies to get a seat in the top gallery just to hear her sing 'Sally in Our Alley.'

Her name is Lydia Titus Yeaman, and she was the most popular variety star in England. On her blouse is a pin given to her by King Edward VII with the notes from 'Sally' in diamonds. Ask her to show it to you. She, too, was paid a thousand dollars a week. She, too, now works as an extra for seven fifty a day."

I got up and went to my portable dressing room. It wasn't cold out, but I had a violent chill. I could see myself some future day sitting on a curb, wearing a ragged dress and an old battered hat, waiting for some movie star not yet born to arrive on the set in a new Packard town car, wearing a new mink coat.

That day was a big one in my life. I didn't give up buying clothes or even cars, and in less than a year John and I joined the big-home crowd with the purchase of a sizable estate of our own in Bel Air, but I saved money, too, against the day when I might not be able to earn it any longer.

Of all the houses that were built by Hollywood stars, Harold Lloyd's Green Acres came the closest to being my dream house. When Harold and Mildred Davis had been married about a year, they bought eighteen acres in Beverly Hills. The gardens were laid out first—surely the most extravagant and beautiful gardens in all Southern California. There was a nine-hole golf course so tough Bobby Jones had to play it three times before he could break par. Harold was a champion squash player, so he built a champion-size squash court. Mildred had a greenhouse where she grew her own orchids for corsages—to me, the height of elegance.

The swimming pool was Olympic size. The fountains by the house were patterned after some of those at Italy's famous Villa d'Este, spilling thousands of gallons of water down the hill. A large waterfall cascaded over a cliff into a stream designed as a canoe course.

All of this was man-built, as in all of Southern California there isn't a waterfall—and what water there is is so scarce and expensive one feels guilty about leaving any in a glass. As a neighbor with only two acres, knowing what my water bill came to each month just for watering the lawn, I used to look at Harold's place and goggle.

But Harold obviously knew what he was in for and prepared for it. When the gardens, which cost a million dollars, were finished, I asked him when the house would be built. He said not until

*I received critical acclaim for my per-
formance in the role of Selina in* So Big,
*but I was not encouraged to pursue a
career as a dramatic actress.*

he had enough income from his investments to pay for the upkeep of the whole place.

The first plans were drawn up by Webber, Staunton and Spaulding for a house three stories high with two elevators. Harold said he wanted something not so grand. After all, there were only Mildred, the baby Gloria, and himself. He took pencil and paper and drew his idea of a house. That was what was built.

When the plans were finished, Harold and the architect went to the hilltop and laid out the house in string. Against the big outdoors it looked awfully small. After it was built, Harold and Mildred stood in the drawing room looking around and at each other. Mildred shook her head. "This house is awfully big. It looked so cozy in string."

When things were going full blast at Green Acres, the Lloyds (who by that time had another baby—a son) had thirty-three servants, including gardeners and a gatekeeper—all paid for out of the income from money Harold made in films before he was thirty!

But then most of us made our money before we were thirty or even twenty-five, so I suppose we may be forgiven for devoting the same wholehearted concentration to spending it that we did to earning it and, since we were almost constantly on display, for displaying ourselves in as grand a manner as we could. I suppose we even thought the public expected it of us.

Certainly we were the center of a great deal of attention—our public and private lives dissected, our personalities explored, our tastes emulated, our clothes and hair styles copied.

Jetta Goudal, a C. B. De Mille star, was the first to wear her dark hair drawn back from her face into a bun at the nape of her neck— a style later made popular by Kay Francis and Nita Naldi. Jean Harlow started a worldwide trend for platinum hair. Marlene Dietrich made men's slacks part of every girl's wardrobe. Garbo made the polo coat and floppy hat a glamour duo. Joan Crawford made Paris accept the wide shoulders created for her by Adrian at M-G-M. Loretta Young made very wide, full skirts the thing for evening wear.

(One day, while I was making a film called *Her Wild Oat*, I saw among the extras the most beautiful little girl I had ever seen. I suggested we make a test of her. When I saw the test the next day with the studio brass, I was elated. She was even better than her promise. To my shock, the bosses, even John, said, "But her teeth stick out in front." I said, "For heaven's sake, she's only fourteen years old. Haven't you ever heard about braces?" So they signed her to a contract and sent her to a dentist. Convinced now they had another Corinne Griffith on their hands, the bosses wanted to change her name to something more romantic than her own name Gretchen Young. So I named her—after the most beautiful doll I had ever had. Loretta.)

Lilyan Tashman, who was our best-dressed woman, started the practice of wearing lapel pins on suits. Lilyan had more clothes than most of the rest of us put together. She never wore the same dress twice, and such was her devotion to making the right appearance, she once repainted her dining room dark blue for one of her famous Easter Sunday brunches so it would contrast with her golden hair.

The flapper clothes started in Hollywood—made by a young dressmaker just out of school who had a cubbyhole shop on Hollywood Boulevard. Her name was Irene.

Howard Greer of Paramount made his "lady" clothes the talk of the fashion world. His were the first untheatrical clothes used in movies. Conservative, elegant, subtle in design, they started a new trend on screen as well as off it.

(Howard had started his career with Madam Lucille in London and Paul Poiret in Paris. One day he received a letter from Poiret saying he was coming to Hollywood for a visit. Wanting to impress his old boss, Howard asked his good friend Betty Compson, a Paramount star, if he could borrow her big town car and chauffeur to meet Poiret at the station. Driving back to Howard's salon, Poiret brought out a cigarette. He fumbled around, looking for the lighter. Howard, not knowing where it was either, also fumbled around. Poiret said, "Isn't this your car?" Howard said, "Certainly, but I always use the sports car, seldom this one.")

While I was vitally interested in the clothes Colleen Moore wore on the screen, I never paid much attention to my own wardrobe, going around most of the time in skirts and sweaters and saddle shoes. One time the famous New York dress designer, and my good friend, Janet "Foxy" Sondheim came to visit me. She stood it for two days. Then she burst out, "Someone has to tell you, so I suppose it might as well be me. You're the worst dressed woman in Hollywood, and that's saying a lot, because this is certainly the land of ruffles and buttons and bows, and you have more of them than anyone. Now I've said it, shall I pack?"

I hugged her. "Pack? Are you crazy? Help me buy some clothes."

I didn't buy a stitch. I took every dress she'd brought with her except for three which Jean Harlow, who was standing there during this conversation, managed to latch onto. Poor Foxy went back to New York with only the suit on her back.

After that, Foxy took pity on me and would regularly send me not only a dress she'd designed, but shoes, hat, and a bag to match—all numbered so I wouldn't get things mixed up. Each time a box arrived, there was a note in it saying, *Have you thrown away the saddle shoes?"*

A box arrived on my birthday. Inside was a lovely pink chiffon evening dress with black dots. I was disappointed Foxy had forgotten to send the slip to go with it, but since I had one that fitted it, I wore the new dress to a party that night, where I received many compliments on it. When I wrote Foxy to thank her for it, I got a phone call from New York. "Evening dress? That's a nightgown!"

One lady who didn't think much of Hollywood or its clothes was the actress wife of a prominent European director who came to Hollywood with her husband to star in a picture he was making for First National about the legendary Helen of Troy. One morning I heard a big commotion outside my studio bungalow and looked out to see the lady, her face taut, her beautiful figure clad only in a diaphanous chiffon gown, striding toward her set followed by two beseeching assistant directors and, bringing up the rear, her maid, holding up a pair of underpants and wailing, "But, Madame, this is America. You must wear your pants!"

The end of the story was reported to me—and to everybody else in the studio—in short order by the movie's wide-eyed crew. When Madame arrived on the set, everybody joined in the chorus trying to get her to put on more clothes. She finally became so angry she put her hand up to her bosom and with one majestic sweep of her arm ripped her gown off. Then she stalked off to her portable dressing room stark naked.

Another lady who did not think the sun rose and set in Hollywood was Mrs. Patrick Campbell, who came to us from London, where for over forty years she had been one of the most celebrated actresses in the theater, achieving her first success in 1893 in the title role of

Sir Arthur Wing Pinero's *The Second Mrs. Tanqueray*, going on to play, among other roles, Juliet, Lady Macbeth, and Ophelia to Sir Johnston Forbes-Robertson's Hamlet, Mélisande to Bernhardt's Pélleas in Maeterlinck's play, and, in 1914, creating the role of Eliza Doolittle in Shaw's *Pygmalion*, which he wrote for her.

George Cukor, the director and an old friend of Mrs. Campbell, gave a party in her honor. As usual, everybody who was anybody in Hollywood turned out for the big affair.

Looking at Mrs. Campbell, who was then almost seventy, I found it hard to believe she'd been a great beauty in her youth. She was fat, with her hair dyed black, and with lots of teeth. When I was introduced to her, she purred to me, "You're such a pretty little thing. You should be in the movies."

In all innocence I said, "I am."

Douglas Fairbanks was introduced next. When she gave him the same sort of line, he said, "If you don't know who I am I'd better fire my press agent."

On and on Mrs. Campbell went, giving the same line to all the stars, until Bebe Daniels put an end to it. When Mrs. Campbell said to Bebe, "You're so beautiful, you should be in the movies," Bebe said, "And what did you say your name is?"

Drawing herself up regally, Mrs. Campbell boomed out, "I am Mrs. Patrick Campbell."

"Oh," Bebe said, "of the Campbell soup family?"

But if Mrs. Campbell felt that way about us, other distinguished visitors did not.

A few years ago the American press and public were considerably taken aback over the fuss Russia's Nikita Khrushchev kicked up about going to Disneyland, yet in the 1920s whenever any foreign notables came to the United States, the first place they wanted to go was Hollywood, and the three people in America they most wanted to meet were Mary Pickford, Douglas Fairbanks, and Charlie Chaplin.

The guest list at Pickfair reads like Who's Who of the World. The Crown Prince of Japan—he's now the Emperor. Alfonso XIII, ex-King of Spain. Marconi. Lindbergh. Einstein. Amelia Earhart. Sir Austen Chamberlain. The King and Queen of Siam. Crown Princess Frederica of Prussia. The Duke and Duchess of Alba. The glamorous Lord and Lady Mountbatten, who spent part of their honeymoon visiting Pickfair. The great authors, painters, politicians—all found their way to the hill.

I once asked Mary how it felt to entertain royalty, and she told me about the time she gave a dinner party for the King and Queen of Siam. The young couple liked tennis, so Douglas invited them to come up in the afternoon for a few games.

They were on the court playing when the little queen, going after a far ball, slid into some mud, splattering it all over her.

Mary took the queen upstairs to her bedroom, went into the bathroom and ran water in the tub, and then stood outside the door saying to herself, "Imagine you, Gladys Smith of Toronto, Canada, with the Queen of Siam in your bathtub."

People in Hollywood were just as honored to be entertained at Pickfair as the world's great. Mary Pickford and Douglas Fairbanks were our undisputed leaders. Mary was also one of the few movie people who took part in outside activities. (Louis B. Mayer, a pillar of the Republican party, was another, and Harold Lloyd, an active Shriner and a member of the Los Angeles Chamber of Commerce, still another). It was Mary's participation in one of those outside activities that led to her greatest service to the motion picture industry itself.

In addition to selling war bonds in 1918, Mary organized a benefit performance at the Grand Opera House which raised $40,000 to buy ambulances as gifts from motion picture people. The war ended before the money could all be spent, leaving $27,000 in the treasury.

At a meeting Mary called at the old Triangle Studio, someone suggested the money be prorated and sent back to the donors. Mary had a better suggestion—that the money be used to start a Motion Picture Relief Fund "to care for our own people who need help," her dream a country home where our old could live in pride and dignity.

Together with Mrs. Ann Lehr, whose husband ran the Goldwyn Studio, Mary raised $200,000. Mary's cousin, Sonny Shaliff, who was in radio, suggested that if actors would donate their services to a weekly radio show, at least $10,000 a week could be raised. Jules Stein, then head of MCA and now the largest stockholder in Universal, sold the idea to Campbell Soup, and the money started rolling in. The studios asked everyone to give one half of one per cent of his salary to the cause, and almost everyone did.

With all this money coming in, the Motion Picture Home was

built—a series of beautiful bungalows, attractively furnished, situated around a main house containing a lounge, a dining room, and a theater. All the new films are shown there before they reach the movie houses. A modern clinic and hospital have been added with the finest medical care available. Is it any wonder that Mary Pickford was and is Hollywood's first citizen?

To young matrons in Hollywood like me, Mary Pickford was also the symbol of the perfect marriage. She and Doug were never separated. Once when Doug was on location about three hours' distance away, Mary, after finishing work at the studio, would get in their trailer and be driven to the location to stay the night with Doug. At dawn she'd get up, then sleep in the trailer while the chauffeur drove her back to the studio. For more than fourteen years they were our great love story.

Then we heard that Doug was in Europe alone, that there was another woman in the picture—the beautiful blond Sylvia, wife of Lord Ashley. Gossip columns hinted there would soon be a showdown between the most famous movie star of all times and her athletic actor husband.

It was unbelievable to us. We thought Doug must have lost his senses and should be locked up until he recovered them. Even if they wanted to, how could the Fairbankses let the world down by divorce? It would ruin both their careers. Hollywood buzzed with rumors and speculation. Mary said nothing.

Years later, when Mary and I became friends, she told me she and Douglas had had it out before he left for Europe. He swore he wasn't going. She believed him, until she found his steamship tickets.

In a huff, Mary took the Santa Fe *Chief* to New York to consult her lawyer. Sitting alone in her drawing room, she brooded about what course of action to take. The train had just pulled out of Albuquerque after an hour's stop there, when a knock came at her door. When she opened the door, there, bag and baggage, stood Doug, smiling and looking mischievous. Mary gasped. "How did you get here?"

"A friend flew me over," Doug answered.

Mary told Doug to get out of her drawing room and find space for himself somewhere else. He said there wasn't any other space, and he'd told the conductor he was sure his wife would let him share her room. She laughed and let him stay. He kept her laughing all the way to New York. When he wasn't making her laugh, he was vowing his undying love, swearing that Lady Ashley meant nothing to him.

In New York he got on the boat and sailed for England. Mary returned to Hollywood brokenhearted.

Hollywood now became a bristling community with the whole town on Mary's side. The strain on Mary, who still remained silent, was almost unbearable. She, the world's sweetheart, one of the great beauties of all time—cameramen said hers was the one perfect photogenic face in Hollywood—had lost her husband to another woman.

The person closest to Mary was her mother Charlotte. Mary poured out to her all of her unhappiness and her fears of ruining her career by scandal. Charlotte told her her happiness came first and her career second, to forget about public reaction and think only of her own feelings.

One day Mary told a woman newspaper friend in confidence what was going on. The woman betrayed her trust, and headlines were splashed around the world that Douglas Fairbanks had a new love.

Doug cabled Mary, saying he had been named corespondent in a London divorce suit. In England a man so accused is supposed to marry the lady mentioned or be considered a cad. Doug asked Mary what she was going to do. She told him she would file for divorce.

That wasn't what Doug wanted. He sent a long cable to his former wife Beth, who was happily remarried to musical comedy star Jack Whiting, begging her to intercede for him with Mary. Beth tried, but it was no use.

In California it takes a year before a divorce becomes final and the parties involved can marry again. Eleven months after Mary filed, Doug returned from Europe and begged Mary on his knees not to pick up the final papers. Her heart was breaking, but her pride had been so wounded by front-page publicity around the world, she refused.

Doug and Lady Ashley were married and moved into the beach house formerly occupied by Doug and Mary. Before long Mary began getting phone calls from Doug asking if he could just come up to Pickfair and sit by the pool and be quiet. They'd sit there together, peaceful, saying little. Once Doug said, "What a mistake, Mary."

She answered, "I'm sorry."

Two years later Mary married Charles (Buddy) Rogers, her leading man in *The Girl Friend*. This time it really was the perfect marriage. Just like the movies, they've lived happily ever after.

And just like real life, Mary got the last word.

Except for Marion Davies, Mary had the finest collection of jewelry in Hollywood—matched sets of emeralds, of rubies, of sapphires, and of diamonds, each stone in each set of superb quality, the earrings in her diamond set enormous pear-shaped drops which had belonged to her mother.

Shortly after the divorce Mary took a plane trip to Washington, D.C. She had just boarded the plane and was sitting in a seat by the window, her jewel box on her lap, when who should flounce in but the new Mrs. Douglas Fairbanks. She sat down beside Mary and, seeing the jewel box, said, "Pickey, dear, let me see your jewels."

Mary told me no one in all her life had ever called her Pickey, but she said nothing. Then the devil in her came out.

Sylvia's passion for jewels was well-known. Very innocent-eyed, Mary turned to her and said, "Of course. I want you to see them, because Douglas gave them all to me." Taking out each jewel, one by one, she would say, "This was for my birthday, and this one was for nothing at all—just a Tuesday present."

Sylvia's eyes popped, especially when she came to the diamond eardrops.

Mary, still looking innocent, said, "Let me see your jewels, Sylvia."

Sylvia mumbled something about not having been married very long and showed Mary a very ordinary pin she was wearing, made of large but second-rate stones.

Sitting with the new Mrs. Fairbanks all the way across the country had made Mary so distraught that when she left the plane in Washington she forgot her jewel box. She had just realized it was missing when the phone rang. It was Sylvia calling from New York. "Pickey darling," she said, "I want you to know your jewels are safe with me. I'll hold them for you until you get to New York."

Mary thanked her, thinking what a delicious scene there would be when Doug tried to explain that the fabulous earrings were not a present from him, and that he had not bought the rubies either—Mary had paid for them herself. An ex-wife does sometimes have her moments.

There was another woman in my marriage, too, but it wasn't the kind of situation either the press or people in Hollywood could have made anything of, except to think I'd lost my senses, too. John's mistress wasn't a flesh and blood woman. She was Colleen Moore.

As production head of the First National studio, John had to see all of the pictures made there and follow through on them. Our lives began to separate more and more. He stayed nights at the studio looking at rushes. Since I had to get up early, I went home alone, often had dinner on a tray in bed, reading. But there was a separateness between us far more damaging than that dictated by the hours of our work.

One of the drawbacks of success in Hollywood, as elsewhere in public life, is the spotlight of attention which is continually focused upon you. Actors are grateful, of course, for the support of the public and the press. Without them we would be nothing. (I reached a point where my fan mail came to over ten thousand letters a week. A staff of four secretaries handled the mail, answering every letter with a form letter which appeared to be a personal letter from me, telling about my newest film, asking them to be sure to inquire at their local theater as to when the picture would be shown there, and signed with my name—all four secretaries could copy my signature perfectly.) But the lack of privacy is sometimes nerve-racking.

One time after completing a picture, I was tired and nervous and not feeling well. A young cousin of mine, Maran Johnstone, was visiting my parents, and Mother suggested that Maran and I go to Yosemite for a few days, so I could get some rest.

We arrived in the evening, and after checking in went to the lodge for dinner. I stopped on the porch, where there was a phone booth, and called John to tell him we had arrived safely. A crowd gathered around the booth listening to every word I said. Maran reported to me later that the person nearest the booth would call out to those behind, "She just said she loves him," and this word would be spread through the crowd. Then, "She says it's colder than she expected," and so on and on until I hung up. They followed us into the dining room and sat around watching us eat. I smiled and smiled until the smile just froze to my weary face. We didn't finish dinner, but made a track-winning run back to our cabin.

In the free time John and I did have alone together, I wanted to get away from the movies for a while and discuss things with him as wife to husband—the books I was reading, current events, ideas. All he wanted to talk about was Colleen Moore and how to make her the biggest box-office attraction in America.

One Sunday afternoon I suggested to John that we have a child. He looked at me in dismay. "A child?" His voice was full of fear. "What would you do with a child? You're only a little girl yourself."

I stared at him in disbelief. I was a twenty-two-year-old woman with a husband and with the responsibility of a home as well as a career. Colleen Moore was only a part of my life.

She was all of his. He ran my films over and over again, obsessed with the idea that Colleen Moore was his creation, telling me I would be nothing without him.

It came as a shock to me when I finally faced it, though I suppose I'd known it all along. John didn't love me, Kathleen Morrison McCormick. He was in love with his dream girl, Colleen Moore. He wanted no part of the woman I had become. He wanted no discussion, no equality. He wanted a young, innocent, amusing little girl who would sit at his feet and call him Daddy, a child wife who would be totally dependent upon him.

If a husband and wife don't grow together, their marriage doesn't have a chance. I was growing and changing, but I was doing it alone.

Another specter shadowing our marriage was John's drinking, which was getting worse all the time and with which I was increasingly unable to cope. It took me some time to recognize the onset of a drinking spell—the taut nerves, the white line of strain that would appear around his mouth—and disappear into a rosy glow of lightheartedness and relaxation when he started to drink.

That would have been fine if relaxation was as far as it went, but once John started drinking, he couldn't stop until, usually after three days of all drinking, no eating, he was shaking so badly he could no longer lift the glass to his mouth. Then he'd go to a doctor and be taken to a hospital to dry out.

During the year of our engagement he had had only two of these drinking bouts—at least, as far as I knew. During the first few months of our marriage he had had only the two brushes with them—on our wedding night and on Christmas morning. But gradually the rumors my mother had heard about his being a periodic drinker proved all too true.

At first—and with alarming regularity—John's periods of drunkenness came about every two months. Then as time passed and the pressures of being studio production head mounted, they came about every six weeks.

After a drinking bout—and the drying out—he would return to the studio—where I'd strained my imagination thinking of excuses to explain his absence, trying to protect his job for him—pounds thinner and filled with a feverish energy, his perception of story values sharper, ideas coming so fast it was like a dam breaking.

He also returned filled with remorse, bringing me an expensive present, usually a jewel. I think the reason jewelry has never meant anything to me is because I earned almost every piece John ever gave me.

This was the man who wanted me to be totally dependent on him.

There was one man I could depend on, did depend on. He became my closest and my lifelong friend.

I met him at the end of 1924, when I was making *Sally*, adapted from the Ziegfeld musical in which Marilyn Miller had appeared on Broadway. It seems strange now, the idea of adapting a musical comedy into a silent film, but we did it all the time, supplying the theaters with a cued score for the orchestra or organ, or, in some smaller theaters, piano, incorporating into the film the story and all the dance numbers, omitting only the singing.

Since musical comedy stories in those days were invariably thin, we fattened them out with gag sequences. One day early in the filming of *Sally*, Al Green, the director, brought a young man over to me—a young man a little taller than I who was about my age but looked fifteen, with large blue eyes, a sensitive mouth, and very fair skin. Al said, "This is Mervyn LeRoy. He has a great sense of humor. I think he can invent some funny gags for this picture."

He did—and inadvertently set up the best gag sequence we had off-screen, too. In *Sally* I played the role of a dancer, my biggest

My public preferred to see me in the sort of role I played in We Moderns, *a film with glossy settings and madcap antics. Here I am with another actor.*

scene one in which, dressed in a Russian costume, I squatted down on my heels and danced the getzolski. Only I couldn't do it. So Mervyn suggested I be put in a harness attached to invisible piano wire, with a man up in the rafters handling the wire, enabling me to kick my legs out and back with all the flashiness and apparent ease of a born and bred Cossack.

The day we shot the scene the Notre Dame football team visited the set. The team, which included the famous Four Horsemen, had just won the 1925 Rose Bowl game and was being everywhere feted. I was thrilled to be visited by these men, and when the orchestra started playing, I went into my dance with great confidence, watching them, hoping to make a big impression on them.

I did. The man in the rafters was watching them, too—so much so that he forgot what he was supposed to be doing and pulled the wire high. Legs flashing, I went sailing right over their heads, knocking down scenery and lamps as I flew.

Mervyn invented the gags for many of my pictures after *Sally*— invented, too, a screen credit for himself as Comedy Constructor! (And said to me one day on the set when I asked him if he thought comedy or drama was harder for an actress to do, "Comedy. An onion can make any actress cry, but the vegetable has yet to be grown that can make her funny." I agree. Both comedy and drama are hard, but in a tragic scene you can dig down into your emotions, whereas in comedy there's no depth of experience in life to call upon. Similarly, in drama the director becomes an actress' audience and, if there is a rapport between them, the wellspring of her emotional outpourings. But in comedy you're on your own, taking only from the director's intellect.)

But as important as Mervyn was to me in my career, he was even more important to me in my personal life. We became almost inseparable. He knew all about John's drinking—he and John were good friends, too—and whenever the drinking got me down, I'd talk it out with Mervyn.

Mervyn had a better understanding of John's sickness—because of course it was a sickness—than I did, but then Mervyn didn't have to live with John. I did, and I began to fight his drinking with bitter words and sarcasm, which didn't help.

John fought back, saying if I were tolerant like other wives and let him have one martini before dinner every night, he wouldn't have a drinking problem, that it was my insistence on no drinking at all that drove him mad.

I agreed to try it his way.

That night he had one drink before dinner. He never got to the table. He ran away. The next I heard was from a policeman in Beverly Hills, who phoned to say he had found John sprawled in his Rolls-Royce, the car sideways across Wilshire Boulevard. He'd taken him to a bungalow at the Ambassador Hotel. I thanked him and called the doctor.

When we arrived, the bell captain sent two boys with us, saying John had become dangerous. We went to the bungalow and found it locked from the inside. Looking through the window, we saw he'd broken every piece of furniture in the room. The bellboys broke down the door and with the help of my chauffeur, who was wiry and strong, they got John on the floor and held him fast, so the doctor could give him a knockout shot. Then we took him to the hospital.

I had had enough. The next morning I was sitting in the bedroom of my bungalow putting on make-up, determined to leave him, knowing I couldn't go on this way. To appear on the set every day and try to be funny when my heart was breaking wide open was getting beyond my strength.

The door from the living room opened, and in came a small Scottie dog. Attached to his collar was a balloon. Written on it was, *"Please let John come home."*

I couldn't help but laugh.

My maid Katherine shook her head at me, saying, "He'll laugh you back again." He did. He was standing outside the door, waiting to hear if I laughed, knowing if I did I was lost.

This time he wasn't filled with remorse. He became very excited, telling me we were going to New York to make *Naughty But Nice*, and we'd go to the theater every night and to the Stork Club and other fun places. We'd have a second honeymoon. Only this time no press, no exhibitors. Just us at night painting the town. He also said he'd negotiated a new contract for me—$10,000 a week for the next two years.

His eyes were very blue and shining, his handsome, smiling face full of love. I melted and said, "Okay."

The train trip across country was fun, because all of my gang was along. When we arrived in New York, Mervyn and the director and John and I and my maid Katherine checked in at the Hotel Ambassador on Park Avenue.

Our first day's work was on top of a Fifth Avenue double-decker bus. That evening Mervyn and I went back to the hotel to pick up John so we could all go to the Stork Club for dinner. When we arrived in the sitting room of our suite on the sixteenth floor, John was standing before an open window. He looked around at us, glassy-eyed, without recognition.

Furious, I lost my temper, crying out, "I hate you, you weak, dumb idiot. You're ruining my life and destroying your own career. How long do you think it will be before the New York office hears about your disappearances? I can't save your job for you forever." I learned later that the New York office had warned John about his drinking that afternoon.

He turned and, grabbing me to him, tried to throw me out the window. I screamed with fright, but I was no match for him. Mervyn rushed over and kicked him, pulling me free. Then he grabbed my hand, and we ran out the door.

All night long Mervyn walked me around the streets of New York, me crying, he comforting me, neither of us wanting to return to the hotel for fear John would kill me. By dawn we were a couple of bleary-eyed kids.

When we went back to the hotel John was gone.

He stayed away for three days. The director, knowing John was doing one of his disappearing acts—his drunken spells were studio jokes by this time—said nothing. Merv thought he could persuade John to take a cure. He said he would talk to him when he sobered up, letting him know that if he didn't stop drinking he was going to lose a wife.

Three days later John walked into our hotel room sober and cross, with no apology. Just seeing him standing there indifferent to the fact that he was destroying me infuriated me. I lashed out at him, ending up telling him I was going to divorce him.

He gave me a taunting look. "You can't divorce me. You're a Catholic. You're tied to me for life." And he laughed.

I stared at him, shocked by the realization that he was so sure I wouldn't defy my church that he felt free to do as he pleased. I'd always be there. For the first time the full meaning of "for better, for worse" got through to me. I loved my church. I wondered if I would have the courage to defy it.

I also still loved John, although it was getting harder and harder to prevent my image of him from shattering completely.

By the time we returned to Hollywood to shoot the interiors for *Naughty But Nice*, the gossip about John had taken a new turn—the bosses were going to fire him as head of the studio.

John never said a word to me, but I heard, and my heart ached for him. He was a proud man, and I knew this would break his pride. I wanted to help him. I was now in a position where I could.

In the fall of 1926 John's goal for Colleen Moore had been realized. *The Exhibitor's Herald* poll showed that over twenty-five hundred theater owners had voted me the number-one box-office attraction in the country. (Number two was my teenage idol, Tom Mix.) My films were bringing more people to the theater than those of any other star, and that included Mary Pickford, Norma Talmadge, and Gloria Swanson.

My films were also making millions for First National. I picked up the telephone and called Dick Rowland in New York. "This is Mrs. John McCormick speaking," I said. "I just called to say hello."

Adela Rogers St. Johns was with me when I made the call. Later when she wrote an original story from which the picture *A Star Is Born* was made, she used my gambit. In the final scene of the picture, the star arrives at a premiere and, wanting to keep the memory of her now-dead husband alive and to declare her love for him to all the world, she steps up to the radio microphone and says, "This is Mrs. Norman Main."

It was a very effective scene, and though its original was for a somewhat different purpose, it, too, was effective. John's job was saved.

But the strain of his ordeal had been too much for him. He started drinking again, this time right in his office. His secretary sent word down to me on the set. Merv and Henry Freulich, our still photographer, went up and got him on his feet and, practically carrying him, took him out the back way to Hank's car and drove him home. An hour or so later our butler, Ben Fukeshima, called to tell me John had disappeared.

A week later John called me from the hospital where he was drying out, and I went over. I don't know where he'd been, and I'm sure he didn't remember, but he looked as if he'd had a rugged time. On one cheek was a scar, as if he'd been cut with a knife.

As I came near the bed, he grabbed my hands, the tears running down his face. He was weak and trembling.

I couldn't say a word. I pitied him, but there was no welling of love in my heart this time. He was like a lemming bent on his own destruction, and because I was so closely associated with him professionally, he was at the point of destroying Colleen Moore with him—more nearly so than even I realized at that moment.

The next picture I was scheduled to make was *Smiling Irish Eyes*. It was to be Mervyn LeRoy's first picture as a director, the culmination of the dream he and I shared—Mervyn directing me.

A week after his return to the studio, John came to my bungalow and said, "We're leaving tonight for New York."

I stared at him. "But the picture—"

"We're not making *Irish Eyes*. You're walking out on it."

"But why?" I asked.

All he said was, "I've done all right for you before picture-wise, haven't I? Trust me that what I'm doing is for your good."

He always had done all right for me professionally, so there was nothing I could say. But Mervyn now had no film to direct. I was walking out on my best friend.

As soon as John left, I called Dick Rowland in New York and said, "Don't ask me any questions, Dick, because I don't understand what's going on, and as you know, I'm in John's corner. But for old times' sake, please give Mervyn some other picture to direct."

Dick said he understood, and he would, and that he was sure everything would be straightened out when John and I got to New York.

I didn't know what to make of that last remark, but I found out when we reached Kansas City. There I received a wire from the New York office saying they were suing me for one million dollars for breach of contract. Bewildered, I asked John what had happened. He said he was quitting as head of First National. He was going to make a new deal with them in which he would produce only my pictures. I knew then what had happened. He'd been fired.

When we arrived in New York we checked into an enormous suite at the Ritz-Carlton Hotel on Madison Avenue, where my brother Cleeve joined us. John had wired him to come, thinking, I guess, that I needed a friend. I did.

Even thinking back on it now makes me as ill as it made me then. In those days a million-dollar lawsuit was big news. The papers were filled with the controversy. Nothing I ate would stay down. My weight dropped to ninety-nine pounds. I became so weak from hunger and nervousness Cleeve finally sent for a doctor to give me a prescription.

John was drinking heavily, but because of the magnitude of the situation he managed to keep himself from going off the deep end. He bought tickets on the *Mauretania*, telling all the reporters we were going to Europe to make films.

When that word hit the papers I couldn't go anywhere at all, because process servers started looking for me to prevent me from leaving the country. For days I moped around in the living room

We Moderns *in which I typified once
more the audacious flapper daughter of
rich aristocrats, complete with a butler,
doesn't seem very modern now.*

of our suite at the Ritz, until one day a dear little old lady appeared at the door saying she loved Colleen Moore and wanted her autograph. When I took the paper she held out to me, she turned and fled, leaving me staring after her wondering why she hadn't waited for the autograph she wanted so much.

The injunction served, the lawyers started negotiating. John won a new contract for $100,000 a year as the producer of my films only. The press took pictures of Dick Rowland and me burying the hatchet, but the pictures should have been of John and Dick Rowland. I had no fight with First National. I knew John had used me to gain what he wanted, at the expense of my health and happiness. I began to wonder if I, as a human being, had ever existed for him.

Still, when we returned to California, he seemed so happy over the new arrangement and went around telling everybody how he was going to have time now to enjoy life, I began to believe it myself, thinking that with the responsibility for the entire studio off his back, he'd be able to relax, and maybe the drinking would stop.

One of my mother's favorite maxims was "It's always darkest before the dawn." All I could think was it had been a long, dark night.

CHAPTER 10

BUT CAN SHE TALK?

One day in 1928, while I was filming George Gershwin's hit musical, *Oh Kay!*—my dream-come-true film, because Mervyn was directing it—John came on the set and told me he wanted to speak to me in private. We went to my portable dressing room, and he said, "How would you like to have a film shown on Broadway twice a day at two dollars a throw?"

Just as Hollywood's big grosses aren't a thing of today—*The Birth of a Nation* grossed sixty million, *The Big Parade* over twenty-five million—neither is the two-a-day reserved-seat showing a modern phenomenon. Griffith started it, the way he started almost everything else, with *The Birth of a Nation*.

In my years in Hollywood, when the ordinary price for a movie was about thirty-five cents, a successful film given a two-a-day showing was more than a moneymaker. It was a mark of prestige for its star.

John had already achieved just about everything else for his dream girl Colleen Moore. I had won the exhibitors' poll as number one box-office attraction not only in 1926, but again in 1927. On December 19, 1927, Sid Grauman having decided I rated the big cement job,

I had put my hand- and footprints in the forecourt of his Chinese Theater. (Determined to have my feet look properly dainty instead of my own size six—now eight—I bought a pair of very tiny shoes with spike heels. Feeling like a Chinese girl with bound feet, I hobbled over to the wet cement and made the prints. When I was in Hollywood recently I went to look at them, and my feet are smaller than my hands!)

The only thing I hadn't achieved other than the two-a-day showing, and something I had been quite hurt about, was to be asked to join the Motion Picture Academy at the time of its founding in 1927. The night of the big banquet I asked John why we hadn't been included. He only gave me a cross look and stalked out of the room. Years later when somebody showed me a program from that first banquet, I was dumfounded to see my name listed as one of the founders. Why John didn't tell me, I don't know, but I suppose that after he was dropped as production head of First National, for all his talk about being pleased just to have the responsibility for my pictures, he felt he was no longer such a big shot, and the idea of appearing at the banquet with his wife still a top star and so many of his former associates still the big shots they had been rankled him.

The two-a-day showing presented no conflict, since it didn't involve me as his wife but only as his screen property.

Answering his question, I said I thought it would be great and suggested he start looking for a story. He told me he'd already found one and bought it—Jane Cowl's stage hit, *Lilac Time*. He'd also persuaded George Fitzmaurice, who produced his own pictures for First National, to direct it. Adela Rogers St. Johns was going to do the treatment, adapting the story to fit me, Carey Wilson was to write the scenario, and the picture was going to cost the knee-shaking sum of one million dollars to produce. (If today's big grosses were not unknown to us, today's production costs would have staggered us. *The Birth of a Nation* cost $80,000, *The Big Parade* $200,000, *Flaming Youth* $90,000, most of my starring pictures about $250,000.)

While John was getting *Lilac Time* ready for production, Mervyn and I and the *Oh Kay!* company and crew went to Catalina to film exteriors. In *Oh Kay!* I was supposed to be mixed up with a gang of bootleggers on a rum-running boat. The boat was actually

Another time-consuming activity of movie actresses was posing for "stills." I am decked out in this pirate suit for no reason except the purposes of publicity. I'm afraid my face reflects boredom.

When Sid Grauman invited me to leave my footprints on the con-crete sands of time, I wore such small shoes I could hardly walk. Colleen and Sid Grauman in the forecourt of the Chinese Theatre.

a huge fishing boat, and how we managed to film the scenes on it I'll never know. It reeked so of dead fish I longed for a gas mask.

One night at the village movie theater we saw a very good-looking young man named Gary Cooper in a Western. So far John had been unable to find the right man to play opposite me in *Lilac Time*, so I called him and suggested he test Cooper. At that time Gary was under contract to Paramount and had a small part in the as yet unreleased Clara Bow film, *Wings*. John saw the picture, thought he was great, and persuaded Paramount to loan him to us. His role in *Lilac Time* was Gary's first big one.

I found out soon enough when we started filming why *Lilac Time* was going to cost a million dollars. It was a war story, and we used hundreds of extras, blew up a whole village, and destroyed seven airplanes—our aerial dogfights done not with miniatures but with the real thing.

The premiere of *Lilac Time* at the Cathay Circle Theater in Beverly Hills was a gala affair—and, as is the case with so many other things in Hollywood, not so commonplace then as now. All the big spotlights at the studio, and some others rented for the occasion, were used to light up the route to the theater. Great crowds of people lined the street for blocks to see their favorite movie stars arrive. Arrive they did, everyone in formal attire—Mary Pickford and Douglas Fairbanks, Charlie Chaplin and Lupe Velez (who had attended the dinner party John and I gave that evening), Harold and Mildred Lloyd, Ruby Keeler and Al Jolson, Mabel Normand and Lew Cody, Corinne Griffith and John Gilbert, the Conrad Nagels, Laura LaPlante and Bill Seiter, Maria and Alexander Korda, and many more—almost everyone, as usual, who was anyone, not to mention Mother and Dad and Grandma.

When John and I drove up and got out of the car, a great cheer went up—people calling out my name and wishing me luck. It was all quite thrilling, even more so to John than to me. After all, as he loved to point out to me, I was only his puppet. Without him I would be nothing. I wondered, in fact, as we made our way to the entrance, if he shouldn't be the one waving to all the people. Turning to look at him, I saw to my astonishment he was. I was embarrassed for him, but I needn't have been. He was having a ball.

The lobby of the theater was filled with so many flower arrangements it looked like a gangster's funeral. Propped against an easel was John's contribution—a large square blanket made of one thousand American Beauty roses, across the flowers a gold ribbon with the words "*Jamais amour ne meurt*" ("Love never dies")—the theme of the picture as well as our private theme.

My crew had sent another huge square, this one made of white carnations spelling out "*To our Colleen*" in the center of a green shamrock.

New York's fabulous mayor, Jimmy Walker, who was a friend of Dick Rowland, acted as master of ceremonies—a great coup for us, since he was idolized all over the country.

Most important of all, the picture went over well. When it opened at the Astor Theater in New York it ran for six months—an unheard of length of time in those days.

Almost more important to John and me at the premiere, the picture went off without a hitch.

While we were filming *Lilac Time*, we heard that Warner Brothers had come up with a new invention. Sound on film. Not sound per se. Warner Brothers had already introduced that with Al Jolson in *The Jazz Singer* in the fall of 1927, creating a sensation with the public and causing some speculation in Hollywood.

And not sound on the same film with the picture as it is today. Sound on a film played from another projection machine hooked up with the machine running the picture. Properly synchronized, the sound and action would match. Before this time, sound was put on a record disc like a Victrola record.

A merger was under way between First National and Warner Brothers, and John thought it would be a novelty if we could have the musical score for *Lilac Time* put on the new film. Jack Warner agreed to let us be the first to try it.

After *Lilac Time* was finished, it was taken to New York, where a one-hundred-piece orchestra recorded the sound track, producing, so we were told, a much fuller and richer sound than with the old disc method. The films were rushed back to Hollywood, and the morning of the opening we tried them out. The sound film broke three times, while the picture kept on rolling.

Frantic, John contacted the Cathay Circle's orchestra leader, who rounded up his regular musicians, also numbering one hundred, and put them in the pit. Provided with a score, the orchestra was to follow the film, and if the sound film broke, start playing. It cost a fortune, but John was never one to quibble in an emergency.

But, as I said, the picture went off without a hitch—or a break— and we were pleased with the success of our little novelty.

Our little novelty.

As my favorite of all the bosses, dear, gentle Mr. Moe Finkelstein of Minneapolis would have said, no doubt did say, and more than once, "Oi vey."

For an industry whose very livelihood depended on giving the public what it wanted, we in Hollywood not only underestimated the public where sound was concerned, we didn't understand it. After the sensation created by *The Jazz Singer*, did all the other

My role as the heroine in the film version of George Gershwin's hit musical, Oh Kay, *was a dream come true. Mervyn LeRoy became my director for the first time.*

studios in Hollywood rush to jump on the Warner bandwagon? They weren't convinced there was a bandwagon.

John had gone over to the Vitagraph Corporation to look at—no, the new word wasn't look, but hear—a short film in which George Jessel, the important vaudeville star, sang. John came back to our studio impressed, but convinced that talking and singing were good only for the short subjects which filled out the movie bill as "added attractions." He said people liked the dark quiet of movie houses with the organ playing soft music while the hero silently poured out his love to the heroine. Even comedy was better silent with all those hilarious sight gags and skillful pantomime.

I agreed with him. So did nearly everybody else. Let the Warner brothers fool around with this novelty, this fad. The rest of us would go on doing what we had been—making silent films.

It's hard to say now just when or where or how or by whom the boom was lowered on us, but almost overnight, it seems in retrospect, Hollywood was transformed from placidity to pandemonium.

News leaked out one day from M-G-M, where stars were making exhaustive tests, that Greta Garbo's deep voice was the perfect recording pitch for Vitaphone, as this new sound device was called. That night I went to a party at Marion Davies' beach house.

After I'd been cleared by the guards, I left my coat in the ladies' dressing room and went on into the large, pine-paneled drawing room, where many of my friends—girls I'd grown up with in the movies—were already assembled. Every one of them greeted me in deep Garbo tones, "Hello, Colleen, how are you tonight?"

The following Saturday night I went to a party at George Fitzmaurice's. (Fitz and his wife Diana, who was and is one of my close friends, were considered leading hosts in movieland. Fitz was a great gourmet, his dinner parties culinary wonders. He also liked antique porcelain and had a habit of lifting up a plate at someone's dinner table to look at the china mark on the bottom. I once acquired some lovely Derby dessert plates. When Fitz came to dinner, he picked up the plate, as I knew he would, and turned it over. Over the mark I'd pasted a piece of paper saying, "None of your damned business!")

Entering their large, two-story hall, I met several of the same girls I'd seen the week before at Marion's. News had leaked out again, again from M-G-M, that it wasn't Garbo's deep voice, after all, which registered perfection. It was Norma Shearer's high-pitched English voice. This time they all greeted me in piercing English tones, "Darling, how nice to see you."

But if the stars were nervous, and directors and producers at a loss as to how to go about tackling this new medium, the owners of the great theater chains—my twenty-six bosses among them—were in a state of near panic.

In an expansive mood only the year before—and because I was their biggest moneymaker—the bosses had signed a new contract with me for six pictures, giving me $125,000 a picture ($10,000 a week), which was more money per film at that time than any other actress in Hollywood was getting. Now as they rode out to Hollywood

Oh Kay *was about bootleggers on a rum-
running boat during prohibition. We
filmed it on a fishing boat reeking of
dead fish. I needed a gas mask.*

My most famous film was Lilac Time *which ran for six consecutive months at the Astor Theatre in New York. Here I am as Jeannine. This film had an orchestral sound track (1928) and theme song.*

together on the Santa Fe *Chief* to see for themselves what was going on, they considered this aspect of the crisis.

Sam Katz of the huge Balaban & Katz chain in Chicago said, "What about Colleen—suppose she can't talk?"

Bob Leiber, First National's president, said, "I didn't notice she was mute when we signed that last contract."

Sam said, "Yeah. And according to that contract, she doesn't have to talk, even if she can. We not only gave her her choice of directors, casts, and stories, she can even cut a film the way she wants it. She's wangled four secretaries, a maid, a studio bungalow, and a personal press agent out of us. And she can keep all the clothes she wears in a picture."

Colonel Jules Levy from Kentucky said, "I heard she always has one dress trimmed in sables, and when she gets enough she's going to have a coat made. Instead of sables we should call them schnooks —it's our skins she's using."

They all laughed. Then Mr. Ruben from Minneapolis said, "I hear she wants twenty-five thousand more a picture to talk."

His partner Mr. Finkelstein shrugged. "So, what's twenty-five thousand?"

In that remark lay the key to their panic, to the panic of theater chain owners everywhere. What, indeed, was twenty-five thousand?

My bosses made motion pictures only to be sure of having products for their theaters. It was in their theaters that their real interest lay—their interest and their multimillion dollar investments. Now the vast kingdom each had built from a rented store with benches into great, glittering movie palaces filled with works of "art" was threatened with oblivion.

Singly and collectively they damned the Vitagraph Corporation and the four Warner brothers who had opened this Pandora's box called talking pictures. They were going to have to spend millions renovating their theaters. Their expensive projection machines would have to be junked and new ones purchased, new sound equipment installed, the houses wired to handle it. Then suppose, after the novelty wore off, the public lost its interest in talking pictures, and the houses had to be converted back to the running of silent films? The public was fickle and couldn't be trusted.

And if the novelty didn't wear off, if talking pictures were really here to stay, what about all of those sure-fire moneymaking products they'd developed to supply to their movie palaces?

Which brought them right back to where they'd started from. Suppose I couldn't talk?

Mr. Sanger from New Orleans said, "Now let's relax. *Lilac Time* is doing better than any film I've run since *The Big Parade*."

But they couldn't relax. Round and round the vicious circle of their problem they went, every click of the train wheels making them want to chant, "Talk, talk, go away, send it back another day —when I'm dead yet."

By the time they arrived in Hollywood, they were worn and harassed and looking years older.

My voice test was made at Warner Brothers. In the center of a half-darkened stage was a small, totally bare room with glass walls. At one end and above the room was a smaller room filled with machinery. In front of a large steel panel covered with knobs and switches sat a young man. He was about my age, twenty-five. He may have been twenty-eight, but no older. He wasn't a movie person. He wasn't connected with any of the arts. Nor did he know anything about acting. He was a young engineer sent out by General Electric to man this complicated new thing called a sound machine. On this young man's judgment my whole career depended.

I was told to go inside the glass room. I did. Outside, my twenty-six bosses and my producer husband stood watching me with worried faces.

A round thing, about as big as a tennis ball, was lowered on a thick string to the level of my face. A voice boomed from nowhere into the little room saying, "Come closer to the microphone."

Bewildered, I said, "What's a microphone?"

The voice from nowhere said, "That round thing in front of you is a microphone. You speak into it."

I drew nearer to The Thing.

The voice said, "Now say something. I want to take a level."

"What shall I say?"

"Say anything. A nursery rhyme will do."

I felt like Alice and the Looking Glass. I peered out of my glass house, looking for some sort of reassurance from my bosses and my husband. They were no longer looking at me. They were watching the young man high in the booth above me. I swallowed and thought to myself, here goes nothing. "Little Bo Peep has lost her sheep and can't tell where to find them. Leave them alone, and they'll come home wagging their tails behind them."

I could feel the tension on the other side of the glass—twenty-seven men watching the young man in the booth in strained silence. I looked up, too.

He leaned out his window, smiled, and made the now familiar circle with thumb and forefinger meaning okay.

The burst of chatter outside filtered through the glass. John opened the door and came into the room to hug me. Over the others I could hear Sam Katz say, "Thank God, she can talk."

On the same Santa Fe *Chief* bringing the twenty-six bosses to Hollywood were some other men, and women, too, filled not with fear of losing a fortune, but with dreams of making one.

I chose Gary Cooper as my leading man in Lilac Time *after seeing him in a bit part in a Western. This was his first important role, launched his career.*

It all started with Laura Hope Crews, a well-known stage actress who had, as she became older, gone into character parts. Miss Crews not only had a beautiful voice, she had a talent for teaching. At the suggestion of Samuel Goldwyn, Gloria Swanson brought her to Hollywood to coach her in her first talking picture, giving her a one-year contract at $1000 a week—an unheard of sum for a character actor on the stage. When news of this reached Broadway, dozens of actors, many of them with Shakespearean training, headed for Hollywood. It was the gold rush of '49 all over again, only this time the gold lay in the mouths of silent movie actors, whom they all looked down upon in their hearts as a disgrace to the acting profession.

After my voice test, the bosses decided that while I could talk,
I must have some voice lessons. Why I must have them, they didn't
know, but Gloria Swanson had a teacher, so I should, too. Surveying
the field, they picked Constance Collier. The fact that Miss Collier
was one of Broadway's most distinguished actresses didn't influence
their choice. Constance Collier charged more than anybody else—
one hundred dollars an hour. They figured if she could get away
with that, she must be good.

As I said earlier, I never had the time or the patience to bother
about my everyday clothes, but went around the studio looking,
I guess, like a Care package in my sweaters and skirts and flat
shoes. Never thinking of the impression I might make, I arrived
at Miss Collier's house for my first lesson dressed that way.

Miss Collier took one look at me, and her shock was plain to see,
even to me. "Miss Moore?" Her voice was hesitant.

I smiled. "Yes."

"Come in," she said, "and sit down. I want to listen to you
speak."

Her golden tones, her straight, queenly carriage as she beckoned
me into the living room of her rented bungalow awed me. When
I sat down she gave me a kind but curious look. "I am told you earn
ten thousand dollars a week. Is this possible?"

"No, ma'am," I said, "that's not true."

Miss Collier looked relieved.

"I earn twelve thousand five hundred a week." I didn't explain
to her that the bosses had agreed to give me the additional $25,000
per picture for talking.

It was just as well.

She handed me a book of Shelley's poems and asked me to read.
I did. She sat there not looking at me, but listening. Then, raising
her hand in a regal manner, she boomed out, "Stop. I have heard
enough."

I thought she was dismissing me, but she wasn't. "You're from
the South, aren't you?" she asked. "Yet you have a Northern twang
to your l-y endings."

I explained that my parents were from Michigan, but that I had
lived my childhood in the South. I also told her that two English
cousins had lived with us for a while. "Maybe," I said, "that's why
I talk like a bastard."

Lilac Time, *a saga of World War I, was a spectacular in which whole villages were actually blown up and aerial dogfights were photographed using real planes.*

Miss Collier stared at me, and I hastened to say, "I mean, maybe that's why I have a bastard accent."

"Yes, yes," she said. "That explains it. All right, my dear, now say mother."

It was my turn to stare. Then I thought, don't laugh, you ignorant motion picture actress. You're in the presence of a lady from the Land of Voice. Pull yourself together and do as the lady asks. "Mother," I said.

She said nothing. I wondered if I'd flunked mother.

"Your r's," she said at last, "are very bad. There *is* an r in mother. Try it again."

I tried saying it like my Michigan father. "Moth*er*."

Miss Collier shivered. "No, no, dear. Now listen to me. Mother."

It did come out rolling and soft and golden. As the echo of it died away, I tried to say it the same way. Her eyes widened in horror. "No, no! Listen to me. Mother."

For one solid hour I said mother. When she dismissed me she told me to come back the following day at the same hour.

A bit shaken at having learned only one word in my first lesson, I went back to the studio. Going up the steps, I ran into Mr. Finkelstein. "Dollink," he said, "vot did you learn today?"

By now I was almost in tears. "She taught me how to say mother."

He stared at me. "One hundred dollars mother?"

"Yes," I said.

He patted me on the shoulder. "Cheer up, dollink. Tomorrow maybe you will learn a sentence."

The next day I went to my lesson wearing a Howard Greer suit with matching cloche. I looked like a well-dressed movie star or a young matron out of *Harper's Bazaar*. Until I looked down at my feet. I had a brown alligator shoe on my right foot, a plain black pump on my left. The confidence which had returned to me oozed away.

Miss Collier greeted me warmly and said, "Now, let's get started."

Feeling more at ease, I sat down.

"Say father," she said.

I said father. For one hour I said father. When I left I was exhausted. Even Miss Collier looked exhausted.

Once again I bumped into Mr. Finkelstein at the studio. "How did it go today, dollink?" he asked.

At the gala premiere of Lilac Time *at the Cathay Circle in Beverly Hills, New York's fabulous mayor, Jimmy Walker, was Master of Ceremonies. He is standing between my husband, John McCormick, and me.*

I sighed. "She taught me to say father."

He looked at me aghast. "One hundred dollars mother, one hundred dollars father. Oi, oi! Before she gets a vocabulary, we will be broke."

I kissed him and said, "Cheer up, Mr. Finkelstein. I think I've had it. I can understand how Corinne Griffith and Norma Talmadge and all the others who play great ladies on the screen are worried about speaking with a Brooklyn accent or a Midwestern twang or a Southern drawl, but as for me, what kind of roles do I play in the movies anyhow? Waifs coming out of garbage cans. Can you see one of them talking like this?" Drawing myself up in Miss Collier's grand manner, and in my cousins' best English accent, I said, "Dear sir, will you kindly give this small, deserted waif a pound or two for her inebriated father?"

I made six talking pictures. The best of them was The Power and the Glory, *with Spencer Tracy, the finest actor I ever worked with. Left to right: Jesse Lasky, Spencer Tracy, Colleen, and William H. Howard.*

We both laughed.

We didn't laugh—and neither did anybody else—when my first talking picture was released in 1929. Not that there was anything wrong with my voice. Or if there was, by the time "The End" flashed on the screen, the audience was too tired to care.

It was surely the longest, slowest, dullest picture ever made. The name of it was *Smiling Irish Eyes*—the picture I had been scheduled to make two years earlier with Mervyn LeRoy directing, which John had pulled me out of. This time Bill Seiter directed it. Bill made some very fine talking pictures later on, but when we made *Smiling Irish Eyes* he didn't know a thing about the new medium of talk. Neither did John. Neither did I. We made it the only way we knew how—like a silent film.

In silent films the actors anticipated the title by pantomiming it in action. For instance, if the title coming up was, "I'm going to leave you," I would make a broad nod or gesture toward the door and then toward the character the line was intended for. Then I would mouth the line verbatim. After I'd said the first couple of words, the film would be cut and the title inserted. When the picture flashed back on the screen I would be saying the last word, and the action would continue with a little more pantomime about leaving before I actually went out the door.

That was how we did *Smiling Irish Eyes*, the actors pantomiming every sentence, then speaking it, then pantomiming it again. The obvious solution would have been to edit out the repetition. Obvious but, unfortunately, impossible. The sound system we used was the old disc one. Since the film was matched to the record, and there was no known way to cut the record, we couldn't cut the film.

Probably the only funny thing about *Smiling Irish Eyes* was one scene not meant to be funny at all.

Nobody in my family had a singing voice. I least of all. I could barely carry a tune. But in the early talkies, the star always had to sing, so in *Smiling Irish Eyes* I sang—if I may call it that—"Come Back to Erin."

Every morning I got up at six o'clock to go have a singing lesson. My teacher did his best. So did I. But my best wasn't good enough, especially when it came to the high notes at the end of the song. The one-hundred-piece orchestra did its best, too—trying to drown me out, I was so off-key. But my voice carried right through them.

We finally hit on a way out. I was supposed to be singing to my lover across the sea in America, so when I came to the high notes at the end, I broke down, weeping.

John wasn't the only producer nor Bill Seiter the only director who made mistakes in the early talking pictures. A great many mistakes were made. One man, at least, profited by them—M-G-M's Irving Thalberg, one of the smartest as well as most talented men in Hollywood. In spite of pressure from the New York office, Irving refused to be rushed into the new medium. Louis B. Mayer backed him up. While M-G-M's great stars continued to make silent films, Irving sat at the studio every night running the talking pictures made by everyone else. Sat there learning. As a result, when M-G-M made its first talking picture, it was smooth, well directed, and underacted in the way the new medium demanded.

Nor were all of my talking pictures bad. I made six of them, and I learned, too. The last one I made in Hollywood, *The Power and the Glory*, with Spencer Tracy, was in my opinion the best picture I ever made, silent or sound. (Also in my opinion Spencer Tracy was the finest actor I ever worked with, and that includes the great Barrymore. In the scene following my suicide in the picture, I was so moved by him that tears ran down my face, and the scene had to be shot with my head turned away.) The critics agreed with my opinion of my work in *The Power and the Glory*. The public did not.

But my quarrel with the public was still some years away, and it had nothing to do with mastering the technique of talking pictures. Nor did the public do to me what it did to John Gilbert—one of Hollywood's greatest stars of the silent screen and the most tragic victim of the advent of sound.

CHAPTER 11

THREE LITTLE WORDS

John Gilbert—or Jack, as his friends all called him—was one of the few on-screen lovers who was also a big beau off-screen. So many of my friends were in love with him at one time or another, it's hard to keep count. I even had a small flirtation with him once myself.

His first wife was the C. B. De Mille star Leatrice Joy. The great stage beauty Ina Claire was his second wife, Virginia Bruce his third. Jack and I were good friends for many years, but it was between his first two marriages, when he and Greta Garbo were having their big romance, that I saw the most of him.

The occasion at which many of us in Hollywood first met Garbo was a party screenwriter Carey Wilson gave in 1927 in a private dining room in the Beverly Wilshire Hotel. We'd heard about her. We knew she had come to Hollywood in 1925 as part of a package deal Mauritz Stiller had negotiated with M-G-M, that in order to get the famous Swedish director, a reluctant M-G-M had had to take Garbo, too.

But it was the news now leaking out of M-G-M, where Jack Gilbert's new picture, *Flesh and the Devil,* was being filmed, that had us all agog. According to studio gossip, Garbo was so sensational in the love scenes that when the picture was released, a new star would be born (and M-G-M's deal would become one of Hollywood's great ironies, Stiller returning to Sweden a failure, the unknown, umpromising-looking Garbo rising to become one of the screen's all-time greats). People who had seen the rushes said that Jack and Greta were so much in love that when a scene finished, and the blackboard came up, indicating the director had called "Cut," the lovers remained in each other's arms, oblivious to the call.

Most sensational of all, we'd heard that Stiller was also madly in love with Garbo and had threatened to kill Jack.

Garbo almost didn't come to the party. When Carey went to Jack's house to pick the two of them up, she said she didn't have an evening gown and couldn't go. She was wearing a long, dark green dress with a high neck and long sleeves. Carey took a scissors, cut a low back, cut across the front, and whacked off the sleeves. The result may not read like much. It may not have been much, but with Garbo wearing it, who noticed? For she was, when she arrived at the party, all we had heard about and more—a radiantly beautiful woman, a girl-woman, young, shy, unsophisticated, with that same childlike quality about her which has marked so many of the world's great artists.

I remember one time when a group of us were at a dinner party at George Fitzmaurice's, intending afterward to go to a preview of Garbo's latest film. Greta refused to go with us, saying she would wait there until we came back with the bad news.

The picture, previewed at a theater in Glendale, was received with enthusiasm, almost with cheers by the audience, and we rushed back to tell her.

The living room in Fitz's house was about fifty feet long, the floor of dark, double planked, highly polished wood covered with small Oriental rugs. We arrived to find chairs and rugs pushed aside and Garbo sliding from one end of the room to the other on one small rug like a child, having a ball and totally disinterested in either the audience reaction or our comments.

Like my John, Jack Gilbert was an alcoholic, but unlike John, who just drank and got drunk and passed out, Jack became more argumentative and belligerent with each drink.

One day Jack, who lived just up the hill from John and me,

One of the great real-life romances in
Hollywood history was the love affair of
John Gilbert and Greta Garbo. He called
her his svenska flicka (little girl) and
they once planned to be married.

stopped by our house to tell me some exciting news. Greta, his *svenska flicka* (little girl), was going to marry him. "She's going to wear a Swedish dress," he said, "and we're going to be married in the pine grove above my house. She says it's like Sweden there, and she gets homesick for the pines."

I congratulated him, and off he went in a rush of excitement.

The marriage never took place. By the time Jack got to his house he was roaring drunk. Greta said, "I t'ink I go home," and she did. Home to Stiller—her "big man," as she used to call him to infuriate Jack, who wasn't very tall.

After brooding a while—and getting still drunker—Jack got in his car and drove to the Miramar Hotel in Santa Monica, where Garbo and Stiller both lived. He stood in the driveway under Greta's balcony yelling obscenities to Stiller. Then he climbed up the vine-covered drainpipe, à la Douglas Fairbanks. Stiller had had enough. As Jack started to climb over the railing, Stiller came out on the balcony, grabbed him, and threw him down to the pavement three stories below. If Jack hadn't been drunk, he would probably have been killed.

Bruised and cut, he got in his car and weaved over to Carey Wilson's house where Carmelita Geraghty Wilson, my good friend and now Carey's wife, bathed and bandaged him.

Brandishing a gun, Jack said he was going back and kill Stiller. Carey took the gun away from him, but when he tried to stop him from going, Jack escaped.

He didn't make it to Stiller. Roaring down Sunset Boulevard, he was arrested and taken to the Beverly Hills jail, where the captain called Howard Strickling, who handled press relations for M-G-M. Howard, who was a good friend of the captain's, said, "Keep him locked up, Chief, until he's sober, and then I'll come down and bail him out."

The captain also kept newsmen away, so only Jack's close friends knew about the escapade, and they only told their close friends, so by noon the next day the story was all over Hollywood.

Jack used to have a luncheon party every Sunday, mostly for the same group of people—Paul Bern and Jean Harlow, Irving Thalberg and Norma Shearer, King Vidor and Eleanor Boardman, Arthur Hornblow and Juliet Crosby, David Selznick, Herman Mankiewicz, the Barney Glazers, Edmund Lowe and Lilyan Tashman, Carey and Carmelita Wilson, John and myself, and, of course, Garbo.

One time John and I had as house guests our good friends James Montgomery Flagg and Arthur William Brown, both famous illustrators. I called Jack to ask him if we could bring them to his Sunday party. He was delighted.

I was in the middle of a picture and exhausted, but I pulled myself together, and the four of us went up the hill to Gilbert's eagle nest.

John and the artist friends went ahead to the pool, but as I was going through the empty living room, I saw a nice squashy red velvet sofa and thought I'd just lie down for a quick nap.

I was awakened by voices—Greta's and Jim Flagg's. I heard Jim say, his voice vibrant with emotion, "You're my dream girl. I've drawn your face all my life. And here you are come to life."

This was true. The Flagg girl was Garbo, had been since before Greta was born.

Garbo, unable to resist playing the scene that was being handed to her, answered him in a voice as vibrant as his own. "All I want," she said, "is to come and live in your studio. Give me a little cot in a corner with a small curtain, and I'll pose for you all day long."

Jim thereupon went into a passionate declaration of his love for her, Greta egging him on, persuading him her only interest in life was art, me stuck there on the sofa, hardly daring to breathe. Finally they left the room, and, wiping the beads of perspiration off my forehead and by now wide awake, I joined the others at the pool.

Jim never saw her again. He tried in vain to phone her, to find her. For three years he wandered around mooning over his pen-and-paper dream-come-true, sending people to talk to her, to ask her to let him see her just once more. But the elusive Garbo had vanished for James Montgomery Flagg. He used to talk about her for hours on end, beginning to wonder at last if the episode with her had actually happened. I wanted to say to him, "It happened. I was right there on the sofa and heard every word the two of you said." But I never could bring myself to do it.

Following the enormous success of *Flesh and the Devil* after its release early in 1927, Jack Gilbert signed a new million-dollar contract with M-G-M for four pictures. His romance with Garbo ended, he married Ina Claire and, after making his first picture under the new contract, went with her to Europe on a honeymoon.

The new picture was also Jack's first talking picture. When it was shown in the M-G-M projection room, the top brass were elated, convinced that Gilbert would go on to even greater heights in the new medium.

When the picture was shown in the large first-run movie palaces in the twenty-six key cities of the United States in late 1929, stunned theater owners could hardly believe their ears. As the screen's great lover took his leading lady in his arms and spoke to her, the audience started to giggle, ended up laughing.

The title of the picture—*His Glorious Night*—was as unfortunate as everything else about it. Newspapers flashed headlines around the world that John Gilbert, the epitome of male virility on the silent screen, had the high screeching voice of a sissy. Jack went to Europe the idol of millions of adoring women. He returned to America to find them laughing in his face.

I have never believed, then or now, that it was Jack Gilbert's voice that ruined him. Jack's voice was not a deep one, but neither was it a high-pitched one. His voice was in the middle register—the same register as that of Douglas Fairbanks and many other male stars.

What ruined Jack Gilbert were three little words.

Remember, first of all, the era. For all that women in the roaring twenties believed themselves to be emancipated, free to smoke and drink and—most of all—to discuss right out in the open the great taboo of sex, the vast majority of women did nothing of the kind. Nor did the lives they led resemble even remotely, for the most part, the romances fed to them in movie theaters.

Feed on those romances they could and did. In the privacy of a darkened movie house a woman could sit watching John Gilbert in *Flesh and the Devil* pour out silent words of love, seeing not Garbo but herself as the love object, imagining, when a title flashed on the screen, such lines as "Forget you? Not while I live—not if I die," directed to her alone, and, as befitted an idyllic love scene, for her alone to hear.

Then along came *His Glorious Night*. For the first time in her life she actually heard John Gilbert say, "I love you, I love you, I love you," right out loud not only for herself but for all the world to hear. It disconcerted and embarrassed her.

It disconcerted and embarrassed all the women in the audience, those most ordinary but still most profound words that can be spoken

With the arrival of the talkies new faces appeared among the old in Hollywood. In this picture made by Carmel Meyers at a party at her house you see (top row) Colleen, Lily Pons, Ginger Rogers; (center row) Jeanette MacDonald, Claire Windsor, Helen Hayes; (bottom row) Mervyn LeRoy, Ann Harding, Ernst Lubitsch, Wallace Beery.

between a man and a woman. In their embarrassment they giggled.

After *His Glorious Night* it was a long time before any man, no matter what his voice register, said, "I love you," on the screen again.

But the realization by Hollywood producers of the dangers inherent in speaking words of love aloud on the screen came too late for Jack Gilbert. He was finished.

Not in actual fact. His contract with M-G-M called for three more pictures. Jack, sure he could redeem himself in one of them, was determined to make M-G-M honor the contract. Louis B. Mayer was just as determined to make Jack agree to a settlement. Aware of Jack's strong pride and quick temper, he did everything he could to humiliate him, hoping Jack would do what we were all afraid he would do—tear up the contract and throw it in Mr. Mayer's face. Instead, Jack laughed in his face—something Mr. Mayer never could take—and the feud was on.

Louis B. Mayer was a great hater, and the full force of his hatred centered now on destroying Jack Gilbert. In fairness to Mr. Mayer I must say Jack gave him plenty of provocation. He was as vitriolic as Mr. Mayer himself, and there were many bitter scenes between them as Jack reminded Mr. Mayer that he had to make the remaining pictures even if they were a total loss.

They pretty much were. For all the hatred between Jack and Louis B. Mayer (brooding and drinking too much, Jack reached a point in his hatred where he hired a bodyguard to keep him from killing Mr. Mayer) it was the critics and the public who destroyed Jack. As each picture failed, Jack's confidence drained away. His acting became uncertain and less and less like the Jack Gilbert of old.

The last picture made, Jack retired to his eagle-nest house to brood some more, while Louis B. Mayer heaved a sigh of relief.

It was premature.

Garbo was about to start *Queen Christina*. The sets were ready, the costumes made. After testing one leading man after another, M-G-M had imported Laurence Olivier from England to play opposite her. But Garbo wasn't happy. She went to see Mr. Mayer and said she couldn't make the picture. She didn't like her leading man. He wasn't suited to the part.

Mr. Mayer told her she could have anybody she wanted. Just name him.

She said, "I want Jack Gilbert."

Mr. Mayer yelled so hard he nearly blew the roof off the studio. Jack Gilbert, whom he'd finally just got rid of?

Garbo only nodded and said, "Jack Gilbert."

I have always loved Garbo for this last, wonderful gesture—to try to give Jack his career again. We all loved her for it. It should have worked—these two famous lovers of *Flesh and the Devil* together again in a picture. But it was too late. Their scenes no longer caught fire. Jack was only ordinary in his part.

Nothing and no one could help Jack. His marriage with Ina

Claire broke up. His third marriage, to Virginia Bruce, didn't last very long either. In a few years the combination of frustration and bitterness and drinking took its toll, and Jack died on January 9, 1936, at the age of thirty-eight.

Garbo never married at all. Shortly after her breakup with Jack, she asked Lilyan Tashman to help her buy some new clothes. She was going to Sweden for a visit, and, as she confided to Lil, she wanted some beautiful outfits to "startle Stiller." A few days before she was to leave a cable arrived saying Stiller had died.

Unable to face the prospect of seeing herself grow old, Garbo retired from the movies while she was still a young woman. Today she lives alone on the East Side of New York, her future her past. When her films are shown at one of the small art theaters, she can usually be found sitting somewhere in the back, wearing her polo coat and slouch hat, watching and weeping over the Garbo of long ago.

Every year she receives offers, fabulous ones, to make a screen comeback. A couple of years ago Sam Bronston, who was making a spectacular in Spain, sent his assistant, Ralph Wheelwright, who knew Garbo at M-G-M, to New York to offer her a million dollars if she would play the dowager empress in *Twenty Days in Peking*. The story would be rewritten around the empress and the part made to please Garbo. She turned down the offer.

"If you needed the million, would you do it?" Ralph asked.

"Less than ever then," she said.

CHAPTER 12

BOY LOSES GIRL

When I was a little girl living in Florida I made a paper doll house, cutting pictures of furniture out of magazines and pasting them against the wallpaper samples I used as rooms. My house had an indoor and outdoor swimming pool, an enormous ballroom, a greenhouse filled with orchids, and a day and night nursery and a schoolroom for the children. It even had a yacht—one room with portholes that opened, and, pasted behind the openings, the sea. Where I got such ideas of grandeur I don't know, but it looked like something out of Cecil B. De Mille.

The house John and I bought in Bel Air in 1927 was not nearly so grand as my paper doll house, but with the help of Harold Grieve—he who had asked Peggy Hopkins Joyce what was so valuable about an old shoebox—it became my dream house.

Spanish in architecture, it was half-built when we bought it. I was wondering where to get a decorator to furnish it after it was completed when I bumped into Carmelita Wilson one day standing in front of the Brown Derby with a young man. She said, "This is my friend Harold Grieve. He used to be art director at the Marshall Neilan Studio. Now he's starting in business for himself."

I looked at this tall, thin young man with a pixie grin on his Scottish face, and feeling like a movie star, I suppose, and thinking of Cecil B. De Mille, I said, "How nice. I'd like to have you do my bathroom for me."

He gave me an amused look. "Either I do your whole house, Miss Moore, or nothing."

I was so taken aback I said, "Okay. Do the whole house."

That was how Harold, now a big-time decorator and at one time national president of the American Institute of Interior Designers, landed his first private customer. But he didn't just decorate and furnish the house. By the end of the afternoon I had fired the architect, and Harold took over the whole job.

He pushed out walls, closed in the sixty-five-foot loggia. Off the loggia, between the U of the house, he built a large flagstone patio. At one end of the U he added a guest house, at the other end a theater. We bought another acre below the house and put in a tennis court and swimming pool with a pool house between.

There was also a guest suite upstairs in the main house between John's suite at one end and mine at the other, each with sitting room, bedroom, and bath. In my suite there was also an office off the bedroom for my secretary.

Harold did my suite in yellow and turquoise, with heavy silk-pile turquoise carpeting made in China, which really did make me feel like a movie star. The bathroom was done in yellow onyx and mirrors, some of them with scenes painted behind the glass. Years later, when I was renting the house, Greta Garbo came to look at it. When she saw the bathroom she said, "Ah, Colleen, those were the good old days."

(After doing my house, Harold did Jack Gilbert's. He used to claim that just re-doing the guest bedroom and bath there paid his office rent each year. Hoping to marry Garbo, Jack had the bedroom done in European style with painted Venetian furniture, the bathroom in black marble with gold fixtures. When he married Ina Claire instead, the bath was torn out and redone in pink marble, the bedroom in peach color with French furniture. After Jack married Virginia Bruce, the pink marble was replaced with white, the bedroom done in pale blue and white with Early American furniture.)

John was as interested in his suite as I was in mine. He kept turning down the light, bright color schemes Harold and I sub-

My father, tired of a divided family, had moved his business to California. Here I am, reunited with my beloved male relatives on a boat we chartered for a cruise. Left to right: my cousin, Jack Stone; my brother, Cleeve; Colleen; and my father, Charles Morrison.

mitted to him, saying he liked dark blue on the purple side. That's what Harold finally gave him. Harold and I hated it—we used to call John's suite the chamber of horrors—but John thought it was beautiful.

John's bathroom had a steam room attached—handy, he said, in case he got fat. Also handy for hangovers, I wanted to add, but I held my tongue.

Held my tongue and crossed my fingers, because John, whose periods of drunkenness now came not every six weeks but, in spite of the reduced pressure on him at the studio, every three or four, went on the wagon as the house neared completion—so taken with the house that every evening after work we drove over to see what had been accomplished that day.

One night after we'd been to a party at Corinne Griffith's, John suggested we stop to see it on the way home. When we pulled up in the driveway, he took a box from his pocket and said, "Hold out your wrist." I did, and he put a bracelet on it. The bracelet was a simple strand of jeweled flowers arranged to spell out "dearest"—a diamond flower, then an emerald one, an amethyst, a ruby, another emerald, a sapphire, a topaz—the flowers connected by diamonds. It was one of the few jewels he ever gave me that wasn't a peace offering, and I treasured it.

Finally, almost a year and a half after we had bought it, the house was finished, the last ashtray in place. Harold said we could move in. There was only one problem. John had disappeared again.

A few days later, the doctor called to say he was drying out in the Hollywood Hospital. This time I didn't go to the hospital. I moved into my dream house alone.

I called John's parents in San Francisco, asking them for help. They came down at once. When John's father went to the hospital to bring John home, he was so upset at seeing the condition his son was in, he could hardly speak.

I had explained to both of his parents how John was wrecking my career as well as my life, telling them, as one example, what he had done to my picture *Her Wild Oat*.

After the shooting on *Her Wild Oat* was completed, my brother Cleeve, my cousin Jack Stone, and I had chartered a boat for a six-weeks' cruise, so I could get away for a rest. John stayed on at the studio to finish up the picture and preview it for audience reaction.

When I returned and saw the cut version I nearly died. The film, which had been very funny in the rushes, wasn't funny at all now. I asked Al Hall, our cutter—later a very well-known director of such hit films as *My Sister Eileen* and *Here Comes Mr. Jordan*— what had happened. He said John had been drunk all the time I was away and had insisted on cutting the picture himself. The tops to all the gags—*Her Wild Oat* was a silent film—had been cut so short, the laughs had been left on the cutting-room floor.

Al told me to keep John away. He'd put the film back together again. He did, and at the next preview, the laughs came in all the right places.

When John and his father came home from the hospital, the doctor came with them, and we had a long family discussion. John said he would like to take a cure. The doctor suggested the gold cure, which he said had worked for many alcoholics and which could be taken at home under the supervision of a male nurse, thus assuring no publicity.

After the doctor left, John's mother came to me saying, "The doctor said his liver is gone, and he can't live long. Please don't divorce him. He needs you so. Stay a little longer for me." (Actually he lived to his mid-sixties.)

I loved John's mother very much. I said I would stay and see the cure through. Then if John was able to stay on the wagon, we might be able to salvage our marriage.

My in-laws went home, and the male nurse arrived. The cure was drastic and, for me, horrible to watch. The nurse would give him a shot glass filled with a brown liquid which made him deathly ill. He would turn blue and go into spasms. All the time this was going on, the nurse kept repeating, "This is what will happen to you if you ever take another drink."

Already pale and thin from his last binge, John became so weak he could hardly walk from his bed to a nearby chair. He would look up at me, his lips blue, his body doubled in pain, and say, "I am trying hard, Alanna." I was so shaken I would burst into tears and have to leave, wanting to tell the nurse to stop for fear John would die before he was cured.

Three weeks later the doctor said he was now okay. His stomach returned to normal, and he started eating again. He seemed fine, and I had great hope, especially when he said that even the thought of another drink was horrible to him. He was on the wagon for life.

He dressed, and I took him by the hand, and we made a tour of the house. When we came to the front door, he looked at me with tears in his eyes and said, "I'm sorry I wasn't here to carry you across the threshold. Let me do it now." He was too weak to lift me.

I think now I made a mistake in having our suites on opposite sides of the house, not only because John needed someone near so he wouldn't feel so alone, but because in a marriage husband and wife should be together. Separate sleeping makes for separate lives.

My excuse then, and I suppose it still holds, was that he was drunk so much of the time, and I had to get my rest in order to be at the studio every morning to go to work.

The picture I was working on at that time—we moved into the

Bel Air house early in 1929—was my second talking picture, *Foot-lights and Fools,* with Fredric March playing opposite me, and Bill Seiter directing. Although Bill had learned from the mistakes we made in *Smiling Irish Eyes,* he was so accustomed in silent films to laughing at the gag sequences in order to give his actors the feel of an audience, he would forget we were working with sound and burst out laughing in the middle of a scene, and the scene would have to be retaken.

John, his cure complete and his strength restored, resumed his duties at the studio as producer of the picture. For a while he seemed to be getting along all right, though he still wanted me to be "his little girl" at home—I was now twenty-six years old—and call him Daddy. I couldn't and wouldn't, until I saw the white line of strain begin to show around his mouth. Then I started calling him Daddy like mad, feeling a complete fool, but terrified of the consequences if I didn't.

Two weeks later he fell off the wagon. This time he didn't disappear. He went home, called the nurse he had had when he was taking the cure, and paid him to watch him so he couldn't get a drink.

I don't know why he bothered. Unknown to me or the servants, John had cached away case after case of Scotch. Bottles were hidden in bushes in the garden, on top of window valances, in the top of his toilet, under chair cushions. As I drove up to the front door one day, I saw a bottle on a string outside his bathroom window. It was hopeless. John got drunk right under the nurse's eyes.

Got drunk and stayed drunk and sat around all day in his dressing gown staring into space and not making much sense when he talked. One night when I came home he said, "Why have you hired that yellow taxi that keeps going around the block? You're trying to keep my bootlegger away, aren't you?"

"I haven't hired any yellow taxi," I said.

He rushed over to the window and pointed. "There it is now."

I went over and looked out. There was nothing there.

Another time I said to him, "You make it tough on me having to go to work every day and be funny."

He weaved over to me, a wild look in his eyes, and said in a menacing tone of voice, "You're nothing without me. I made you a star, and I can break you just as easily."

Except for the time in New York when he had tried to throw

me out the hotel window, I had never been afraid of him when he was drunk. He used to say he had never hit a woman in his life and never would. That much of his manhood he wouldn't violate. But I was afraid of him now.

I went over to my side of the house, took off my make-up, and sank down on the bed. Not to cry. I was past that.

The next day was a day I had looked forward to for weeks. Louis B. Mayer and William Randolph Hearst were hosting a big luncheon at M-G-M in honor of Winston Churchill. Not only was I a big fan of Mr. Churchill's, the affair was a must on everybody's social calendar. I went to John's room early in the morning, hoping he would be sober enough to go to the luncheon, thinking if people saw him there, the stories going around about him might stop.

My hope died the minute I saw him. Dressed only in shorts, shoes, and socks, he was sitting in his chair staring straight ahead of him, dead drunk. Furious, I took off one high-heeled shoe and began hitting him on his bare chest and arms with the heel of the shoe, making D welts on his fair Irish skin. He just sat there looking down at the welts, and then he said, "D—that stands for dummy. That's me—damned dummy. You've branded me correctly."

The way he said it, it was funny, but I was past laughing, too. I went to the luncheon alone, telling people John was ill.

The luncheon was held on a big sound stage at M-G-M. At the end of it was a huge set for a new musical Busby Berkeley was directing, and during lunch we were treated to a spectacular song and dance show from the new picture.

After the lunch and the entertainment, Mr. Churchill rose and made a beautiful speech. When he sat down, Conrad Nagel, who was the master of ceremonies, said, "We loved your talk so much, Mr. Churchill, we would like to hear it again." To the amazement of all of us, Mr. Churchill included, we did—from the big sound boxes on the stage.

Mr. Churchill's reactions to the playback—a microphone had been hidden in the flowers in front of him to record the speech—provided the best show of all. He would laugh and then turn to Mr. Mayer in disbelief. From his expression, I judged this was the first time he had ever heard his own voice.

When the luncheon was over, I went to see Harold Grieve at his office. He knew all about John. We'd had some big decorating

This picture was made in New York in the long-skirt era, when Mickey Neilan directed The Social Register *at Astoria, Long Island. Left to right: Arline Donne (my stand-in), Pauline Frederick, Mickey, and myself.*

arguments when John was drunk. Harold said he had heard First National wasn't going to renew my contract because John was too undependable. Maybe John was brooding about that.

This was news to me. Worried, I called home and learned that the nurse had sent for the doctor. The doctor came to the phone and said John was out cold. There was nothing to be gained by coming home. So Harold and I went out to dinner together.

When I got home about nine o'clock, John was still out. There was a full moon outside, and I walked downstairs and out onto the patio and sat in a swing looking at my garden below with the blue pool shimmering in the moonlight, the palm trees around it reflected in its water.

I looked at my garden and looked at my life. My great ambition to be a movie star had been realized. I had built the house of my dreams—the grownup version of my paper doll house. I had a million dollars in the bank that I had earned myself. I had everything a woman could ask for, except the one most important thing in a woman's life.

It had always been easy for me to pretend. Whenever I played a movie role I identified with the character so much that for the time being I would lose my own identity—and get scared sometimes that I wouldn't be able to find it again. In the same way I had pretended about John—made him fit my image of him, believed that one day he would wake up and say, "I'm never going to take another drink," and mean it, went on believing it even after I knew better.

I couldn't pretend any more. I sat there empty and alone, the man I was married to lying upstairs in my dream house a hopeless, drunken mess.

I went upstairs, packed my clothes, and moved to my parents' house.

But I was not yet ready to admit failure to the world. Except for Harold Grieve, nobody knew I had moved out. I went to the Bel Air house every day after work to see how John was getting along.

The word that my contract would not be renewed after I finished *Footlights and Fools* was true, but I did nothing about it. I didn't know what to do. John had handled all of my contracts with First National for me.

In one of his sober moments I asked John what was happening. He said he was working on a deal for us to make our pictures at United Artists with Joe Schenck. I don't know now whether there was any truth to that or not. Not long ago Jack Warner told me that when Warner Brothers took over First National, he offered John a new contract for me at $15,000 a week because of the enormous success of *Lilac Time*, but John turned it down. I didn't know anything about it at the time, because John didn't tell me. But I know why he turned it down—because the contract didn't include him.

The day my contract was terminated, John moved out of his office, and I moved out of my studio bungalow, sending the furniture to the guest house at Bel Air. It depressed me to leave that happy little house, but the move from First National was harder on John. He was in bad shape, and I left him to his nurse.

The day that was to be the turning point of my life came a couple of weeks later on a Thursday afternoon. I went to the Bel Air house as usual. The servants were off, as well as John's day nurse. The night nurse was due at six. Why I took my chauffeur inside the house I will never know. But I did, asking him to wait in the hall for me while I went upstairs to John's room.

John was sitting in his large, gold brocade overstuffed chair, his face red and bloated, his mouth hanging loose, his eyes blank and staring straight ahead. He bore no resemblance to the man I had married six years before.

Sitting on the edge of the bed taking in this picture, I said, "John, I want a divorce."

As the words sank in, he turned to look at me. Getting up from his chair, he came over to me and grabbed me by the throat, pushing me back on the bed, shouting, "You'll never divorce me!"

Before I could make a sound, his hands closed tight around my neck. The room began to spin. In the hall below, the chauffeur heard John's shout. He rushed upstairs and pulled him away from me. Gasping for breath, I tore down the stairs, the chauffeur following. When we got in the car I was trembling so I couldn't speak.

I was still shaking when we arrived home. My mother made me drink some brandy, saying, "You must never go back again." Then she went to the phone and called our lawyer, telling him to file for divorce.

Two days later we met at the Bel Air house with my lawyers, his lawyers, and my parents. California has a community property law, but John signed a property settlement saying what was mine belonged to me, and what was his was his own. Since I had bought and paid for the house (he had paid for the maintenance of it), he had packed his clothes and other belongings the day before and sent them to the Beverly Wilshire Hotel.

Sober and quiet, he hardly looked at me during the proceedings. When they were over, he asked me if he could speak to me alone in the hall. I went out, and he said, "Tell me it's a lie I tried to choke you. I've never touched a woman in my life."

I said, "You nearly killed me, John."

He stared at me for a moment, then looked away.

"You must realize now you need help," I said.

Still not looking at me, he nodded. "Do one thing for me, will you? In your divorce suit, don't mention drunkenness." He shrugged. "You can find enough else."

"All right," I said. The charge, when it was drawn up, read "noncompatability of temper."

That night he sent me twelve dozen American Beauty roses, with a card attached saying, "*Love never dies.*"

Before she was a newspaper columnist, Hedda Hopper was a stage and screen actress. She played with me in a film called Orchids and Ermine *in which Mickey Rooney also had a part.*

CHAPTER 13

FROM
A FAIRY CASTLE
IN FAIRYLAND

One of the big moments in my life in Hollywood came when John and I had been married about three years. We were invited for a weekend at the Hearst ranch at San Simeon. Mr. Hearst's secretary phoned to say the private train—not a private car, mind you, but a private train—would be leaving at seven o'clock Friday night and for us to be at the Southern Pacific Railway station at six-thirty. We had heard about the unbelievable parties given by Marion Davies and Mr. Hearst at the ranch. My Uncle Walter Howey, who went there all the time to see Mr. Hearst on business, had told me about the swimming pools, the private zoo, and, most of all, about the castle itself. I could hardly wait.

John didn't make it. It wasn't that he was drunk. The doctor had a theory at that time that maybe John drank because he was allergic to some food, and John, trying hard to cure himself, was in the middle of making tests. So I went alone, but I went. I wasn't going to miss San Simeon.

Once aboard the train, I had plenty of company. Hedda Hopper, who hadn't yet discovered the excitement of writing a column, but was still a stage and screen actress (in 1927 she played in my film

Orchids and Ermine, in which Mickey Rooney also had a part) was there. Julanne Johnston, who had played the beautiful princess opposite Douglas Fairbanks in *The Thief of Bagdad,* and would later appear with me in that dismal *Smiling Irish Eyes,* was there. Constance Talmadge with her department-store-heir husband Townsend Netcher. King Vidor and Eleanor Boardman. Adolphe Menjou and his wife Kathryn. Eileen Percy and her brewery-heir husband Eric Busch. Bebe Daniels and Jack Pickford. Jack Gilbert. Irving Thalberg and Norma Shearer. Carey and Carmelita Wilson.

Arthur Brisbane, whose Hearst column was the most famous in America, was there. So were a number of other writers from Eastern magazines, Hollywood magazines, and some of the other Hearst newspapers. There were some French diplomats and some titled English people. Even a lady painter from England who had been John Singer Sargent's love and who later painted my portrait as a Chinese girl. It all added up to a very glamorous and exciting weekend for me.

A little after midnight the train was put on a siding at San Luis Obispo. The next morning after breakfast aboard the train, we climbed into a fleet of limousines and were driven north along the Pacific Ocean—a beautiful ride in the bright morning sunlight. About an hour later we turned into the small Spanish village at the foot of *La Cuesta Encantada* (The Enchanted Hill) where workers on the ranch lived. Looking up, I could see outlined against the sky on top of the mountain an enormous castle—a beautiful pale fairyland castle poking through clouds to sparkle in the sun.

The first gate we went through was a letdown—a plain wire cattle gate found on any Western ranch, with a small shack, very temporary looking, at one side. The motorcade had to stop while the cowboy there checked us over and then phoned up ahead to say we were en route.

As we drove up the mountain toward the next gate, we passed hundreds of white-faced Hereford cattle feeding on the lush grass. The ranch consisted of two hundred and fifty thousand acres, and Mr. Hearst had one of the largest herds of cattle in California.

The second gate was Western style like the first. Another cowboy came out of a shack, looked us over, and also phoned ahead. Driving through this part of the ranch, we passed a herd of white camels. I thought I was seeing things. Suddenly a large herd of buffalo went racing up the mountain, followed by zebras and deer. Ibex and gnu roved around. We even passed two large giraffes. (Later on the female giraffe died. The mate was so stricken, he pined away, refusing to eat, until he, too, died. This was a bit unusual for Hollywood, and long after their deaths the tale was told—a sort of Tristan and Isolde of the animal kingdom.)

We had driven many miles up the mountain when the castle came in view. Just the size of it was enough to stagger the imagination. An enormous white-stoned twin-turreted structure with red tile roofs, it towered over the cluster of guest houses surrounding it and the beautifully manicured trees and shrubbery of the formal gardens like a stately Spanish cathedral. At one corner of the grounds was a large T-shaped blue tile swimming pool flanked by a white marble colonnade.

The guest cottages—anywhere else they would have been called haciendas, they were so big were also of white stone with red tile roofs. The cottage I was assigned to by the housekeeper who greeted us—we were about fifty in all—housed twelve people. This particular cottage was built against the side of the mountain, so that only the top of its three stories was visible from the great stone patio in front of the castle.

My sitting room was filled with Spanish antiques and paintings—I remember a Velázquez and a Goya—and the bedroom had been lifted in its entirety, including the carved and painted ceiling, from a castle in Spain. The enormous four-poster bed was so high I had to make a jump to get up there.

The bathroom was black marble with gold fixtures. Getting undressed to bathe for lunch, I stepped into the tub feeling like Cleopatra.

Marion and Mr. Hearst were in the large salon waiting to greet all of us. Then we went into the one-hundred-foot-long dining room which had once been a whole church in Spain. Mr. Hearst bought it to get the ceiling, which was carved in wood with life-size saints in full relief. Wondering which saint I would be seated under, I found my place and looked up. I'd drawn St. Sebastian, with all the arrows sticking in him. He was so unappetizing, I never looked up again.

The table was a long, narrow trestle type, with Mr. Hearst and Marion in the center across from each other. The glasses were beautiful blue Venetian ones, and the plates lovely china, but the napkins were paper, and down the center of the table were bottles and jars, with the labels still on them, of catsup, mustard, pickles, jellies, etc. I guess Mr. Hearst had to prove his palace was only a ranch, after all. (We used to wonder what became of the bottles and jars that were left half full at the end of the meal, because at the next meal there were always new ones freshly opened.)

After lunch that day a group of us ran to the huge sofa in front of the big walk-in fireplace. We were gossiping and giggling when Mr. Hearst came over saying we must get some fresh air and exercise and to put on our riding habits or blue jeans. The horses were waiting.

We had no choice. A little old Mexican hand named Pancho helped us onto our horses, and off we went. A few minutes later I got the shock of my life when Pancho, riding at the head of the group, turned and called out, "Willie, come up here and ride with me. I want to show you a pasture." In all the years I knew William Randolph Hearst I was so in awe of him I never called him anything but Mr. Hearst. We all called him that, except Marion, of course, who called him W.R. Now I couldn't believe my ears. *Willie* to the great Mr. Hearst! I found out that night that Mr. Hearst and Pancho had been raised together on the ranch and had been close friends since childhood. The beautiful Spanish house we had passed that morning in the village below had been built for and given to Pancho by Mr. Hearst.

After my first visit to San Simeon I went back many times. I remember it was at the ranch that we discovered bridge. Soon all of us were taking lessons like mad. Marion was very good, but Constance Bennett and Bebe Daniels always won all the money. Sometimes after dinner we would play hide and seek—a great game when you have a huge castle at your disposal. Golden chests from Venice make a great hiding place, especially with a beau. Not so the suits of armor belonging to knights of old. I almost smothered one time inside Charles of Burgundy, besides getting a scolding from Mr. Hearst when I lost my balance, and Charles and I went crashing to the floor.

One of Marion's favorite pastimes was jigsaw puzzles. The puzzles set out on two big tables in the salon were always crowded with people trying to put them together. Sometimes they were so large it took months to complete them.

Before dinner we gathered for one cocktail—Mr. Hearst didn't approve of drinking. (If you swallowed fast, you might get another.) Then we were hustled into the dining room. During dinner Marion would do imitations of people for Mr. Hearst, making him break up with laughter. Or if not imitations, something else. She always seemed to have some stunt to amuse him. Looking at them made me think of Louis XV and Madame Du Barry. In fact, the whole place resembled a court of long ago.

Marion's parties were famous, whether at the ranch or at Santa Monica, where she had the largest house on the beach—and I mean the beach from San Diego to the Canadian border. It was a colonial house about two hundred feet long, with a pillared porch all around the front. After Marion died it was turned into a hotel, so you can see how large it was.

Mr. Hearst's birthday was always the occasion for a great costume party. At one birthday party at the beach house the double tennis courts were tented over and a real merry-go-round with hurdy-gurdy music set up inside. I don't remember what costume I wore to that particular party, but I remember what Mr. Hearst wore, because he always wore the same one to all of them—a Buster Brown suit right out of the comic strip. It was a sight to see.

Marion's own fabulous art collection was hung in the beach house. I remember one Sunday when Lord Duveen, the famous art dealer, had sent six pictures on approval to Mr. Hearst. Four of us girls were there with Marion, and Mr. Hearst asked us to come look at the pictures, which had been propped up against the wall in the sun room. As Marion perched on the arm of his chair, he said, "Pick one out for yourself, Marion."

She studied hard, then chose the famous portrait of Lady Hamilton by Romney. Mr. Hearst gave her an amused look. "Why is it you always pick the best painting?"

She grinned at him, her eyes dancing with mischief. "Because you taught me what's best."

Marion herself taught something to all of us, Mr. Hearst included —that money can't buy stardom. Mr. Hearst lost untold millions trying to make a star out of Marion Davies after he brought her to Hollywood. He put her in expensive costume stories where her

John and I bought this house in Bel Air to keep up with my rising star. The house had two acres of gardens, orchards, an Olympic-size swimming pool and a baronial air.

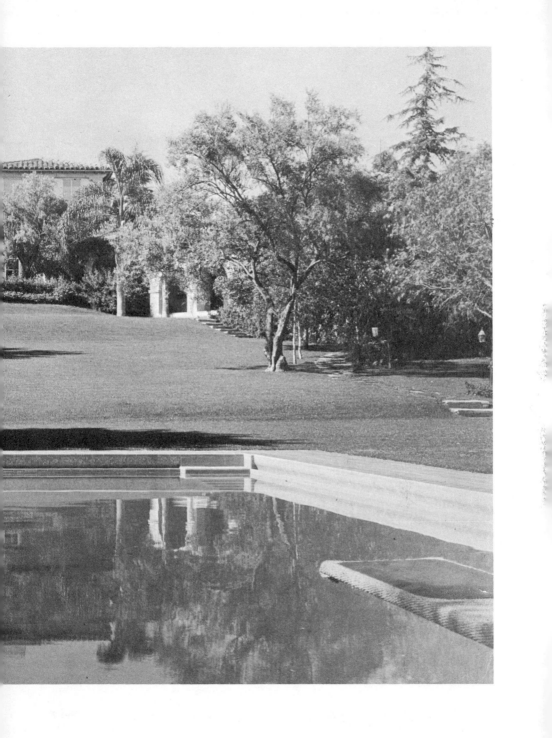

beauty was displayed. The Hearst papers staged great advertising campaigns for her films. But the public passed her over until she made *Little Old New York* in 1923, the picture in which she displayed her true talent, that of a comedienne. She became a star—on ability alone.

Marion was indeed a beauty, blond and blue-eyed, with milk-white skin and natural color in her cheeks and with small, even features, but in Hollywood beauty was a fairly common commodity. It was Marion's mind and personality that endeared her to her friends. She had a quick wit, but one that wasn't barbed. Her humor was never at someone else's expense. She was, in fact, one of the kindest, most thoughtful, most sensitive persons I have ever known.

One time a group of girls was at the ranch, all of us stars with big incomes, except for one girl who was having a hard time. This girl's coat was thin and worn, but she was too proud to take help from anyone. After lunch we were all sitting around the fire when a deliveryman came in with several large boxes, each containing a beautiful winter coat with a fur collar. Marion had sent to San Francisco for them, and she had one for each of us—all so she could give a coat to the girl who needed one without hurting her pride.

During the forties, when Mr. Hearst was on the verge of bankruptcy, I was in New York, and Marion asked me to tea. She told me she had given Mr. Hearst a million dollars that morning and all of her jewels. Stuttering the way she always did when she became excited or self-conscious, she said, "After all, he gave them to me, and he needs the money now."

Theirs was a great love affair, and a beautiful one, lasting thirty-five years, until Mr. Hearst's death in 1951.

Another time in the later years I took my daughter Judy to spend the night at San Simeon. There were only six guests altogether. Mr. Hearst was an old man, his health not too good. Marion was no longer the little girl amusing the king. She was a woman in love looking after her man.

Not knowing how to explain the situation to my child, I said, "Miss Davies is Mr. Hearst's adopted daughter, and she's our hostess."

Bunkie Hearst, a grandson about Judy's age who was also there

Here I am, playing Lady of the Manor, under my portrait by Garan in the stair-well of the Bel Air house. That house had so many rooms I'm not sure I ever saw them all.

This champagne supper included from left to right, Douglas Fairbanks, Jr., Gloria Swanson, Michael Farmer, and Colleen, who seems to have put on weight.

visiting, took Judy around the grounds. When Judy returned she said, "Miss Davies isn't Mr. Hearst's daughter. They're in love."

For a moment I was stopped cold. Finally I managed to stammer out, "Why do you say that?"

"I saw them walking and holding hands," she said. "And they stopped and kissed."

All I could think was, out of the mouths of babes.

This time, as we had done so often in years past, we went into the theater after dinner to see a movie. A small electric heater was brought in, and Marion adjusted it so the heat was directed toward Mr. Hearst. She wrapped a blanket around his knees, then took his glasses to polish them with her handkerchief, turning to grin at me and say, "I'm the glasses polisher." They were holding hands when the movie began.

That visit was the last time I saw Marion. She asked me if I missed the movies and life in Hollywood. I said truthfully I didn't miss a thing. I was so busy I didn't have time. I asked the same question of her. She said she had never been as happy. I believe it. I had never seen her look so well or so young and carefree.

I asked her what she did to occupy her time up there on the mountain. "A little sewing," she said. "And a little washing and ironing."

I couldn't help but smile. Du Barry and the Petit Trianon. A little washing, a little ironing in a castle staffed by fifty servants, including her own personal maid. But she was happy. Gone were the trainloads of guests for the weekend. Now only a few were asked. She and Mr. Hearst were alone together in their fairy castle on the mountaintop.

The idea for my own fairy castle—a miniature fairy castle— came not from Mr. Hearst but from my father, though my doll house has the same feeling about it as San Simeon. When Hedda Hopper first saw it, she turned to me and said, "It's plain to see you've been to the Hearst ranch."

The first doll house I ever had was one my mother and father made for me out of cigar boxes when I was two years old, though I know now they didn't make it for me so much as for the fun of doing it. They even made the furniture.

Through my childhood Dad made four more doll houses, each more elaborate than the last.

Toward the end of my marriage to John, Mother and Dad and I went to Hawaii for a few weeks in the hope that my being away from John for a while would straighten out his drinking problem. One day on the boat going over, Dad said, "Why don't we build a fairy castle to house your collection?"

Kathleen's Collection, started those many years ago by my aunts, had, with additions by me and by friends in late years, grown into a really fine collection.

"This time," Dad went on, "let's get an architect and artists and build a work of art."

We hardly saw the beach at Waikiki. We couldn't wait to get home. Horace Jackson, who designed the sets at First National, was our choice for architect. He was enchanted with the idea. It was his suggestion that the architecture be unreal, making the castle look as if it had come from the pages of a storybook. Harold Grieve was consulted as decorator. He said the name of the period for the furniture should be Early Fairie. He went on to say that the princess who lived in the castle must like antiques. She would go to the antique shops of fairyland to find her furniture—King Arthur's round table for the dining room, Sleeping Beauty's bed for her bedroom. This was the premise on which we furnished the house.

I had the best time I had ever had in my life when we were creating the doll house, as we then called the castle. Dad was in his element bossing every nail and joint as chief engineer. He rented an empty shop in Glendale to do the work, saying this doll house must be engineered so the rooms came apart and not end up like doll house number four. Number four was built in the attic play-room. When we moved, we couldn't get it through the door. He also said it mustn't be built like doll house number five, which warped in spite of the wood being plied four times. This house must be made of aluminum, because aluminum was light as well as strong. (Even so, the fairy castle, which measures nine feet square, its highest tower twelve feet from the floor, weighs close to 2000 pounds!)

The plans were drawn, the scale one inch to the foot. When Horace Jackson was seen wandering around the studio with a far-away look on his face, people would say, "Don't mind Horace. He's just getting rid of his suppressed desires in Colleen's fairy castle." The whole studio knew about my folly, as I also then called it. Much of the work was done by miniature workers at First National—men who made the scaled-down objects often used in movies for depicting fires, floods, earthquakes, and other great and otherwise too costly catastrophes.

Each room was built in wood first, then cast in aluminum. We were told this was the first time aluminum had been used for cast-ing. It was done through what is called the lost wax process, which permits very fine detail in carvings. When each room came back, a jeweler polished off the rough edges and made it ready for paint-ing. Finally we had the complete shell. Next it had to be decorated and furnished.

The fairy castle is fantasy throughout. We would say, "What wouldn't people have?" Dad would say, "People wouldn't have a

My father inspired and engineered the building of the fairy-castle Doll House I had always dreamed of. The scale of this building is 1 inch to the foot. It is 9 feet square and the tallest tower is 12 feet high. It weighs a ton. The Doll House is now in the Museum of Science and Industry in Chicago.

drawing-room floor made of rose quartz and jade." I sent a sketch to Yamanaka's in New York, the famous collectors of Oriental art, and they sent it to Peking, China. Nine months later my floor came home.

News got about that I was building a completely mad doll house. My friends James Montgomery Flagg and Arthur William Brown were in California again, so I took them to see it. Hanging in the unfinished drawing room was a small brass chandelier trimmed with crystal beads. Jim said, "That's no fairy chandelier. If it were, it would be made of gold and hung with diamonds."

Delighted with the idea, I took the brass one to Mr. Crouch, a Beverly Hills jeweler who had great imagination, asking him to copy it in gold. Then I held out a handkerchief filled with my jewels. "And please put these on instead of the beads."

He looked at me as if I were from another planet, then, fingering the emerald bracelet, the Oriental pearl chain, the square cut diamond ring, the necklace, he said, "It could be very interesting." He took the jewels out of the handkerchief but handed me back a chain from which hung a six-carat pear-shaped diamond. "Take this home," he said. "You must keep something."

Two weeks later he called me and said, "Bring back that pear-shaped diamond. I need it for the drop at the bottom of the fixture." He had joined the club. The Goofus Club, we called it, because everyone who worked on the castle went slightly balmy.

I wanted real electric bulbs for the chandelier. Everyone said this was impossible, because no globes were made to my scale. I went to a surgical supply company and asked if there wasn't an instrument which I'd read about in *Time* magazine for photographing the interior of the stomach which used a globe the size of a grain of wheat. They showed it to me—a tiny bulb which screwed into a socket. I took the name of the manufacturer, the Chicago Miniature Lamp Works, and wrote to them. When they received my letter, they phoned me to say they would love to work on the lighting, that they not only made grain-of-wheat bulbs but other small ones, and if necessary, they'd invent some new ones for me. They, too, had joined the club.

Sidney Hickox, my cameraman, came over one night with spotlights and laid out the indirect lighting effects. Jerry Rouleau, a

The theme of the Doll House is fantasy
throughout. The drawing-room floor is
rose quartz and jade. Chandeliers are
solid gold with precious stones and light
bulbs the size of a grain of wheat. It has
running water and its own electrical system. It contains more than 2000 small
objects. This is a view of the Great Hall
and stair.

master electrician, carried out the plan. More than two hundred people worked on the house at one time or another.

And everyone had ideas. "Punch a bigger hole in the weeping willow tree in the garden," someone would say. "It isn't crying fast enough." "Aladdin could never get through that trap door," somebody else would point out. "It's too small. His shoulders are a good two inches wide." Nothing was too expensive, nothing too difficult to get. From start to finish, the fairy castle took seven years and cost almost half a million dollars.

The castle, which comes apart into two hundred pieces—with each room a separate unit—fits together like a Chinese puzzle. It has a complete waterworks system. Distilled water is released from a tower on top of the castle and circulated over and over through the use of centrifugal pumps. A complete electrical system lights the house, with the electrical and waterworks systems also coming apart at each room. Inside the castle are nearly two thousand small objects from all over the world—many of them added in the years since its "completion."

To give you an idea of the fairy castle, let me describe the bedroom of the fairy princess. The room is about two feet long and a foot and a half wide. The height is almost two feet. We discovered, after throwing away a couple of models, that in miniature rooms one has to go overscale in height to give the appearance of reality. To the eye, the height of the room looks about fourteen inches at most.

The big problem was what to use for a floor. It had to be a romantic floor that would be right for a tiny princess to walk on in her bare feet. At church one Sunday I looked down at the cover of my childhood prayer book and found the answer. A floor was made of small pieces of mother-of-pearl with a gold inlaid border.

The walls are a very pale pink. Over the door leading to the crystal and silver bathroom is a mural of Peter Pan. In the back wall there are two stained glass Gothic windows picturing happy songbirds, the windows very tall and narrow and of different heights to give a storybook look. Between the windows stands a tiny ivory spinet.

The boat-shaped bed which belonged to Sleeping Beauty is made of gold, the bedspread the golden spider web which covered her during her hundred-year sleep.

By the bed is a pair of red satin slippers with leather soles and heels. They were made by an Italian shoemaker who wanted to see if a pair of shoes could be made size double zero. Even for fairyland this is small. He, of course, qualified for the club.

The dressing table is made of carved ivory. On top is a gold toilet set, with the handles of the mirror and brush made of platinum set with diamonds, and on the back of each a wee platinum crown. I had difficulty finding anyone who could make a set as small as our miniature scale required. The bristles of the brush presented the greatest problem. Even a human hair was too coarse. Finally Guglielmo Cini, a well-known Boston jeweler, undertook the job.

One day his wife came home in the late afternoon and stood for a moment in the doorway, the sun hitting the fox fur piece she was wearing. Cini looked up and yelled, "Don't move!" With a scissors he trimmed off the very fine white guard hairs, using them for the bristles in the brush.

The complete toilet set consists of comb, brush, mirror, nail file, and two boxes each smaller than the nail on my little finger—one for powder, the other a jewel box. When Mr. Cini handed me the jewel box he said, "Look inside. I've given the princess a present." Inside was a minute engagement ring with a full-cut diamond, not a chip—the smallest full-cut diamond he could find in the markets of the world. The ring is so small it won't go all the way down on a common pin. Mr. Cini had also joined the club.

In the front of the princess' bedroom is a small ivory table with a chair on each side. When I was showing the castle once to a prominent jeweler in Des Moines, Iowa, I pointed to a pair of diamond and emerald clips I was wearing and said, "Everything I own in jewelry is in the castle except these clips."

He said, "They don't look like clips to me. They look like chairs."

I took them off, and he turned them into platinum chairs with backs of diamonds and emeralds. Those are the chairs by the table.

Nearby is an ivory spinning wheel—the one Sleeping Beauty pricked her finger on. An ivory harp is, of course, "the harp that once through Tara's halls." The other chairs in the room are of Battersea enamel—the ones given to me by the aunts when I was a child.

The castle is rich throughout in the lore of fairytales. In the

The Bedroom of the Fairy Princess has a floor of mother-of-pearl inlaid with gold. Walls are pale pink with Peter Pan murals. The canopied bed, boat-shaped, is gold and the dressing table is carved ivory. Between the windows is a tiny ivory spinet piano. Chairs are Battersea enamel. Windows are stained glass.

courtyard stands Cinderella's coach. In the great hall the goose that laid the golden eggs sits on a tiny gold and enamel table, a gold mesh basket holding several golden eggs beside her. Under a glass bell on a rosewood table nearby stand the chairs belonging to the Three Bears. Each chair rests on the head of a pin, the largest chair weighing only 150,000th of an ounce. Next to the chairs are Hans Brinker's silver skates and Cinderella's glass slipper. Tall, etched glass windows overlooking the garden tell the stories of Jack and the Beanstalk, Prince Charming, and the Princess and the Seven Swans. Mother Goose characters adorn the walls of the kitchen. The copper stove there is the one in which the wicked witch locked Hansel and Gretel.

The library is filled with tiny, tiny books. In the mid-1800s the printing of miniature books from real type was a widespread hobby. I have collected nearly a hundred of these small treasures. Included in the collection is the smallest Bible in the world, printed in 1840 and given to me by Antonio Moreno after he played opposite me in *Her Wild Oat.*

My modern library is my most cherished possession. I have had made up scores of beautifully bound books with blank pages not quite an inch in size. Many of my friends have been helpful in getting their author friends to handwrite in these small books. Robinson Jeffers wrote an original Irish poem—quite gay and laughing in contrast to his dramatic *Roan Stallion* and *The Women at Point Sur.* Sinclair Lewis made up a small story about Arrowsmith going to Hollywood to try to break into the movies. There are books by Conan Doyle, Louis Bromfield, Booth Tarkington, Elinor Glyn, Willa Cather, Clare Boothe Luce, John Steinbeck, Thornton Wilder, Adela Rogers St. Johns, Edna Ferber, Fannie Hurst, Daphne du Maurier, Irving Stone, Edward Albee, and, of course, F. Scott Fitzgerald. And many more—nearly a hundred of the most famous authors of our time.

The library also contains a postage-stamp size autograph book. I am very snobby about this book. Each name in it is that of someone who has made a real contribution to twentieth century history. Orville Wright for aviation. J. P. Morgan for finance. Henry Ford for business. (Remember when he startled the world by doing so radical a thing as to pay five dollars a day to labor!) Wally and the Duke of Windsor, the romance of our age. Admiral Richard E.

The Dining Hall of the Doll House has a table based on the Round Table of the King Arthur legends. The shields of Arthur's knights are on the backs of the chairs. The walls are hung with real tapestries of very fine petit point. Fine English porcelain in perfect miniature scale is displayed in this room.

This is the Library of the Doll House, which is filled with tiny books, in the original handwriting of such authors as Sinclair Lewis, Scott Fitzgerald, Willa Cather, Thornton Wilder. An autograph album here is signed by Churchill, De Gaulle, Nehru, Einstein, Henry Ford, Orville Wright, five Presidents, and Queen Elizabeth II.

*Prince Charming's Bedroom in the Doll
House has a vaulted frescoed ceiling and
carved furniture and a fine icon. Perhaps
the most interesting thing in this room
is the white fur rug. The rug was made
by a taxidermist from the skin of a
single ermine and the ferocious teeth in
the head once belonged to a mouse.*

Byrd for adventure. All the Presidents since Hoover except Kennedy (I thought I had time—he was so young). Einstein, Churchill, Eisenhower, Pershing, Nehru, De Gaulle, Queen Elizabeth II, the Crown Prince of Japan, and many others.

In the drawing room are several music scores handwritten by their composers—among them Rachmaninoff's *Prelude*, Gershwin's *Rhapsody in Blue*, Stravinsky's *Firebird Suite*, Rodgers and Hammerstein's *Oh, What a Beautiful Mornin'!*, Irving Berlin's *Alexander's Ragtime Band*, and a special favorite of mine, *West Side Story*, by Leonard Bernstein and Stephen Sondheim—Stephen being the son of my longtime friend Foxy Sondheim.

The scores are displayed on a grand piano made of rosewood with ivory legs—a piano which actually plays! On the mantel of the fireplace nearby stands a tiny gold clock set with diamonds and emeralds which actually keeps time—it's wound every day.

Of the many stories connected with furnishing the fairy castle, one of my favorites concerns the rug on the floor of the prince's bedroom. I took an ermine skin to a taxidermist and asked him to make it into a bearskin rug, head and all. He said he could make the bear's head, but not with his mouth open, because he couldn't think of any way to duplicate the bear's teeth in miniature (this was before the age of plastic). When I went to pick up the rug I was astonished to see the bear's mouth yawning wide and filled with white, wicked-looking teeth. The taxidermist beamed at me. "I caught a little mouse," he said, "and used his teeth."

We decided not to put any figures in the doll house. When we tried, the dolls looked static and dead. With an empty castle and a full imagination, it's easy to people the rooms with running, laughing elves and fairies. (I have often asked children looking at the doll house what they liked best, and often the answer has been, "I liked best the little fairy who was baking a cake in the kitchen," or "I liked best the little fairy who was playing the organ in the chapel.")

The castle was started in 1928 and finished in 1935. I had built it for my own amusement—and amazement—regarding it as a beautiful toy, an extravagance, a folly, even, but one which had brought me more happiness than I'd ever known before.

Certainly there was not much happiness in my personal life at that point.

After the breakup of my marriage to John in 1929, I moved

back into the Bel Air house. It seemed big and empty to me. It was, all sixteen rooms of it, not to mention the guest house and the pool house and the theater and the servants' quarters—all for just me and the servants.

I sat in the swing in my garden a lot looking at the blue pool and the California sky and listening to the birds, thinking about my life and my career. Why my career had never held much glory for me I didn't know, unless it was because of John, but it hadn't. I don't mean the work. I had loved every minute of that. But it seemed to me there had to be more to life than just work.

I wondered if the success I had had in my career had to be compensated for by not having much personal happiness. I began to wonder about the "private" people—people like my mother and father, who had such a good understanding between them and shared so many things.

Virginia Valli and Charlie Farrell were friends of mine. One day Virginia called to ask if they could bring a friend of theirs— a "private" person from New York—over to swim. They arrived with a good-looking guy about my age who was fresh, flip, and funny. His name was Albert Parker Scott, and he had a seat on the New York Stock Exchange.

We swam, and they all stayed to dinner. For the first time in a long time I found myself laughing and having fun. Al was filled with enthusiasm and the joy of living. He was different from anyone I'd ever known. He kidded all my movie sacred cows. He even kidded Louis B. Mayer. At that time Mrs. Mayer was ill in a hospital, while Mr. Mayer, who loved to dance, was being seen nightly at different clubs dancing with some pretty girl. Al said, "I hear Mrs. Mayer's illness has gone to Mr. Mayer's feet."

His kidding of the world I had regarded with a feeling close to reverence my whole life staggered me at first, but gradually it endeared him to me, and I began to see him for dinner almost every night.

John, meanwhile, had taken a house at Malibu Beach next door to Adela Rogers St. Johns. He heard about Al and me, and one afternoon, drunk and despondent, he started swimming out to nowhere. Adela was in her study on the second floor and just happened to look out. She saw John and ran down to the beach calling for help. Jack Gilbert, who had a house on the other side of John's, ran to her, and they rowed out and pulled John in just as he was going down. (Adela also adapted this incident for use in the story which became *A Star Is Born.*) Next day she phoned to say she was trying to help John, but he'd said he was going to kill Al. Maybe it would be a good thing if I could get away for a while.

I wanted to get away anyhow, so when Edgar Selwyn offered me a play written by my friend Barney Glazer—a play with the appropriate title *On the Loose*—I accepted and went to New York. I took a suite at the Plaza while the play was in rehearsal, seeing Al nearly every night.

On the Loose was destined for Broadway, but it was such a flop at its opening in Cleveland and everywhere else we played for the six weeks of its out-of-town tryout that it folded on the road. Nevertheless, the experience was a revelation to me. To be able to start a story and finish it in sequence in a few hours seemed so easy. I understood then what Lionel Barrymore had meant when he said, "An even performance given by a movie star is a miracle, considering the bits and pieces in which a film is taken. And the wonder of Hollywood is these miracles are being performed every day."

When the play closed, Al and I were married. This time I had the kind of honeymoon I'd dreamed about before. We went to Niagara Falls, just like all the other brides and grooms.

Our hotel suite had a large living room with a phone on a cord reaching into all the rooms. One afternoon Al said, "Let's call your Aunt Lib in Paris."

We put in the call, and after I introduced him to her, he said, "Do you want to hear Niagara Falls?"

"Oh, yes," she answered. "It would be a sound from home."

"Wait a minute," he said, "and I'll put the phone out the window." With that, he took the phone into the bathroom, held it inside the toilet bowl, and flushed the toilet.

Aunt Lib said, "How wonderful. I can hear the falls perfectly."

We spent the afternoon calling up people all over America. They all fell for the gag.

Since my first play had been a flop, I wanted a chance to try again. Early in 1932 I was offered the lead in the West Coast company of the hit play, *A Church Mouse*, in which Ruth Gordon was starring on Broadway. It was a big success in San Francisco

Albert Parker Scott was my friend before he was my husband and we're still friends. We went to Niagara Falls on our honeymoon.

and an even bigger one in Los Angeles. M-G-M signed me to a year's contract, and I was back in the picture-making business again.

The trouble was, Al was in the brokerage business in New York. When he could get away from the Stock Exchange, he lived with me in my Bel Air house. When I could get away from California, I lived with him at the Sherry-Netherland in New York.

One time when I was in Europe and Al was at the Bel Air house for a few weeks, he called Harold Grieve and said, "I want to do over this bedroom of John's as a surprise for Colleen."

Harold was elated. At last this dark, somber room which John had adored and we hated could be done in light, gay block linens. At least, that's what Harold thought, until Al said, "McCormick and I have only one thing in common besides being married to Colleen—this room. I think it's beautiful. I want you to duplicate it exactly." Harold even had to have one piece of material hand woven.

When Al left for New York, he said to Harold, "I'd never say this to Colleen, but this is the only perfect room in her house."

One time in 1932 when Al was in California, we entertained a group of visiting Olympic athletes with a buffet supper. A friend had sent an enormous salmon—so enormous it wouldn't fit in our oven, so I took it to the Beverly Wilshire Hotel to have it cooked. The chef made that fish a masterpiece. The Olympic flags from all nations were done in aspic all over its back. It was so beautiful no one would cut into it.

The next day Al bumped into an old friend from the New York Stock Exchange and asked him to come up to the house for lunch. The man said, "I don't want you to go to a lot of trouble." Al assured him it wouldn't be any trouble at all, it would just be a pickup lunch.

When the fish masterpiece from the night before was served, the man's eyes popped, but he said nothing. But when the ice cream discus throwers were served for dessert, he said, "My God, Al, do you always live like this?"

Al said, "You should come sometime when you're expected."

Al helped straighten out my tangled financial affairs and soon my portfolio was filled with securities that were sound.

Al and I were friends in a way that John and I had never been, and we have stayed friends to this day. But we didn't stay married very long. Our lives were too separated, our interests too different, our feeling for one another as husband and wife not strong enough to make the good times we had together the basis of a permanent relationship.

So I was alone once again. Wondering once again about my life and my career.

The public took care of the latter.

While I was still under contract to M-G-M, I was loaned to Fox to make *The Power and the Glory* with Spencer Tracy. As I said earlier, I thought it was the best film I ever made, and the critics agreed with me. But the part I played in it was a heavy dramatic one in which I went from a young girl to a woman of sixty. The public didn't care for me in that kind of part. They wanted me to go on being a wide-eyed, innocent little girl.

I was too old for that—and too tired of it in any case. So I bowed out.

Now all I had to wonder about was my life and what to do with it.

I thought a lot about my mother's old maxim, "God opens many doors for us in our lives," wondering if there were any more doors left for me. I was beginning to doubt it when the most exciting door in my life thus far opened for me.

I discovered America.

CHAPTER 14

"IN MY FATHER'S HOUSE ARE MANY MANSIONS"

When I was making *The Desert Flower* in 1925 I broke my neck. We were in Barstow, California, shooting the exteriors for the film, in which I played the daughter of a railroad man who headed a work gang repairing the road bed. The opening scene showed me pumping a handcar along the tracks, something that was physically impossible for me to do, so the usual piano wire was attached to the car, and the car was to be pulled along by a group of men off camera. The men were Mexicans, and either they didn't understand English or they misunderstood the director's instructions. In any case, they gave a sudden jerk to the wire, and I fell off the car onto the tracks.

The only damage so far as I could tell was a stiff neck, which prevented me from holding my head up straight, making me look very coy in all the scenes.

Some cowboys from a nearby ranch said there was a bone setter in the district who could crack my neck to get rid of the stiffness. God was on my side, because the bone setter was at a distant ranch setting the leg of a cowboy who'd been thrown from a horse. Had he cracked my neck he would have snapped the spinal cord, killing me instantly.

When John saw me upon our return to the studio, he said I'd better see the doctor and find out what could be done, since I couldn't very well finish the picture with my head on one side.

The doctor met me at the Hollywood Hospital and took some X rays. I was sitting there with my cocked head waiting to be told to go home when he came in with another doctor and a nurse, all of them looking at me in awe.

My doctor came over and, taking my hand, said, "Now, Colleen, you're going to be all right, but you've had a little accident to your neck. We have to set it and put you in a plaster cast for a while."

Telling me to walk carefully without moving my head, the three of them steered me into the operating room and put me on the table. When I came to I was all plastered up, looking like a cross between a nun and Red Grange.

I stayed that way for six weeks—and John stayed sober for six weeks. (And First National, who had to keep the entire company on salary in order to hold them together, no doubt stayed dour for six weeks.) Finally the big day arrived when I was to be cut out of the cast. John, never one to miss a publicity stunt, had newsreels there to record the event. The doctor cut through the cast. Then he said, "Now, Colleen, move your head up and down." I did. He told me to move it sideways. I did that, too. "Thank God!" he exclaimed, and my mother burst into tears.

I didn't know what it was all about until the doctors told me they had doubted I would ever be able to move my head again. When I heard that, the newsreels got a better show than they had counted on. I fainted dead away.

It was during my six weeks' stay in the hospital that I became interested in crippled children. I made a promise to myself that someday I would do something to help them. Ten years later, looking at the extravagant toy I had built for my amusement, I remembered that promise.

I called the Children's Hospital in Los Angeles and asked the volunteer ladies association if they would like to have a castle-viewing tea at my house some afternoon to raise money for the hospital. A friend of mine, Jerry Fitzgerald, was the public relations man for the May Company department store in Los Angeles. When I told him of the proposed tea, he said, "How would you like to raise a million dollars for crippled children?"

I clapped my hands. "Jerry, I'd love it! But how?"

He laid out the idea for exhibiting the fairy castle in a nationwide tour of department stores. The stores would pay my expenses. The money collected from a small admission charge would go to the local crippled children's charity.

Enchanted with the idea, I engaged a young man named John Hewlitt, who had done such fine work in publicizing the new Grace Line passenger ships.

Hewlitt came to California, saw the doll house, talked to Fitzgerald at the May Company, and made a deal whereby the May Company agreed to underwrite my expenses for the entire tour if two stipulations were met—one, that the doll house be shown first at Macy's in New York, because Macy's was the acknowledged leader among retail merchants, and what it did, other stores would do; two, that the doll house be shown in all six May Company stores.

Hewlitt went back East with photos of the house. Paul Hollister, the public relations man at Macy's, called me, saying, "Do you swear the house is like these photos?" I swore they were exact. Macy's booked the house, making the New York Hospital Fund, Children's Division, the beneficiary.

We had the doll house insured for four hundred and thirty-five thousand dollars. Much, such as the books, couldn't be insured.

Because of its value, the castle was transported in a private car on the Santa Fe *Chief* with an armed guard supplied by Railway Express. My dad and mother accompanied Hewlitt and me—Dad to see how people in New York liked his "child," Mother to look after the furniture.

When we arrived in New York the doll house was set up in a corner of Macy's luggage department, scheduled to go on display on Monday morning. On Sunday Macy's advertised the doll house in four pages of pictures in the local papers. By Monday afternoon the crowds were so great, the entire floor had been put out of business. Before the store opened the next morning the crowds were already a block long, with ramps set up to contain them. Before the week was out, every department store in America was begging for the doll house.

From New York we went to Los Angeles and from there to Chicago, where the little castle was shown for six weeks in the toy department at the Fair Store. People who came to see the doll house bought so many toys the buyer had to reorder four times. One Monday from nine A.M. to nine P.M. twenty thousand people were clocked going past it. (In 1966 over one and a half million people—more than four thousand people a day!—visited the doll house at the Chicago Museum of Science and Industry, where it is now on permanent display.)

Several different children's charities were the beneficiaries in Chicago, and it was there, as I met the many women who served on the boards of these various organizations, that a whole new world opened up to me—a world where women gave not just money, but gave of themselves as well. They worked in settlement houses, as hospital aides, in orphanages, at the Art Institute. They didn't have much time to even think of themselves, they were so taken up with those who needed their help. I could hardly believe it.

From then on as I toured the country I met many more women doing this same thing. Many men, too. They worked for better government, for Boys' Clubs, for camps for poor children. I spoke at men's and women's luncheons, many of them Rotary Club luncheons. In Hollywood the dirtiest name you could call anybody was a "Rotarian." I wanted to go home and tell my friends that the finest things we have in America are the Rotary Clubs.

Almost everywhere I went the mayor presented me with a small gold key to the city. I have hundreds of them mounted in a shadow box. To me they are wonderful souvenirs—the keys to the doors that opened America for me.

I am very proud of today's Hollywood, where all the stars work for some charitable or civic or cultural endeavor. But as I mentioned earlier, in my day hardly anyone but Mary Pickford did a thing, so it's no wonder I felt like Columbus.

My discovery of America, of this world of the "private" people, made me yearn to be a part of it, to have a husband and a home, to be able to give as they were giving, to know the satisfaction which comes in making one's community a better place in which to live—to find the kind of happiness they had found.

I wasn't a part of their world. I was only an onlooker, a visiting celebrity, my life a continuous chain of trains and hotels and department-store reception lines. As the tour progressed, I became a very tired visiting celebrity. And I was lonelier than ever.

I began to wonder if now, with the success of the doll house added to the success of my movie career, I had used up all my doors. (I didn't quite reach my million-dollar goal, but Mary Jane Burns, who took John Hewlitt's place after two years and who stayed on with the tour long after I left, managed to bring our total to almost six hundred and fifty thousand dollars for children's charities all over America—and this in the darkest days of the Depression, when even a ten-cent admission charge was often hard to come by!) Then I remembered a passage from the Bible: "In my Father's house are many mansions." To me this meant there had to be more doors.

I remembered something else from the Bible: "Ask and ye shall receive."

I asked. I said, "Please, God, let me have just one more opportunity for 'boy meets girl.' I'm almost thirty-three years old, and I know it's a lot to ask when so much has been given to me already, but please, just one more chance."

In 1936 we took the doll house back to Chicago for a return showing. While I was there I met Homer Hargrave, a widower who was a broker—and would soon become one of the original partners in Merrill Lynch, Pierce, Fenner & Beane (now Smith). He was everything I'd dreamed about. He even had a bonus of two children—Judy, aged five, and Homer, Jr., twelve.

We were married the following year. After the ceremony he took me to Chicago's Riverview Amusement Park. We rode on the roller coaster, had a wedding supper of hot dogs. My wedding present was a pennant on which was written, "*Riverview Park, 1937.*" Then we went to Europe.

After my marriage to Homer, I went back to Hollywood many times. My parents were there, as well as most of my closest friends. There was, too, the matter of my house in Bel Air, which I had been renting whenever I was away from Hollywood for a long period of time, and which I continued to rent—sometimes to some pretty extraordinary people.

My first big tenant, and the best housekeeper who ever lived there, was Marlene Dietrich, who rented the house for a year when she first arrived from Germany.

In 1937 I married Homer Hargrave of Chicago, a widower with two young children, Judy and Homer, Jr., and then my true happiness began. Here I am with my family, left to right (back row) Homer Hargrave, Jr.; Homer Hargrave; Roger Coleman; (center) Alice Pirie Hargrave; Grandma Colleen; Judy Hargrave Coleman; (front row) Charles Pirie Hargrave; William Coleman; Kathleen Moore Coleman (namesake); William I. Hargrave; in 1964.

We had all been enchanted with her performance in *The Blue Angel*, but no one knew her. After she came to Hollywood, brought there by Joseph von Sternberg, her director, people in Hollywood still didn't know her. No one even saw her except her co-workers at the studio. Her co-workers and one other. My gardener, Fujita. He went with the house. So I had a pipeline to the activities of our newest glamour girl.

Fujita said to me one time when I was out in Hollywood visiting my parents that while he hoped I would return soon, nevertheless he was very happy, because Miss Dietrich was a wonderful cook. Or, as he put it, "Miss Dietrich big cook, make many cakes Saturday, we eat slice each one, also make good thing in cabbage wrappers." This was the first time a big-time glamour girl had ever been known to set foot in the kitchen except for publicity pictures.

Fujita then went on, "Family all eat in the dining room, food all on table at once, send servants to basement so can't hear talk, but they speak German, us speak Japanese, so really not problem."

Another interesting tenant was the Countess de Frasso. She was a wealthy American, the former Dorothy Taylor of New York, who had married into one of Italy's most aristocratic families. The Villa Madama, where they lived outside of Rome, had been restored by Dorothy to its former glory, and it was such a fabulous gem of a house—the ceiling in the drawing room was done by Leonardo da Vinci—that Mussolini later confiscated it for his important visitors.

Dorothy wasn't able to work the same kind of magic on the elderly count, and when Gary Cooper arrived in Rome with a letter of introduction from Mary Pickford and Douglas Fairbanks, she took one look at him and promptly arranged an African safari.

A few weeks of hunting big game with him in the romantic African veldt, with all its danger and closeness, put some big ideas in Dorothy's head. When Coop, as everybody called him, returned to Hollywood, she followed him, ostensibly to visit her friends Mary and Doug.

The story going around Hollywood was that Coop felt he was being smothered as well as trapped. When he brought Dorothy to a Sunday party at my house in Bel Air I could believe it. She was somewhat more than pleasingly plump and looked much older than he, which, as a matter of fact, she was. After seeing all the thin actresses, she promptly reduced and became a glamour girl herself, but by that time it was too late. Coop had flown the coop and married Roxanna Balfe.

But Hollywood had other charms for the countess, and she took to spending long months there, always in rented houses.

The time she had my house was during prohibition, when the gangsters were running loose, not only in Chicago, but on and off the screen in Hollywood. One of them, a handsome, dapper fellow by the name of Bugsie Siegal, was paying court to Dorothy. While the whole FBI was looking for him, where do you think he was hiding? In my guest house. Later, when Dorothy ran back to Rome to put a stick of wood on the home fires, Bugsie was shot as he was sitting at the window of another rented house.

One time when I had returned to California for a week to get the house in order, I was sitting on the patio having lunch with Tyrone Power and a couple of friends when the real estate man came by bringing Bruce Cabot to look at the house.

Bruce wanted to rent it for six months, sharing it with two friends. One of the friends was Freddy McAvoy, a well-known playboy, and an international one at that. The other man was an Englishman whose name I can't remember. I only remember that his father owned ten-cent stores.

Tyrone said, "Colleen, you're mad to rent your house to those men. There won't be a stick of furniture left when they move out." But Bruce was charming, and I wanted to return East, so I signed the lease.

Since it was summer, I figured my tenants would concentrate on outdoor activities, sparing the house and its contents. For the most part I figured correctly. The first person I heard from was my next-door neighbor, who had a twelve-year-old son. She said the goings-on around my swimming pool never stopped, day or night. She also said there was one thing she could thank my tenants for. She no longer had to worry about telling her son the facts of life. She kept dragging him and his friends out of the bushes where they were watching slice after slice of it being given them by Cabot's guests.

One constant visitor was Errol Flynn. One morning I opened the newspaper to see the headline ERROL FLYNN ACCUSED OF RAPE. After stating the pertinent facts, the article went on to say that all of this had happened in his Bel Air house on St. Pierre Road.

Hollywood will always hold a piece of my heart and I cherish the friends I made there when we were young and gay. Here is a picture of Mervyn LeRoy and me, reliving old times. No matter how it looks neither of us has changed a bit!

I nearly flipped. My house in a scandal. I prayed they'd keep calling it Flynn's house and not mention my name.

The whole case rested on the statement by the young girl—young only in years—that Flynn had raped her upstairs in the bedroom which had belonged to John, locking the door so she couldn't get out. My housekeeper testified that the lock on the door had been broken for some time, so the door couldn't have been locked.

But the best testimony, in my opinion, came from my gardener, who was now an Englishman and a milk-toast sort of man. In a letter to me he said there was a lot of excitement at the house that day. A young lady, stark naked, came running down to the rose bed where he was working, put her arms around him, and began making love to him. It frightened him so, he said, that he went home, even though it was only two o'clock in the afternoon. He would make up the time later.

One time when I was out in Hollywood seeing about the house (which I finally sold)—the time that I remember best—I had a phone call from a producer friend who wanted me to make a movie.

It was a tempting offer and a tempting part, but I knew what my answer was going to be before he finished asking.

I had made a total of sixty motion pictures—one as a bit player, fifteen as a leading lady, nineteen as a featured player, and twenty-five as a star. I had given up my girlhood in order to pursue my burning ambition. If I had had it to do over, I didn't doubt that I would have done exactly as I had before.

But I wasn't a girl any longer. And I had learned a number of things along the way which were more important to me in the long run than how to make successful movies.

I thought back to that night in Tampa when my mother had acted on her double-barreled belief that while God opens many doors for us in our lives, opportunity only knocks once. Opportunity, I had learned, knocks more than once. The trick is to know which of those many doors it's knocking at.

It seemed now to be knocking on the door to a possible new career in Hollywood. Seemed to, but I knew better.

Back in Chicago I had the husband and the home I had prayed for. I had two children who needed me. I had experienced there the satisfaction which comes from helping to make a community

When television turned time backward and offered a re-run of Ella Cinders, I had the opportunity of viewing myself in a new medium. You can see how serious I was about the whole thing.

a better place in which to live. Most important of all, I had found there the happiness I had searched for so long.

I had learned that it is the woman who keeps a marriage together, whose job it is—and a full-time job—to make a home a place of warmth and refuge for a man, and a place of security and inspiration —and fun—for their children. It's a difficult job sometimes, requiring imagination and patience and, above all, a giving of self. But the rewards are a companionship and a feeling of belonging worth far more than all the fame in the world.

The opportunity I wanted most in life had been given to me when I met Homer. With him and with our children I had found the right door—the golden door—for me.

I had become at last a "private" person.

THE END

*The text of this book is set in lino-
type Janson. The typography, lay-
out, and binding were designed
by Earl Tidwell.*